Economics as Social Science

There is a growing consensus in social sciences that there is a need for interdisciplinary research on the complexity of human behaviour. At an age of crisis for both the economy and economic theory, economics is called upon to fruitfully cooperate with contiguous social disciplines. The term 'economics imperialism' refers to the expansion of economics to territories that lie outside the traditional domain of the discipline. Its critics argue that in starting with the assumption of maximizing behaviour, economics excludes the nuances of rival disciplines and has problems in interpreting real-world phenomena.

This book focuses on a territory that persists to be largely intractable using the postulates of economics: that of primitive societies. In retracing the origins of economics imperialism back to the birth of the discipline, this volume argues that it offers a reductionist interpretation that is poor in interpretative power. By engaging with the neglected traditions of sociological and anthropological studies, the analysis offers suggestions for a more democratic cooperation between the social sciences.

Economics as Social Science is of great interest to those who study the history of economic thought, political economy and the history of economic anthropology, as well as the history of social sciences and economic methodology.

Roberto Marchionatti is Professor of Economics at the University of Turin, Italy, where he teaches economics, history of economic theory and economic anthropology.

Mario Cedrini is Assistant Professor of Economics at the University of Turin, Italy, where he teaches macroeconomics, international economics, history of economic thought and economic anthropology.

Routledge Advances in Social Economics

Edited by John B. Davis, *Marquette University*

This series presents new advances and developments in social economics thinking on a variety of subjects that concern the link between social values and economics. Need, justice and equity, gender, cooperation, work poverty, the environment, class, institutions, public policy and methodology are some of the most important themes. Among the orientations of the authors are social economist, institutionalist, humanist, solidarist, cooperatist, radical and Marxist, feminist, post-Keynesian, behaviouralist, and environmentalist. The series offers new contributions from today's most foremost thinkers on the social character of the economy.

Publishes in conjunction with the Association of Social Economics.

For a full list of titles in this series, please visit www.routledge.com/Routledge-Advances-in-Social-Economics/book-series/SE0071

19 Poverty and Social Exclusion
New Methods of Analysis
Edited by Gianni Betti and Achille Lemmi

20 Social Capital and Economics
Social values, power and social identity
Edited by Asimina Christoforou and John B. Davis

21 The Economics of Values-Based Organizations
An Introduction
Luigino Bruni and Alessandra Smerilli

22 The Economics of Resource-Allocation in Healthcare
Cost-Utility, Social Value and Fairness
Andrea Klonschinski

23 Economics as Social Science
Economics imperialism and the challenge of interdisciplinarity
Roberto Marchionatti and Mario Cedrini

Economics as Social Science

Economics imperialism and the challenge of interdisciplinarity

Roberto Marchionatti and Mario Cedrini

Routledge
Taylor & Francis Group
LONDON AND NEW YORK

First published 2017
by Routledge
2 Park Square, Milton Park, Abingdon, Oxon OX14 4RN

and by Routledge
711 Third Avenue, New York, NY 10017

Routledge is an imprint of the Taylor & Francis Group, an informa business

British Library Cataloguing in Publication Data
A catalogue record for this book is available from the British Library

Library of Congress Cataloging in Publication Data
Names: Marchionatti, Roberto, 1950- author. | Cedrini, Mario, author.
Title: Economics as social science : economics imperialism and the challenge of interdisciplinary / Roberto Marchionatti and Mario Cedrini.
Description: Abingdon, Oxon ; New York, NY : Routledge, 2017. | Includes bibliographical references and index.
Identifiers: LCCN 2016023181| ISBN 9781138909298 (hardback) | ISBN 9781315694047 (ebook)
Subjects: LCSH: Economics. | Interdisciplinary research.
Classification: LCC HB71 .M283 2017 | DDC 330—dc23
LC record available at https://lccn.loc.gov/2016023181_

ISBN: 978-1-138-90929-8 (hbk)
ISBN: 978-1-315-69404-7 (ebk)

Typeset in Times New Roman
by Swales & Willis Ltd, Exeter, Devon, UK

Contents

Acknowledgements

The volume embeds the authors' long-standing concern, and resulting reflections, on the issue of interdisciplinarity. The perspective here adopted combines the history of economic ideas with an epistemological and methodological approach to the limits of economics imperialism. The book builds on some previous works, and in particular: *Gli economisti e i selvaggi* (*Economists and Savages*) by Roberto Marchionatti (Milano: Bruno Mondadori, 2008); 'The Economists and Primitive Societies. A Critique of Economic Imperialism', by Roberto Marchionatti, *The Journal of Socio-Economics*, 41(5), 2012: 529–40; 'On the Theoretical and Practical Relevance of the Concept of Gift to the Development of a Non-Imperialist Economics', by Mario Cedrini and Roberto Marchionatti, *Review of Radical Political Economics*, forthcoming 2016, and 'Just Another Niche in the Wall? How Specialization Is Changing the Face of Mainstream Pluralism', by Mario Cedrini and Magda Fontana, a revised version of the Department of Economics and Statistics 'Cognetti de Martiis' Working Paper 2015/10, University of Turin.

This book has benefited greatly from the suggestions of several colleagues and researchers working in the field of economics, anthropology and history, as well as from feedback received at a number of conferences and workshops. Special thanks go to Marshall Sahlins and the participants in the second edition of the workshop 'Revisiting the Boundaries of Economics. A Historical Perspective', held at Collegio Carlo Alberto, Moncalieri (Turin), on 19 May 2011. We also thank Matteo Aria, conveners of the conference 'La produzione sociale dell'altruismo: il dono del sangue tra dono, stato e mercato', held at Sapienza University, Rome, on 27–29 November 2013, and the conference participants. We are grateful to colleagues of the Department of Economics and Statistics 'Cognetti de Martiis' of the University of Turin for their participation in a seminar held on 8 May 2014. We are indebted as well to Michael Perelman and participants in the Annual Conference of the History of Economics Society, held in Montreal on 20–22 June 2014. Finally, we thank Gianluca Cuniberti and participants in the conference 'Dono, controdono e corruzione. Ricerche storiche e dialogo internazionale', held at Fondazione Luigi Einaudi, Turin, on 3–4 December 2015.

Introduction

Origins, evolution and metamorphoses of economics imperialism, or the need for an interdisciplinary research programme on human behaviour

In a recently debated article in the *Journal of Economic Perspectives*, Marion Fourcade, Etienne Ollion and Yann Algan (2015) have documented the ongoing insularity of economics within social sciences, mainly in the United States. Economists believe in their 'superiority': they show greater confidence, with respect to other social scientists, in their own practical mission – fixing the world's problems, in Fourcade and colleagues' terms. And economists believe, coherently with the 'economics imperialism' narrative, in their disciplinary autonomy. Despite the existence of many schools of thought inside economics, they easily conceive their field to be unitary and integrated; there is more consensus, in less prosaic words, than in other social sciences. In his qualified defence of economists' work as against accusations of reductionist approach to social phenomena (Rodrik 2015), Harvard economist Dani Rodrik (formerly Albert O. Hirshman Professor at the School of Social Science at Princeton University) has recently contested, with some reasons, Fourcade and colleagues' characterization of today's economics as a rigid and homogeneous discipline. He points out in particular, not without reason, that "economics is a collection of models that admits a wide variety of possibilities" (Rodrik 2015: 178), and draws attention to the pluralism of research programmes currently pursued in the discipline. Still, it seems difficult to deny that, as these latter argue, interdisciplinarity – which, following Choi and Pak's (2006: 359) definition, "analyzes, synthesizes and harmonizes links between disciplines into a coordinated and coherent whole", while multidisciplinarity "draws on knowledge from different disciplines but stays within the boundaries of those fields" – is much less valued than in sociology or political sciences. According to a recent study (Gross and Simmons 2007), economists are the only social scientists who tend to disagree with the idea that interdisciplinary knowledge is better than knowledge obtained from single disciplines. This is hardly surprising. The story of economics' relationships with other disciplines appears essentially as one of imperialism – be it the imperialism of economics towards social sciences or the more recent and ambiguous "reverse imperialism" of other disciplines towards economics.

This introduction to the present volume is devoted to discussing economics imperialism and its evolution over time, with special concern for its relevance in the current troubled times for both the economy and economics as discipline.

We maintain that the traditional narrative dating economics imperialism back to the 1970s, when Chicago economists started popularizing the use of the term, is in truth misleading, and needs profound revision. Lionel Robbins's 1932 essay 'The Nature and Significance of Economic Science' is admittedly a milestone in the story of economics imperialism. Still, in a reconstruction of the story of the uneasy relationships between economics and social sciences expressly centred upon the problem of economics imperialism, Ben Fine and Dimitris Milonakis (2009) consider the marginalist revolution as the key passage. Marginalism, they argue, allowed economists to shift the boundaries separating their own discipline from other social sciences, and to colonize the subject matter of sociology, anthropology and political science. Fine and Milonakis (2009: 1) regard the "desocialization and dehistoricization" of economics occurred with the passing from the political economy of the fathers of economics to the marginalist revolution as the conditions that made economics imperialism possible. To the contrary, we advance the thesis that an imperialist orientation characterizes economics since the dawn of the discipline with Adam Smith. We thus devote a substantial part of this book to showing how economists' early analyses of primitive societies – a fundamental issue in the foundation of political economy – can be taken as shining illustration of the pugilistic attitude of economics towards other social sciences.

Economics imperialism is usually defined, today (see Mäki 2009), as a form of economics expansionism that would allow the application of economic approaches to human behaviour to territories that lie outside the traditional domain of the discipline of economics. In the last fifty years, in effect, neoclassical and mainstream economics have greatly expanded their scope of inquiry as well as their spheres of influence over other social sciences.

In a highly influential and authoritative paper, the American economist Edward Lazear (2000: 99) attributes this expansion to the fact that economics has "a rigorous language that allows complicated concepts to be written in relatively simple, abstract terms", starting from the basic assumption of maximizing behaviour. This language permits economists "to strip away complexity", which, although it may add to the "richness of description", nevertheless "prevents the analyst from seeing what is essential" (ibid.: 99–100). Herein lies, Lazear maintains, the power of economic science and its comparative advantage over the other social sciences. The role of the other social sciences is to identify issues, that of economics is "to provide specific, well-reasoned answers" (ibid.: 103). We can therefore observe, borrowing from Uskali Mäki's (2009) epistemic perspective, that the justification for economics imperialism rests, first and foremost, on its supposed capacity of explanatory unification:

> most scientists and most philosophers of science believe that one respectable, if not the most respectable, species of scientific achievement amounts to expanding the domain of phenomena explained by a given theory, or, even better, by an increasingly parsimonious theory. Most economists seem to share this conviction.
>
> (Mäki 2009: 3)

Economics imperialism is “an implementation” (ibid.) of this view. In truth, the discipline’s imperialism has come to be associated not so much to parsimony of theories, as to an ever-growing scope for the discipline itself. In this regard, Mäki adopts the notion of full consilience, which John Davis (2013a: 205) synthetizes as “a unity of knowledge idea that counterbalances the virtue of a theory simply having wide scope”: full consilience seems particularly appropriate in the case of economics imperialism, which rests upon supporters’ confidence in the unexpected possibility to apply the theory to new phenomena. Hence the metaphor of economics imperialism as colonization of other disciplines: expansionism occurs in territories that are already occupied by other social sciences. But if the ambition to explain more by unifying could justify economics imperialism, we must not lose sight of the fact that economics imperialism occurs “without any invitations” (Stigler 1984: 311) on the part of other social sciences.

The term ‘economic imperialism’, or, better, ‘economics imperialism’, was coined by Marshallian New Zealand economist Ralph Souter (Souter 1933),[1] to be then diffused in the 1970s and 1980s by Chicago School economists (see, for example, Stigler, 1984; Radnitzky and Bernholz, 1987).[2] In using the term, these latter referred, in particular, to works by Gary Becker, who, from the end of the 1950s onwards, relentlessly applied himself to build an “economic approach” (see Becker 1976a) suitable for the interpretation of a wide variety of social phenomena. An overview of the expansion and reorientation of economics since Becker’s fundamental contribution is presented in Grossbard-Shechtman and Clague (2001a, 2001b). But the historical roots of economics imperialism lie in the theoretical and methodological revolution of the 1920s and 1930s, accomplished by Frank Knight, Ludwig Mises and, above all, Lionel Robbins – a revolution that laid the foundations for the mainstream of economic science in the second part of twentieth century. This change was essentially the result of criticisms of the ‘classical situation’, represented by Marshall’s work and legacy, that a new generation of economists raised while calling for a reconstruction of the economic science along different lines. They conceived economic theory as the field of application of exact logic and formalism, and widely adopted the methods of natural sciences, which they thought would alone guarantee the clearness and rigour necessary for both theory and empirical research in economics (see Marchionatti 2003). Many economists expressed doubts and objected to this new approach: Keynes was an undisputed leader of such critics. He considered economics essentially as a moral science, and not the natural science appearing in Robbins’s systematization. Keynes meant that economics belongs to those disciplines that deal with human beings in their social environment, with their “motives, expectations, psychological uncertainties” (Keynes 1973c: 300), with values and introspection; economics belongs, in other words, to human sciences (Marchionatti 2002 and 2010).

Robbins’s definition of economics as the science that studies human behaviour as a relation between ends and scarce means that have alternative uses made it evidently possible to include issues and fields traditionally pertaining to the domains of other social sciences among the *explananda* of economics. The theoretical fertility of economics’ expansion into new areas, and as corollary its relationships with contiguous social sciences, have been widely discussed after economics imperialism had entered the mainstream.

In Lazear's perspective, economics would provide well-reasoned answers to issues identified by other social disciplines – Lazear shares Harold Demsetz's idea that evidence of economics' success comes from "the strong export surplus economics maintain in its trade in ideas and methods with the other social sciences" (Demsetz 1997: 1). A huge debate has developed around this claim. Critics belonging to both the orthodoxy and the heterodoxy of the discipline have severely and widely criticized economics imperialism for impoverishing our ability to understand phenomena outside the traditional boundaries of economics. Ronald Coase's contribution in this regard is particularly relevant. The winner of the 1991 Nobel Prize in economics expressed the view that economics expands its boundaries when economists look "for fields in which they can have some success" (Coase 1978: 203). Imperialists believe that economics is "more developed", or "more advanced in its theoretical development" (Buckley and Casson 1993: 1041), so that, Demsetz (1997: 2) argues, this primacy can be established "even if economics had never influenced other social sciences". To the contrary, Coase believes that economics' primacy owes to its greater analytical generality, as well as to the explanatory power that derives from the "measuring rod of money" (Coase 1978: 209). Yet this also means that once other scientists will have discovered "the simple, but valuable, truths which economists have to offer" (ibid.), these latter will simply lose their comparative advantage. As Fine and Milonakis (2009) argue, Coase is here exposing the problems affecting neoclassical economics, which is victim, so to speak, of an inevitable tension. On one side, neoclassical economics counts upon the presumed universal applicability of its "open-ended set of concepts . . . most of which are derived from a common set of assumptions about individual behavior [that] can be used to make predictions about social behavior" – as Chicago school economist Richard Posner (1987: 2), a leading figure in the field of law and economics, maintains. On the other, it suffers from "the practical implication of thereby being rendered unrealistic or vacuous from the perspective of other more rounded disciplines and methodologies" (Fine and Milonakis 2009: 7). Economists, Coase maintains, will likely "study other social systems . . . not with the aim of contributing to law or political science, but because it is necessary if they are to understand the economic system itself" (Coase 1978: 210). They will realize that property rights help disclosing the means by which markets function, that the family and educational systems influence supply of labour and consumption patterns, and so on. In short, economics expansionism will have as its purpose that of deepening the understanding of the economic system. Therefore, Coase's argument denounces the intrinsic limits of the "economic approach to human behavior" which Lazear and Demsetz praise the virtues of in defending standard Chicago imperialism.

Due also, perhaps mainly, to its imperial attitude, economics has been growing in size and diversity since the heyday of economics imperialism. The development of the theoretic-information approach and the advent of neo-institutional economics seem to have somehow damaged the compactness of mainstream economics, which now includes a variety of different research programmes significantly deviating from the neoclassical core. The rise and coexistence within mainstream economics of evolutionary game theory, experimental economics, behavioural economics, evolutionary economics, neuroeconomics and complexity theory might signal a transition "from neoclassical dominance to mainstream pluralism" (Davis 2006). Unprecedented specialization in a more and more fragmented discipline (see Cedrini and Fontana 2015, and the references there cited) has increased awareness of the 'decreasing returns' of economics imperialism (see Frey and Benz 2004, Marchionatti 2008 and 2012, Fine and Milonakis 2009) and opened up the possibility of cooperation with other disciplines. These latter (psychology *in primis*) have in effect established "limited intellectual 'colonies'" (Mäki 2013: 336) in economics, their 'reverse imperialisms' (see Frey and Benz 2004, Davis 2013) being at the origins of virtually all the research programmes currently populating the mainstream of the discipline. Greatly criticized for excluding rival disciplines, economics imperialism has thus been variously reformulated, in the attempt to produce a less pugilistic economic approach to intrinsically complex behaviours and facts.

For sure, mainstream economics is changing face (see Colander 2000; Colander, Holt and Rosser 2004; Hodgson 2007, Gintis 2007, Davis 2008a and 2008 b, Cedrini and Fontana 2015) and exploring new research paths. The rise and success of complexity economics and evolutionary game theory promote a new conception of social interaction, one that involves heterogeneous agents endowed with limited/bounded rationality, helps focus on institutional structures, and draws attention on unpredictable, emerging properties of social systems shaped by interactions themselves. Collaboration with other disciplines is a crucial but critical factor of this transformation. Geoffrey Hodgson (2007: 20) points in fact at the scarcity of truly interdisciplinary dialogue as an obstacle to such progress, and advocates a "reconsideration of the nature of and boundaries between the social sciences, and their possible reorganization on different lines". Remarkably, various 'mainstream reformers', so to speak, believe that the desired post-neoclassical mainstream of the discipline will result from reconciling the competing non-neoclassical research programmes in today's economics, many of them born under the influence of other social disciplines. Thereby, it is argued, economics will be able to help solve the "scandalous" (Gintis 2007: 15) problem of today's "social sciences pluralism" (Colander 2014), by contributing to developing a common model of human behaviour.

The American economist and behavioural scientist Herbert Gintis (see Gintis 2007 and 2009) finds in "both mathematical models and common methodological principles for gathering empirical data on human behavior and human nature" (Gintis 2007: 15) the preconditions for constructing a unifying framework for behavioural sciences. He observes that recent laboratory and field research (see, respectively, Fehr and G*ä*chter 2000, Henrich et al. 2005) have emphasized the importance of cooperation and reciprocity, upon which sociologists have traditionally focused their attention, and revealed the biological-evolutionary roots of the concept of preference consistency. The main analytical tools of the new theoretical framework (that should replace the flawed traditional model of individual choice behaviour) are thus an evolutionary perspective (gene-culture coevolution), and game theory ("the universal lexicon of life"; ibid.: 8).

Yet Gintis insists on the continuing relevance of "the most important analytical construct in the behavioral sciences operating at the level of the individual" (Gintis 2009: 222), that is, the rational actor model, based on choice consistency, to represent behaviour; he even resurrects general equilibrium theory in presenting his suggestions for a renewed sociology (Gintis and Helbing 2015). Although the new framework includes an implicit condemnation of economics imperialism, it is remarkable that Gintis assigns the task of leading the reform to biology in particular, to be joined by the 'new' post-neoclassical economics which might arise from today's "mainstream pluralism" (Davis 2006). Edward O. Wilson's sociobiology is admittedly an influence on the proposal (see Getty 2007), while the affinity with Jack Hirshleifer's 'economics imperialism' project of the late 1970s through the early 1980s – proclaiming the impossibility "to carve off a distinct territory for economics, bordering upon but separated from other social disciplines. Economics interpenetrates them all, and is reciprocally penetrated by them . . . There is only one science", with economics as its "universal grammar" (Hirshleifer 1985 [1967]: 53) – might be a matter of concern.

It has been argued that a "new" form of economics imperialism has developed with the advent of the information-theoretic approach in the 1980s, treating the "social" (explained on the basis of methodological individualism) as a "rational" response to imperfect market relations (Fine 2000: 14), with the result that, while economics "takes the social seriously as something distinct from the economic", it nevertheless "provides a rationale for it" (ibid.). In this regard, Gintis's new framework, allowing room for other disciplines while at the same time requiring them to respect an imperative of consistency and compatibility, may represent significant progress. But, as evident from some ambiguities in Gintis's own framework, the pluralistic essence of today's mainstream economics might fail to provide sufficient conditions for truly democratic exchange between social disciplines. This requires enhanced understanding of the historical origins of such imperialistic attitude, in particular, and the removal of its deep roots, so as to avoid that such dialogue be victim of the above-mentioned presumed comparative advantage of economics. After Robbins's tremendously influential definition of economics as the science of rational choice, in fact, the refusal to make assertive a priori hypotheses about human behaviour other than the requirement that they behave consistently – as though they were maximizing something, this "something" to be named after empirical observations of human behaviour (see Binmore 2005) – continues to exert an almost irresistible appeal.

The first two sections of this book focus on a territory that persists to be largely intractable if explored by using the postulates of economics: that of 'primitive' societies.[3] Primitive societies represent one such territory, and a fundamental one, due to the historical difficulties experienced in handling their dynamics by using the conceptual tools of economic theory. The importance of the subject lies in that primitive, 'savage' societies are those that Western thought traditionally considers to be the furthest from modern market societies – 'the others' *par excellence*. Firstly, the book discusses in historical perspective the various representations of such societies offered by economists since the dawn of the discipline, from Adam Smith to contemporary economists. It is claimed that the general economic approach to the study of such societies configures a fundamental case of economics imperialism, which excludes the alternative strand of anthropological and sociological reflections on the topic. It concludes that when applied to primitive societies, economics imperialism rests on the ideological (not scientific) hypothesis that the primitive man is already, at least in embryo, a *homo oeconomicus*. In the third section, it is shown that in developing the so-called 'economics of unselfishness', the discipline has not succeeded in removing the theoretical and methodological foundations of the *homo oeconomicus* paradigm and economics imperialism. The main thesis the book aims at analysing in depth and generalizing is that the explanatory power of economics imperialism in territories that are traditionally occupied by other disciplines shows 'decreasing returns'. Economics imperialism offers a reductionist interpretation of primitive economies that, however seductive, is truly poor in interpretative power.

By retracing the origins of economics imperialism back to the birth of the discipline, our analysis offers suggestions to current 'economics reformers'. The attempt to construct a theoretical framework to make compatible the heretofore alternative approaches of behavioural disciplines requires economists to address the original sin of economics imperialism, if economics is to participate in the formulation of a new, unified framework to analyse human behaviour. We thus maintain, in the fourth section and in the conclusions, that it is only by approaching the neglected tradition of sociological and anthropological studies on the socio-political foundations of our societies that economics can hope to contribute to a democratic cooperation between social sciences. It is only on these bases, therefore, that it can aspire to participate in the launch of a new, interdisciplinary in essence, research program on human behaviour. With this aim in mind, the book ends with proposing the possible lines of a research programme on the foundations of a non-imperialist economics.

The book explores in particular the concept of gift and gift exchange, around which primitive societies are structured. While a great part of the anthropological-sociological literature has considered gift-giving as the foundation of a radically different sociality from the one underlying the contested economicist paradigm of "rational fools" (Sen 1977), economics has substantially failed to participate in the interdisciplinary debate organized by social sciences around the gift throughout the twentieth century. We show that by tacitly establishing the universality of economics on the hypothesis that the primitive man is already a *homo oeconomicus*, economics has refused to address the complexity of the gift. We thus argue that the reintroduction of the concepts of gift and gift exchange into the economic discourse can encourage an innovating discourse on economics, contributing to laying down the foundations of an anti-imperialist turn. Having highlighted the central role played by the gift in organizing an important transdisciplinary debate on the socio-political foundations of modern societies, we elaborate on the legacy of Marcel Mauss's pioneering study (and the literature it has inspired) for a redefinition of economics on non-imperialist bases. Last, we throw light on the political essence of Keynes's late plans of global reform, thereby providing a concrete illustration of the still-to-be-explored potential offered by a rediscovery of the 'political anthropology' of the gift in today's economic discourse.

A note on the quotations in this volume

We use both single and double quotes in the book, the former for concepts, the latter for direct quotations. We thus diverge from the usual UK style, but also remove any possible cause of confusion that might arise in the text.

Notes

1 It should be reminded that Souter did not use the phrase 'economic imperialism' in the sense usually meant. In his criticism of Lionel Robbins's Essay, he wrote that the "salvation of economic science . . . lies in an enlightened and democratic 'economic imperialism', which invades the territories of its neighbours, not to enslave them . . . but to aid and enrich them and promote their autonomous growth in a very process of aiding and enriching them" (Souter 1933: 94n).

2 Focusing on the University of Chicago, which is considered as the historical epicentre of economics imperialism, Nik-Khah and Van Horn (2012), situate Chicago economics imperialism in the context of a wide political project started in the 1950s, led in first instance by Aaron Director and George Stigler, aiming at forging a new liberalism.

3 Following the tradition in economics, we use the term 'primitive' to refer essentially to those societies that ethnologists call 'hunter-gatherer' societies. Traditionally, this latter category of hunter-gatherers is used for societies whose subsistence was based on the hunting of wild animals, the gathering of wild plant foods and fishing; recent research has produced a more nuanced understanding of hunter-gatherer societies. In particular, the original 'hunter-gatherer versus agriculturalist' approach to classifying human cultures has been supplemented by a more sophisticated analysis that reflects a continuum of such activities, rather than a dichotomy. It is now recognized that hunter-gatherers use a variety of strategies allowing them to manage the resources on which their subsistence relies (see Lee and Daly, 2001; Fowler and Turner, 2001).

Part I

At the roots of economics imperialism

Classical and neoclassical economics and the issue of primitive societies

Part I is devoted to economists' explanatory models of primitive societies in the history of economic thought.

Chapter 1 deals with Smith's classical model of the "early and rude state of society" and Marx's analysis of pre-capitalistic societies in his philosophical and economic works. Smith and Marx are shown to share the idea that primitive societies are affected, as Smith puts it, by the absence of division of labour, which is the engine of growth. The analyses of the two great classical economists are preceded by an excursus on the interpretations of savage peoples by philosophers from Montaigne to the Enlightenment, the purpose being to understand the intellectual context of the analysis of the economists.

Chapter 2 deals with the neoclassical-formalist model of rational choice applied to primitive man. The model was developed in the 1940s and 1950s by the anthropologists Raymond Firth and Melville Herskovitz; Robbins's and Knight's neoclassical economics clearly influenced their approach. Firth and Herskovitz described the primitive economy as a locus wherein rational choice is limited by customs and institutions, compelling individuals to behave irrationally. Increasing attention paid to non-market institutions by neoclassical economists since the 1970s has produced new interpretative models of primitive societies based on transaction costs and information-theoretic approaches. Richard Posner's theory provides the most significant and ambitious model, which explains many distinctive primitive institutions as adaptations to the uncertainty of the environment or to the existence of high information costs. The influence of sociobiology in economics, essentially through the work of Jack Hirshleifer, and in anthropology with the birth of the behavioural ecology of hunter-gatherers, significantly strengthens Posner's thesis of a rational (maximizing in the economic sense) behaviour of primitives.

Part I

1 Classical and neoclassical economics

1 The distant origins of economics imperialism

Classical economists and primitive societies

1.1 Travellers, philosophers and the savages

1.1.1 The travel literature, a source for philosophers' reflections

In the second part of the eighteenth century, when Smith's foundation of political economy took shape, information on the 'savage nations' of North America, Asia, West Africa and the Pacific was rather extensive. At the end of the 1870s, "the Great Map of Mankind" (a phrase used by the English philosopher and political thinker Edmund Burke in a letter of 9 June 1777, to the Scottish historian William Robertson, on the occasion of the publication of Robertson's *History of America*) was considered well known: "the Great Map of Mankind is unrolled at once." This was primarily all the result of the vast accumulation of travellers' accounts over more than two centuries following the discovery of America, the great event that changed the perception of the world by Europeans and caused the encounter with 'other' new peoples. There follows a survey of the most important and influential among them.

In the first part of the sixteenth century, Giovanni da Verazzano's and Jacques Cartier's voyages of exploration in the service of the king of France to the Americas provided the first accounts of the native peoples of North America. Then published were Jean de Léry's (1536–1613) *Histoire d'un voyage faict en la terre du Brésil autrement dite Amérique* (1578) and André Thevet's (1516–92) *Singularités de la France antarctique* (1557) – France antarctique was a French colony established in Guanabara Bay at Rio de Janeiro which existed between 1555 and 1567. These two were the texts at the basis of Montaigne's *essai* on the cannibals. These works testify to France's role in the sixteenth century as an important centre of interest in the non-European worlds, in particular North America. This role intensified in the seventeenth century with publication of some of the most important works from the ethnographic point of view, rich with information on the manners and customs of the Canadian Indians. The first were the *Voyages de la Nouvelle France* (1619 and 1632) by the French explorer Samuel Champlain (1574–1635), "the father of New France", and the *Histoire de la Nouvelle France* (1619) by the author and poet Marc Lescarbot (1570–1641), based on his expedition to Acadia, a colony of New France in north-eastern North America. They were followed by the *Grand Voyage au pays des Huron* (1632) by the French Franciscan missionary

Gabriel Sagard-Theodat (1590–1640). Together with the *Rélations des Jesuites de la Nouvelle-France* – missionaries' reports written in French and Latin, which appeared in print between 1632 and 1673 – these were the most important sources of knowledge on the Canadian Indians.

At the end of the seventeenth century, England already had an empire in the Caribbean and in North America, but it had mainly cross-border relationships with the North American natives. This popularized a superficial and misrepresented image of the Indians, and also a widespread hostility towards them.[1] The first important English collections, Richard Hakluyt's *Divers Voyages Concerning the Discovery of America* (1582) and *Principal Navigations, Voyages, Traffics, and Discoveries of the English Nation* (1589), consisted mostly of non-English sources; but the above-cited contemporaneous French literature was largely unknown in England at that time. Jesuit accounts were not translated into English and they became known only in the 1820s through the works of Charlevoix and Lafitau, the main sources for Adam Smith (and the Scottish philosophers of his time) in his discussion of the savage state of human history in his *Glasgow Lectures*.

The philosopher John Locke (1632–1704) played a crucial role in expanding knowledge about the American peoples in England. A great collector of travel books, Locke contributed to making the American savage the most interesting figure among the primitive peoples known in England at that time.[2] His famous phrase in the *Two Treatises of Government* (1689) – "in the beginning all the world was America" – meant that America was considered the beginning of civilization, a pattern of the first Ages in Asia and Europe: the state of nature, Locke maintained, was an historical human reality which existed in the America of his days. He was one of the promoters, together with the members of the Royal Society, of the printing of the four volumes of the famous collection of travels and voyages edited by Awnsham and John Churchill in 1704. The collection included many narratives printed in English for the first time, and which expanded and completed Richard Hakluyt's collection of 1589. It also included a preface (often attributed to Locke) entitled "The Whole History of Navigation from its Original to This Time". In the early eighteenth century, the Royal Society began to publish travel accounts in its *Philosophical Transactions*, thus enhancing knowledge of the New World and the recently discovered lands. The Churchill collection was reissued, being augmented from four to eight volumes in 1732 and 1747. Also the less original collection published by John Harris in 1705 was reissued in 1740. In 1745–47, Thomas Astley published the four-volume *New General Collections of Voyages and Travels* compiled by John Green and immediately translated into French by Antoine Francois Prévost, well known as Abbé Prévost (*Histoire général des voyages*, 1747–59), becoming the most comprehensive French source of world travel literature.

In the meantime, two fundamental works had been published in France: the above-mentioned books by Charlevoix and Lafitau – respectively the *Histoire de la Nouvelle France* (1722) and *Moeurs des sauvages americains* (1724).

Pierre-Francois-Xavier de Charlevoix (1682–1761) and Joseph-Fracois Lafitau (1681–1746) were Jesuit missionaries in Canada in the two first decades of the 1700s. The book by Lafitau, who was in Canada from 1712 to 1717, is now considered the most important work produced by the French Jesuit community in the first half of the eighteenth century.[3] Lafitau drew upon five years of 'fieldwork', and he furnished a detailed description of Iroquois practices. He rejected the characterization of the American Indians as peoples without religion, laws and government, considered an error committed by the first missionaries. He challenged this stereotype by providing an accurate reconstruction of the forms of government, marriage customs, educational systems, types of dwelling, clothing, wartime and peacetime activities, trade, diseases, funeral rituals, and languages spoken among the Iroquois and Hurons. Lafitau examined all these aspects of social life for traces of ancient times and concluded that there was not even one aspect of the American customs did not have an equivalent in classical Antiquity.[4]

To complete the picture, mention should be made of some other books influential at that time. First of all, the *History of the Five Indian Nations* (1727–47) written by the Scottish-born scientist, and close friend of Benjamin Franklin, Cadwallader Colden; his history of the Iroquois tribes was the first documentary on native American culture written in English and was considered America's first history book. Also important was the *Histoire de la Lousiane* (1751–53, translated into English in 1763) written by the French (or Dutch) historian and naturalist Antoine-Simon La Page du Pratz (1695?–1775) who spent many years in Louisiana under the colonization scheme organized by John Law and the Companies of the Indies, and who had familiarity with the Natchez people. A peculiar but important contribution was made by Louis Armand de Lom d'Arce, Baron de Lahontan (1666–1715), a French imperial officer who lived in New France and studied the Huron, Algonquin and Iroquois peoples. In 1703 and 1704, he published three books, an amalgam of ethnographical analysis and radical social and political criticism which influenced many authors of the Enlightenment: *Nouveaux voyages dans l'Amérique septentrionale*, his memoirs of his sojourn in New France; the sequel, *Mémoires de l'Amerique septentrionale*, and the imaginary dialogue between the author and a Huron chief *Supplément aux voyages ou Dialogues avec le sauvage Adario.* Lahontan's emphasis on the natural lifestyle of savages, and their profound sense of liberty and egalitarianism, greatly influenced the tradition of social criticism of European institutions: in particular, indebted to his idealized representation of Amerindians, which incorporated many of the staple elements of the noble savage figure, was Rousseau's *Discours sur l'origine de l'inégalité* (see Ellingson 2001 and Harvey 2010).[5]

The nineteenth-century knowledge of savage peoples was completed by the voyages of discovery of new lands in the Pacific Ocean, undertaken by James Cook, Louis Antoine de Bougainville (who published in 1771 the well-known *Voyage autour du monde*) and Jean-Francois de La Pérouse, whose world circumnavigations greatly extended the hitherto scant information available on that part of the world. The two-volume work produced in 1756 by the French *érudit* Charles De Brosses, *Histoire des navigations aux terres australes*, had contained what may be the first occurrence of the words 'Polynésie' and 'Australasie'. It furnished information that was useful for Cook's and Bougainville's explorations – and drew a new map of the world.

These descriptions of the peoples of new worlds, became the empirical foundation for a general rewriting of human history crucial for the Enlightenment project of a world historical science of mankind (see Rubiés (2002). These travel accounts influenced philosophical reflection from Montaigne to Rousseau, Diderot and the Scottish Enlightenment philosophers – and we have already mentioned Locke. Travel accounts and this philosophical reflection upon them were Smith's sources on primitive societies. As regards the former source, as far as we know, Adam Smith had extensive knowledge of this travel literature. His library contained the most important collections of voyages (see Bonar 1932): Hakluyt's, Churchill's, Harris's; the *Philosophical Transactions* volumes, and other more- or less-known travellers' accounts. He possessed Pierre-Francois-Xavier de Charlevoix's *Histoire de la Nouvelle France* (1722) and Joseph-Francois Lafitau's *Histoire des découvertes e des conquetes des Portugais dans le Nouveau Monde* (1733). Lafitau's *Moeurs des sauvages americains* (1724) was not included in Smith's library; however, we know that he was familiar with that text because Lafitau's *Moeurs*, together with Clarlevoix's *Histoire,* are the sources mentioned in his discussion of the savage stage of human history in his *Glasgow Lectures*. In general, these works were the ones most used and appreciated by the Scottish Enlightenment philosophers.[6] In regard to the latter source, to which Smith himself, as a philosopher, contributed, Montesquieu's reflection was crucial in the organization of his theoretical position (as well as that of many others).

1.1.2 Montesquieu's philosophy of history and savage nations

Charles-Louis de Secondat, Baron of Montesquieu, one of the great political philosophers of the Enlightenment, was the author who, in the mid-nineteenth century, more than any other, contributed to defining the issue and the method of analysis of the societies different from those of the West. In his great work *De l'ésprit des lois* (1748), Montesquieu laid the foundations for a philosophy of history.

Montesquieu's starting point was the existence of a multiplicity of laws and customs, so that "the whole seems to be an immense expanse, or a boundless ocean" (Montesquieu 1750: 630), as many authors of the seventeenth century had observed. Unlike those authors, however, Montesquieu thought that he had been able to grasp the connecting 'thread' running through history. When men legislate, Montesquieu maintained, they are not driven by the caprice of fancy: the order of laws is variable, but not artificial. In every law a thought is revealed: when it is uncovered, so too is its meaning, that is, its 'spirit'. Laws vary according to the circumstances: it is therefore not surprising that they are so different.

To grasp its essence, a law must be considered in light of a combination of relationships, Montesquieu explains:

> [Laws] should be in relation to the nature and principle of each government: whether they form it, as may be said of political laws; or whether they support it, as in the case of civil institutions. They should be in relation to the climate of each country, to the quality of its soil, to its situation and extent, to the principal occupation of the natives, whether husbandmen, huntsmen, or shepherds: they should have relation to the degree of liberty which the constitutions will bear; to the religion of the inhabitants, to their inclinations, riches, numbers, commerce, manners, and customs. In fine, they have relations to each other, as also to their origin, to the intent of the legislator, and to the order of things on which they are established; in all of which different lights they ought to be considered.
>
> (Ibid.: 23)

When the relations composing the social organism are discovered, they must be gathered together and classified in order of importance. Montesquieu's method consisted of showing the relationships between a certain particular expression of public and private life and the mentality of a nation as determined by its social necessities. Hence by reconstructing the social frame, understanding connections and concatenations, he sought to unravel the tangle of laws and to grasp its essence. As he writes in the preface of his book:

> I have laid down the first principles, and have found that the particular cases apply naturally to them; that the histories of all nations are only consequences of them; and that every particular law is connected with another law, or depends on some other of a more general extent.
>
> (Ibid.: 14)

Montesquieu thought that he had found an immanent logic which arises through historical events: it is not chance that rules the world, nor God's Providence, he maintained. On the contrary, Montesquieu writes in Book 1, chapter 3, of the *Esprit des lois*, human reason governs the behaviour of all the inhabitants of the earth. Therefore, as mankind becomes conscious of this fact and of the power of reason, it can search for the means to regulate social life and shape its future. In this confidence in power of the reason, Montesquieu, as Ernst Cassirer wrote in his *Philosophie der Aufklarung* (1932), was a true child of his time, a thinker of the Enlightenment.

Like the other nations, also the savage ones are subject to recognizable natural laws. In Book XVIII "Des lois dans le rapport qu'elles ont avec la nature du terrain" (Of Laws in the Relation of their Bearing to the Nature of the Soil), Montesquieu proposed a new definition of "savage and barbarous nations". In the seventeenth century, savage peoples had been often described as characterized by a *défault* of laws, religion and customs. The error of the definition as regards religion and customs was then demonstrated, but the *défault de loix* remained as an issue much debated by scholars. Savage nations, Montesquieu wrote, had a code of laws less extensive than those of nations of traders or peasants. This was due to the fact that "the laws have a very great relation to the manner in which the several nations procure their subsistence" (ibid.: 301). With Montesquieu, the "manner of procuring subsistence" (or mode of subsistence) for the first time acquired an explanatory role.

The "manner of procuring subsistence" of savage peoples consisted in hunting, fishing, gathering and sheep-breeding. This caused the small size of those nations: the peoples who do not cultivate the earth, Montesquieu wrote

> can scarcely form a great nation. If they are herdmen and shepherds, they have need of an extensive country to furnish subsistence for a small number; if they live by hunting, their number must be still less, and in order to find the means of life they must constitute a very small nation.
>
> (Ibid.: 302)

However, this does not prevent them from enjoying a certain abundance, due to the spontaneous fertility of the earth:

> The cause of there being such a number of savage nations in America is the fertility of the earth, which spontaneously produces many fruits capable of affording them nourishment. If the women cultivate a spot of land round their cottages, the maize grows up presently; and hunting and fishing put the men in a state of complete abundance.
>
> (Ibid.)[7]

These peoples are, Montesquieu wrote, "wanderers and vagabonds" (ibid.: 304), and "enjoy great liberty" (ibid.):

> These peoples enjoy great liberty; for as they do not cultivate the earth, they are not fixed: they are wanderers and vagabonds; and if a chief should deprive them of their liberty, they would immediately go and seek it under another, or retire into the woods, and there live with their families.
>
> (Ibid.)

There are few civil laws among these nations, because problems of the division of land do not exist:

> The division of lands is what principally increases the civil code. Amongst nations where they have not made this division there are very few civil laws. The institutions of these people may be called manners rather than laws. Amongst such nations as these the old men, who remember things past, have great authority; they cannot there be distinguished by wealth, but by wisdom and valour.
>
> (Ibid.: 303)

According to Montesquieu, their liberty is based, above all, on the absence of money:

> The greatest security of the liberties of a people who do not cultivate the earth is their not knowing the use of money. What is gained by hunting, fishing, or keeping herds of cattle cannot be assembled in such great quantity, nor be sufficiently preserved, for one man to find himself in a condition to corrupt many others; but when, instead of this, a man has a sign of riches, he may obtain a large quantity of these signs, and distribute them as he pleases.
>
> The people who have no money have but few wants; and these are supplied with ease, and in an equal manner. Equality is then unavoidable; and hence it proceeds that their chiefs are not despotic.
>
> (Ibid.: 305)

Therefore, the "manner of procuring subsistence" establishes the social organization and the laws. It makes possible a liberty guaranteed by the absence of money and by the impossibility of wealth accumulation.

1.1.3. The theory of stages and the ignoble savage: The philosophical and sociological premise of political economy

Montesquieu's discussion of savage peoples influenced all the contemporaneous authors: the entry *Sauvage* in the *Encyclopédie* is nothing but a revival of parts of the *Esprit des Loix*; Helvetius, Turgot, Ferguson, Robertson, Smith, all knew Montesquieu's discussion and used it. The concept of the "manner of procuring subsistence" had a great influence on those authors and it was at the origin of the stages theory. According to Dugald Stewart, pupil and biographer of Adam Smith, author of the *Account of the Life and Writings of Adam Smith* (1793), unlike the majority of politicians before him:

> Montesquieu . . . considered laws as originating chiefly from the circumstances of society; and attempted to account, from the changes in the condition of mankind, which take place in the different stages of their progress, for the corresponding alterations which their institutions undergo. It is thus that, in his occasional elucidations of the Roman jurisprudence, instead of bewildering himself among the erudition of scholiasts and of antiquaries, we frequently find him borrowing his lights from the most remote and unconnected quarters of the globe, and combining the casual observations of illiterate travellers and navigators, into a philosophical commentary on the history of law and of manners.
>
> (Stewart, 1982 [1793]: 294)

Smith, Turgot and many other thinkers of the time, in particular those of the Scottish Enlightenment, interpreted Montesquieu's lesson in this way, and contributed to building what was called the 'four stages theory': a new theory of socio-economic development, which had become part of most writers' stock-in-trade by the end of the 1750s. In its most general form, this theory maintained that the key factor in the process of historical development is 'the mode of subsistence'. More specifically, the theory states that a society naturally progresses over time through four stages, each corresponding to a different mode of subsistence: hunting, pasturage, agriculture, and commerce. Different sets of institutions, laws and customs correspond to each of these modes of subsistence. In light of more or less limited historical evidence, this approach replaced facts with conjectures based on the philosophical analysis of human nature: Stewart called this type of investigation "conjectural history" (Stewart 1982: 293).[8] It responded to the problem: "Whence . . . the different forms which civilized society has assumed in different ages of the world? On most of these subjects very little information is to be expected from history" (ibid.: 292).[9]

According to Ronald Meek (1976: 68) and other scholars, Turgot and Smith – building on a wide tradition in which an important role was also played by the Grotius-Putendorf-Locke line of inquiry into property – were "the two earliest 'inventors' of the four stages theory": "Both men would appear to have been still in their twenties when, quite independently of one another and almost exactly the same time, they first formulated their respective versions of the theory" (ibid.),[10] and it is commonly agreed that Smith gave the clearest form to it in his *Lectures on Jurisprudence* (1762). Moreover, other French and Scottish thinkers of that period developed the theory. The most important of them were Pierre Du Pont de Nemours, Nicolas de Condorcet, Lord Kames, Adam Ferguson, William Robertson and John Millar, all of whom recognized Montesquieu's authority and acknowledged that they owed the concept of mode of subsistence to him.[11]

In the second half of the eighteenth century, two sociological and ethnographic works had major importance in the discussion of savage nations within the stage theory: Adam Ferguson's *Essays on the History of Civil Society* (1767) and William Robertson's *History of America* (1777). Both these authors are considered precursors of ethnological studies, and their works deserve recognition as significant landmarks in the development of cultural anthropology (see Hoebel 1962).

Ferguson's (1723–1816) book clearly identifies the absolute historical novelty of civil society, or the commercial stage. In this stage, Ferguson writes, man is "a detached and a solitary being": "he has found an object which sets him in competition with his fellow-creatures, and he deals with them as he does with his cattle and his soil, for the sake of the profits they bring" (Ferguson 1793: 31). Very different was the situation in the savage societies discussed in Part II of his book, entitled "Of the History of Rude Nations". Ferguson's description of rude nations is based on those of ancient historians (in particular, the Roman historian Tacitus) and on travel accounts (Charlevoix, Lafitau and Colden are the main sources), because, he maintains, "beyond the reach of such testimony, we can neither safely take, nor pretend to give, information on the subject" (ibid.: 126). Rude nations are, Ferguson writes, the barbarous and savage peoples, that is, those peoples who base their subsistence chiefly on hunting, fishing and gathering or who are herdsmen; he calls the latter 'barbarous' in order to differentiate them, because they know what it is to be poor and rich. Ferguson emphasizes two facts about savage peoples: the substantial absence of property and government, and the anti-economical spirit:

> It might be apprehended, that among rude nations, where the means of subsistence are procured without too much difficulty, the mind could never raise itself above the consideration of this subject; and that man would, in this condition, give examples of the meanest and more mercenary spirit. The reverse, however, is true . . . Their aversion to every form of employment which they hold to be mean, makes them pass great part of their time in idleness or sleep; and a man who, in pursuit of a wild beast, or to surprise his enemy, will traverse a hundred leagues on snow, will not, to procure his food, submit to any species of ordinary labour.
>
> (Ibid.: 154–5)

This spirit, Ferguson says, is similar to that of the ancient Romans: "It was not among the ancient Romans alone that commercial arts, or a sordid mind, were held in contempt. " (ibid.: 154). These savage peoples represent the hunting stage of society in the stage theory. However, Ferguson's critical eye describes these peoples with some admiration: as Meek noted, "in Ferguson's view, savage society has certain obvious vices, but it also has certain actual and potential virtues" (Meek 1976: 154), that can be realized when the savage state has been left behind "under the impressions of property and interest".

We find a different approach in William Robertson's (1721–93) *History of America*, first published in 1777. An eminent Scottish historian, Robertson represents the new ethnological and sociological reflection which rejected the 'noble savage' interpretation – Rousseau's version of this idea was particularly challenged – and was ideologically strictly connected with the new science of political economy. Although of good ethnographic value, Robertson's work was considerably indebted to Buffon's and De Pauw's studies, in which ideological statements greatly influenced the argument.

The French naturalist Georges-Louis Leclerc, Compte de Buffon (1707–88), had sought in his *Histoire naturelle* (1749–89) to prove that the American savages were inferior to the Europeans. He maintained that America was a new land where nature was more severe than in Europe: in America, the physical environment was arid and infertile, inspiring fear; mammals were weak and small, inferior to the "usual" size – and so was the man. Buffon supposed that the smaller stature and lesser diversity of quadrupeds in the New World was attributable to an unfavourable climate. Endemic mammals (e.g., the sloth and armadillo) were limited by the climate, while wild animals originating from the Old World (e.g. deer, lynx and bear) and imported domesticated animals degenerated from their original form. Even Native Americans, believed by Buffon to be descendants of Old World humans, had degenerated in the New World. Building on Buffon's contentions, the Dutch philosopher and geographer Cornelius de Pauw (1739–99) in his *Recherches philosophiques sur les Amérindiennes* (1768) – a book which enjoyed an excellent reputation in Europe – argued for the permanent inferiority of American Indians.[12]

Robertson's *History of America*, published in 1777, one year after Smith's *Wealth of Nations*, was the result of many years of work. It is considered "one of the most remarkable ethnological works ever published in the eighteenth century" (Moravia 1970: 254). In Book IV, Robertson dealt with analysis of the "small independent tribes which occupied every other part of America" with the exception of Mexico and Peru: "among these, though with some diversity in their character, their manners and institutions, the state of society was nearly similar, and so extremely rude, that the denomination of savage may be applied to them all" (Robertson 1842 [1777]: 91). In fact, "in America, man appears under the rudest form in which we can conceive him to subsist" (ibid.). These peoples did not know the state:

> Their political union is so incomplete, their civil institutions and regulations so few, so simple, and of such small authority, that they ought to be viewed rather as independent agents, than as members of a regular society. The character of a savage results almost entirely from his sentiments or feelings as an individual, and is but little influenced by his imperfect subiection to government and order.
>
> (Ibid.: 92)

Two main characteristics distinguish a savage, according to Robertson: "the feebleness of constitution" (ibid.) and the limited use of reason. As regards the first point Robertson writes:

> The Americans were more remarkable for agility than strength. They resembled beasts of prey, rather than animals formed for labour. They were not only averse to toil, but incapable of it . . . This feebleness of constitution was universal among the inhabitants of those regions in America . . . and may be considered as characteristic of the species there.
>
> (Ibid.: 93)

As regards the second point, the limited use of reason, Robertson writes:

> In the early ages of society, while the condition of man is simple and rude, his reason is but little exercised and his desires move within a very narrow sphere. Hence arise two remarkable characteristics of the human mind, in this state. Its intellectual powers are extremely limited; its emotions and efforts are few and languid . . . What, among polished nations, is called speculative reasoning or research, is altogether unknown in the rude state of society, and never becomes the occupation or amusement of the human faculties, until man be so far improved as to have secured, with certainty, the means of subsistence, as well as the possession of leisure and tranquility.
>
> (Ibid.: 99)

Notwithstanding such limits, Robertson maintained that "man cannot continue long in this state of feeble and uninformed infancy. He was made for industry and action, and the powers of his nature, as well as the necessity of his condition, urge him to fulfil his destiny" (ibid.: 101). So savages are accepted among humanity.

The theoretical core of Robertson's inquiry is set out in chapter IV of Book IV devoted to the analysis of "political institutions", where the "mode of subsistence" emerges as the fundamental concept: "In every inquiry concerning the operations of men when united together in society, the first object of attention should be their mode of subsistence" (ibid.: 104). Laws depend on it:

> Accordingly as that varies, their laws and policy must be different. The institutions suited to the ideas and exigencies of tribes, which subsist chiefly by fishing or hunting, and which have hardly formed a conception of any species of property, will be much more simple than those which must take place when the earth is cultivated with regular industry, and right of property, not only in its productions but in the soil itself, is completely ascertained.
>
> (Ibid.)

All the people of America belong to the former class. Hunting is their principal occupation. The form of their political institutions may be deduced from this description of the mode of subsistence. The main characteristics of these institutional forms are:

- Small independent communities: "While hunting is the chief source of subsistence, a vast extent of territory is requisite for supporting a small number of people"(ibid.: 108)
- "[N]ations which depend upon hunting are strangers to the idea of property" (ibid.): "peoples in this state retain a high sense of equality and independence. Wherever the idea of property is not established, there can be no distinction among men, but what arises from personal qualities" (ibid.)
- "Among peoples in this state, government can assume little authority, and the sense of civil subordination must remain very imperfect. While the idea of property is unknown, or incomplete conceived, and the spontaneous productions of the earth, as well as the fruits of industry, are considered as belonging to the public stock, there can hardly be any such subject of difference among the members of the fame community . . . Where the right of separate and exclusive possession is not introduced, the great object of law and jurisdiction does not exist" (ibid.: 109).

Robertson emphasizes three other behavioural characteristics connected with this mode of subsistence: the incapacity to engage in regular work, the love of play and the love of war. As regards work, Robertson writes:

> In every attempt towards industry among the Americans, one striking quality in their character is conspicuous: They apply to work without ardour, carry it

> on with little activity, and, like children, are easily diverted from it . . . Their work advances under their hand with such slowness, that an eye-witness compares it to the imperceptible progress of vegetation.
>
> (Ibid.: 121)

This slowness of the Americans in executing work of every kind is imputed to various causes:

> among savages . . . time is of so little importance, that they set no value upon it . . . the tools which they employ are so awkward and defective, that every work in which they engage must necessarily be tedious . . . But, above all, the cold phlegmatic temper peculiar to the American renders their operations languid.
>
> (Ibid.)

As far as play is concerned, the Americans show "an immoderate love of play, especially at games of hazard" (ibid.: 127):

> The Americans, who at other times are so indifferent, so phlegmatic, so silent, and so disinterested, as soon as they engage in play become rapacious, impatient, noisy, and almost frantic with eagerness. Their furs, their domestic utensils, their clothes, their arms, are staked at the gaming-table, and when all is lost, high as their sense of independence is, in a wild emotion of despair or of hope, they will often risk their personal liberty, upon a single cast. Among several tribes, such gaming parties frequently recur, and become their most acceptable entertainment at every great festival.
>
> (Ibid.)

The savages show an "immoderate love" for war as well. The motive for engaging in war, "even in this primitive and simple state of society", is considered, first of all, interest "as a source of discord" (ibid.: 112), but it is not, according to Robertson, the most frequent or most powerful reason for the incessant hostilities among rude nations: "these must be imputed to the passion of revenge" (ibid.).

Twenty-five years after Robertson's book, the French *idéologue* Constantin Francois Chasseboeuf, Comte de Volney (1757–1820), wrote, as an appendix to a study on the United States, a short essay entitled *Observations générales sur les Indiens ou sauvages de l'Amérique du Nord* (1803): it represented a complete reversal of the noble savage perspective put forward by Montaigne, Diderot and above all, Rousseau. Volney's Miami Chief Little Turtle was the answer to Lahontan's Adario. The relationship between the *Observations* and Robertson's work is clear, as has been noted (see Moravia 1970), on the methodological level first of all. Volney's argument was centred around a crucial question: "What is the price they pay for this savage liberty?" (Volney 1803: 426). Savage liberty is a fact – savages have no government – but their social state is that of anarchy, where need and force are the law. Their lives are vagabond and adventurous, but they have no durable provisions and supplies, and their pleasures are limited. Their lives are entirely concentrated on the present and constantly under threat. Savages have been unable to constitute an organic social body. Rather, they are associated in groups and bands, without a spirit of property, preservation, or family; in other words, they have not created a civil society. According to Volney, the savage's way of life is miserable and his social state degenerate in a manner no different from that of the ancient Greek and Italian peoples: Lafitau's thesis thus returns, but this time applying a negative judgement to both savages and ancient peoples. Volney's ethnology breaks with the past, which is evaluated from the scientific point of view of civil society as the lowest state of human progress, and ideally complementing the rising political economy.

1.1.4 Neither noble nor ignoble savages: Montaigne's legacy and Diderot's culturalist interpretation versus the theory of stages

Meek (1976: 97) writes that "there is remarkably little trace of the [four stages] theory in the *Encyclopedia*." And he also notes that "Voltaire and Diderot . . . show few signs of having been affected by the theory, either in the 1750s or later" (ibid.). In fact, the work of the great French philosopher, leader of the Enlightenment and chief editor of the *Encyclopédie*, Denis Diderot (1713–84), more than that of any other philosopher of his times, includes an ethnologically founded description of the North American savages alternative to that comprised in the four stages theory. We refer in particular to the chapters attributed to Diderot in Raynal's *Histoire philosophique et politique des établissements et du commerce des Européens dans les deux Indes* (more often known simply as *Histoire des deux Indes*) (1770, 1774, 1780) on savages.[13]

Edited by the French writer, historian and philosopher, Guillaume-Thomas François Raynal, known as Abbé Raynal (1713–96), the *Histoire des deux Indes* – first published in six volumes in 1770 and then in revised editions in 1774 and 1780 – was a sort of encyclopaedia of liberal ideas in the age of Enlightenment compiled with the help of several collaborators. It provided information about Europe's colonies as well as a critique of their political institutions and, by extension, of the institutions of the European continent as well. It can be considered the first criticism of European imperialism. Diderot was certainly pre-eminent among Raynal's collaborators. His contribution amounted to approximately one-third of the 1780 edition (where the critical position taken by Raynal with respect to the institutions of Europe in the first two editions was radicalized) and it focused primarily upon the New World.[14] Thanks above all to Diderot's contribution, the *Histoire* is not only a historical work but also a philosophical one – a work at once historical and philosophical – and for this reason it is considered a cornerstone of Diderot's thought and the revolutionary will of the Enlightenment's century (Benot 1970). The *Histoire* problematized the main issues of the age of Enlightenment in the context of that first wave of globalization. Among the issues discussed was the relationship between savages and civil societies. Here Diderot's contribution was crucial. We refer to two chapters: Book XV, chapter 4, "Gouvernment, habitudes, vertus, vices, guerres des sauvages qui habitent le Canada" (Government, customs, virtues, vices and wars of the savages that inhabited Canada), and Book XVII, chapter 4, "Comparaison des peuples policés et des peuples sauvages" (Comparison between civilized peoples and savages).

Diderot's interpretation revived Montaigne's view. Montaigne's two essays, "Des cannibales" and "Des coches" have been hailed as an early appeal to cultural relativism; that is, the examination of customs within the context of the culture to which they belong, where no culture is considered superior and they all share a common nature. In fact, Montaigne viewed the inhabitants of the New World as the doubles of the Europeans rather than as wild, sub-human creatures with no form of culture. Montaigne's *Essais* contain "the first and greatest reflections on the impact of the discovery and colonization of the New World upon Europe and early modern consciousness" and offer "the first anthropological speculation on what the New World might be" (Conley 2005: 74).[15] Montaigne declared his cultural relativism from the outset, rejecting the widespread prejudice that everything different from our own way of life may be considered barbarous. He wrote in "Des Cannibales":

> there is nothing barbarous and savage in this nation, by anything that I can gather, excepting, that every one gives the title of barbarism to everything that is not in use in his own country. As, indeed, we have no other level of truth and reason than the example and idea of the opinions and customs of the place wherein we live: there is always the perfect religion, there the perfect government, there the most exact and accomplished usage of all things.
>
> (Montaigne 1877 [1580–88]: 253)

Based on Montaigne's culturally relativist perspective, two hundred years later Diderot offered an analysis of savages that refuted and went beyond the ideas and myths of the noble and ignoble savage.

Chapter 4 of Book XV of the *Histoire*, most of which was written or widely revised by Diderot, is devoted to a description of the government, customs, wars, virtues and vices of the Indian nations of Canada. It is based on many sources of information, from Lafitau and Charlevoix to Lahontan. First described is the environment and the material way of life. The Indian Nations of Canada lived in a rude part of the New World, where woods, springs and mountains abound and "every thing . . . appeared grand and sublime" (Diderot, in Raynal 1780: 121)[16] – "nature here displayed such luxuriancy and majesty as commanded veneration, and a multitude of wild graces, far superior to the artificial beauties of our climates" (ibid.). It was characterized by long cold winters but a pleasant temperature in the rest of the year, with a "pure aerial atmosphere" and "exhaled an air fit to prolong life" (ibid.). Notwithstanding the climate, the natives "were but thinly clad" (ibid.: 122), and "their stature in general was beautifully proportioned" (ibid.: 123), "their features were regular" and "they had more agility than strength and were more fit to bear the fatigues of the chase than hard labour" (ibid.). In fact, their main activity, the lifelong employment for the men, was hunting; but they also knew husbandry – they cultivated maize – and engaged in gathering and fishing. Hunting was "their chief delight" (ibid.: 122), an activity which involved every family in its preparation and conduct, and which explained the nomadic nature of those nations. There were long intervals between their hunting parties; the intervals were used in part to make or mend tools – arrows and bows, snowshoes, canoes, earthenware, and so on – but they were mostly devoted to total inaction and feasts and dances.

Diderot emphasized on the one hand the precarious way of life of savages, and on the other the state of abundance in which they lived. In fact, their way of life implied a succession of periods of abstinence and abundance – "though they lived in a country abounding in game and fish, yet in some seasons . . . this resource failed them" (ibid.: 124). At the same time, Diderot emphasized that the savages were "content with their lot, and satisfied with what nature afforded them" (ibid.: 123). This attitude depended on two elements: the fact that their "wants . . . were few" (ibid.: 124) – note that, in Diderot's analysis, this limitation appears due not to limitation of resources and capabilities but cultural choice: "they know how . . . to live upon little" (ibid.: 130) – and the rule of mutual assistance (ibid.: 124) – which also in this case was a moral duty and not a necessity in order to survive.

The explanation of this social relation lies in the political dimension of the Indian nations of Canada, to which Diderot paid close attention. "They were divided in several small nations whose form of government was nearly similar", Diderot wrote: "some had hereditary chiefs, other elected them; the greater part were only directed by their old men" (ibid.: 127). But, what they had in common was the absence of "coercive power" on individuals: "The will of individuals was not even overruled by the general one" (ibid.). In these societies social order and peace were maintained not by means of coercive power, but by "good manners, example, education, a respect for old men, a parental affection" (ibid.), "without the interposition of government" (ibid.). This absence of coercive power guaranteed, Diderot notes, independence and equality: "Authority never encroached upon that powerful instinct of nature, the love of independence; which, enlightened by reason, produces in us the love of equality" (ibid.).

In other words, the love of independence which characterizes peoples living in the state of nature – in Montaigne's sense[17] – generates the absence of coercive power which, in its turn, guarantees political independence and equality. Whence "arises that regard which the savages have for each other" (ibid.) particularly observable in their National assemblies" (ibid.: 128), these being the community's main institutions by which public affairs are managed. Diderot emphasizes the "disinterestedness" shown by individuals in this management of public affairs. This is "unknown in our government", he says, "where the welfare of the state is hardly ever promoted but from selfish views or party spirit" (ibid.).

The mutual respect shown in the life of community also exists between the nations, "when they are not in actual war". The different nations do not negotiate "for conquest or for any interest relative to dominion", but to protect their independence: "The earth, they say, is made for all men; no one must possess the share of two." From this, it follows that the key aspect of savages' politics "consists in forming leagues against an enemy who is too numerous or too strong, and in suspending hostilities that become too destructive" (ibid.); in other words, they form alliances for war, a frequent phenomenon in those societies, induced by their love of independence. In the international political relations of the savage nations, the ratification of a truce or a league of amity was characterized by the mutual exchange of ceremonial gifts, testifying to "the bond of union":

> When they have agreed upon a truce or league of amity, it is ratified by mutually exchanging a belt, or strings of beads, which are a kind of snail-shells . . . The size, weight, and colour of these shells, are adapted to the importance of the business. They serve as jewels, as records, and as annals. They are the bond of union between nations and individuals. They are a sacred and inviolable pledge which is a confirmation of words, promises, a treaty.
>
> (Ibid.: 128–9)

Here the main role of chiefs – apart from the one that they have in times of war – in savage societies emerges. In fact, "The chiefs . . . are the keepers of these records. They know their meaning; they interpret them; and by means of these signs, they transmit the history of the country to the succeeding generation" (ibid., 129).

This explains why a chief is always a good orator. National assemblies are also the occasions on which the quality of chiefs emerges, that is, their great oratorical skills: "Their speeches in public assemblies . . . were full of images, energy and pathos. No Greek or Roman orator ever spoke, perhaps, with more strength and sublimity than one of their chiefs" (ibid., 126).

Apparent in all these dimensions of savage social life are qualities which, Diderot-Volney notes, "none of the writers who have described the manners of the savages have reckoned . . . among their virtues" (ibid.: 129): "benevolence" and generosity, the great social virtues of savages, the behaviour that guarantees the existence of equality within the community:

> They liberally share their scanty provisions with those whose crops have failed, or who have been unsuccessful in hunting or fishing . . . This generous hospitality, which makes the advantages of a private man a public blessing, is chiefly conspicuous in their entertainments. A savage claims respect, not so much from what he possesses, as from what he gives away. The whole stock of provisions collected during a chase that has lasted six months, is frequently expended in one day; and he who gives the entertainment enjoys more pleasure than his guests.
>
> (Ibid.)

From the social point of view, generosity implies a tendential equality and the ethical rejection of inequality of conditions:

> The inequality of conditions, which we think so necessary for the well-being of society, is, in their opinion, the greatest folly. They are shocked to see that among us, one man has more property than several others collectively, and that this first injustice is productive of a second, which is, that the man who has most riches is on that account the most respected. But what appears to them a meanness below the brute creation, is, that men who are equal by nature should degrade themselves so far as to depend upon the will or the caprice of another.
>
> (Ibid.: 130)[18]

This issue is also the subject of chapter 4 of Book XVII, most of it written by Diderot, devoted to a comparison between civilized peoples and savages. Here Diderot inquires by means of this comparison into a classic issue of the Enlightenment, namely happiness: "whether those untutored nations are more or less happy than our civilised people" (ibid.: 297). The author asks: what does a man want to be as happy as he can be? And answers: "Present subsistence, and, if he should think of futurity, the hopes and certainty of enjoying the blessing" (ibid.). Well, "the savage . . . is not in want of this first of necessaries" (ibid.). What about the civilized man?

> What greater happiness than this does the civilized man enjoy? His food is more wholesome and delicate than that of the savage. He has softer clothes, and a habitation better secured against the inclemencies of the weather. But the common people, who are to be the support and basis of civil society . . . cannot be said to live happy . . . reduced to a state of servitude . . . To what outrages is the civilized man exposed!
>
> (Ibid.: 297–9)

Diderot continues, "even supposing that the dangerous labours of our quarries, mines, forges . . . were less pernicious than the roving life of the savages who live upon hunting and fishing" (ibid.: 300):

> there would still remain a wide difference between the fate of the civilized man and the wild Indian, a difference entirely to the disadvantage of social life . . . This is the injustice that prevails in the partial distribution of fortunes and stations; an inequality which is at once the effect and the cause of oppression.
>
> (Ibid.)

Consequently, the author writes

> if we prefer our condition to that of the savages, it is because civil life has made us incapable of bearing some natural hardships which the savage is more exposed to than we are, and because we are attached to some indulgences that custom has made necessary to us.
>
> (Ibid.: 301)

Apart from this, the savage is "happier than the rich man", because:

> The consciousness of independence being one of the first instincts in man, he who enjoys this primitive right, with a moral certainty of a competent subsistence, is incomparably happier than the rich man, restrained by laws, masters, prejudices, and fashions, which incessantly remind him of the loss of his liberty.
>
> (Ibid.)

1.2 Adam Smith: a conjectural primitive economy, or the model of the "early and rude state of society"

1.2.1 Savage societies, the first stage of human society

In the *Wealth of Nations* savage societies are represented as the opposite, in negative terms, of the civilized societies.[19] The fundamental feature of primitive societies is their state of wretchedness, poverty and distress, as opposed to civilized nations with their societies of "wealth, opulence and prosperity".[20] In regard to the "savage nations of hunters and fishers of North America", Smith writes that

> [they] are so miserably poor, that from mere want, they are frequently reduced, or, at least, think themselves reduced, to the necessity sometimes of directly destroying, and sometimes of abandoning their infants, their old peoples, and those afflicted with lingering diseases, to perish with hunger, or to be devoured by wild beasts.
>
> (Smith 1976 [1776]: 62)

Smith adds that they are in this miserable state even though

> every individual who is able to work, is more or less employed in useful labour, and endeavours to provide, as well as he can, the necessaries and conveniences of life, for himself, or such of his family or tribe as are either too old, or too young, or too infirm to go hunting and fishing.
>
> (Ibid.)

Moreover, "the ninety-nine parts [of the labour of the whole year] are frequently no more than enough to provide them with food" (ibid.: 175). Hence North America societies are unable to produce a surplus, if not only occasionally.

In the four-stage evolution of mankind, these societies are "the lowest and rudest" state of society; that "early and rude state of society which precedes both the accumulation of stock and the appropriation of land", where "skill, dexterity, and judgement with which [labour] is any where directed or applied" are not sufficient to overcome the scantiness of the annual supply. In his *Lectures at Glasgow University* of 1762–63, where Smith put forward a preliminary version of his stage theory, he described this social stage with an example of the method that Dugald Stewart termed 'theoretical or conjectural history' (Stewart 1982 [1793]).

This consists in replacing with explanatory hypotheses those facts which are little known or not at all, but are used also to replace facts not easy to handle from a theoretical point of view: "If we should suppose x or z persons of different sexes settled in an uninhabited Island", Smith writes, "the first method they would fall upon for their sustenance would be to support themselves by the wild fruits which the country afforded": "this is the age of hunters" (Smith 1982 [1762–63]: 14). With an increase of the population, hunting becomes too precarious to support that society. Men are obliged "to contrive some other method whereby to support themselves". The "spontaneous" solution is found in animal husbandry: "Flocks and herds therefore are the first resource men would take themselves to when they found difficulty in subsisting by the chase." But when a society becomes numerous, "they would find a difficulty in supporting themselves" in this way. "Then they would naturally turn themselves to the cultivation of land and the raising of such plants and trees as produced nourishment fit for them", and they would gradually advance into the stage of agriculture. As society progresses, the various activities, "which at first would be exercised by each individual as far as was necessary for his welfare" would be separated, and persons "would exchange with one another what they produced more than was necessary for their support, and get in exchange for them the commodities they stood in need of and did not produce themselves". With the expansion of market exchange, the final stage, "the age of commerce", emerges:

> When therefore a country is stored with all the flocks and herds it can support, the land cultivated so as to produce all the grain and other commodities necessary for our subsistance it can be brought to bear, or at least as much as supports the inhabitants when the superfluous products whether of nature or art are exported and other necessary ones brought in exchange, such a society has done all in its power towards its ease and convenience.
>
> (Smith 1982 [1762–63]: 16)

In the *Glasgow Lectures*, Smith's model of historical growth is extremely straightforward. The basic concept – the mode of subsistence – is derived from Montesquieu's *Esprit des lois*. Population growth brings about a search for more productive modes of subsistence, that is essentially a development of the division of labour. The latter gives rise to exchange. By jointly increasing, the division of labour and exchange generate the most productive mode of subsistence: that of the market societies.

From the standpoint of the civilized societies, savage societies are characterized by the absence of a division of labour and exchange. This explain the state of poverty, which is the key characteristic of primitive societies, and the absence of the "skill, dexterity and judgement" on which the abundance or scarcity of resources in a society depends: "what is the work of one man, in a rude state of society, being generally that of several in an improved one. (Smith 1976 [1776]: 15); "[i]n that rude state of society in which there is no division of labour, in which exchanges are seldom made, and in which every man provides every thing for himself" (ibid.: 276).

Therefore, exchange, the incentive to the division of labour, is scarce in primitive societies, where surplus, when it is occasionally created, is destroyed, thereby hampering the development process:

> Among nations of hunters and shepherds, therefore, whose food consists chiefly in the flesh of those animals, every man, by providing himself with food, provides himself with the materials of more clothing than he can wear. If there was no foreign commerce, the greater part of them would be thrown away as things of no value. This was probably the case among the hunting nations of North America, before their country was discovered by the Europeans, with whom they now exchange their surplus peltry, for blankets, firearms, and brandy, which gives it some value.
>
> (Ibid.: 178)

The absence of division of labour and exchange is the other side of the state of misery.

Smith's anthropology, as Marouby (2007) noted, is conjectural. It is aimed to elaborate a theory of development, but it also has an empirical basis. This causes some problems. On the one hand, a comparison between Smith's ethnographic sources – Charlevoix and Lafitau above all – and his own anthropology reveals "a pattern of selections, of misreadings and interpretative moves, and of outright omissions" (ibid.: 87): the evidence which makes it impossible to maintain the thesis of mere, precarious, unavoidable subsistence is regularly neglected or minimized.[21] On the other hand, Smith emphasizes a positive characterization of the savage man: his mental ability and inventiveness. In fact, on the one hand misery, poverty and absence of the state depend on the absence of the division of labour; but on the other, the absence of the division of labour makes it possible to maintain the unique positive characteristics attributed to the savage society in the *Wealth of Nations*. It emerges from another opposition, that between societies of divided men and societies of undivided men. In savage societies, "the varied occupations of every man oblige every man to exert his capacity, and to invent expedients for removing difficulties which are continually occurring" (Smith 1976 [1776]: 783):

> Invention is kept alive, and the mind is not suffered to fall into that drowsy stupidity, which, in a civilized society, seems to benumb the understanding of almost all the inferior rank of people. In those barbarous societies, as they are called, every man . . . is a warrior. Every man too is in some measure a statesman, and can form a tolerable judgement concerning the interest of the society, and the conduct of those who govern it. How far their chiefs are good judges in peace, or good leaders in war, is obvious to the observation of almost every single man among them.
>
> (Ibid.)

On the contrary, in a civilized society, where there is an almost infinite variety of occupations in overall society, that is, the division of labour is developed, "there is little variety in the occupations of the greater part of individuals" (ibid.), "all the nobler parts of the human character may be, in a great measure, obliterated and extinguished in the great body of the people" (ibid.: 783–4). According to Smith, in fact, the division of labour has adverse effects on men:

> In the progress of the division of labour, the employment of the far greater part of those who live by labour, that is, of the great body of the people, comes to be confined to a few very simple operations; frequently to one or two. But the understandings of the greater part of men are necessarily formed by their ordinary employments. The man whose whole life is spent in performing a few simple operations, of which the effects too are, perhaps, always the same, or very early the same, has no occasion to exert his under standing, or to exercise his invention in finding out expedients for removing difficulties which never occur. He naturally loses, therefore, the habit of such exertion, and generally becomes as stupid and ignorant as it is possible for a human creature to become.
>
> (Ibid.: 781–2)

According to Harkin (2005), savage North American societies constitute a conflicting problem in Smith's stadial theory of progress: the savage, in fact, offers not only an image of wretchedness, but also an admirable alternative to the modern form of subjectivity. Lafitau's and Charlevoix's descriptions of the savage nations of North America evidenced the ethical and social merits of primitives emerged, and they would impress Smith greatly. According to Harkin, there existed in Smith's thought an unresolved mix of attraction and condemnation for the primitive. In regard to this issue, it should be emphasized that the opposition between divided and undivided man, which was then resumed by Marx, was drawn at that time by many scholars, from the already quoted Ferguson to Thomas Jefferson (see his *Notes on the State of Virginia*, 1784), and it related to a tradition of admiration for the savage man that started with Montaigne. Regarding Smith, whilst in *The Theory of Moral Sentiments* (1759) and partly in the *Lectures on Jurisprudence* (1762), criticisms of civil society on the basis of ethnological facts of savage societies are frequent, in the economic discourse of *Wealth of Nations*, the negative aspects of savage society are largely prevalent, and the positive ones are substantially marginal. In order to understand Smith's attitude of minimization of the positive characterization of savages, we must enquire into the theoretical bases of his interpretation of the history, on which the economic discourse of political economy is based.

1.2.2 Market exchange, division of labour and the progress of human society

As shown above, division of labour and exchange are the two concepts on which Smith's theory of human society progress is founded. Their relationship is fully investigated in the *Wealth of Nations*.

In the *Early Draft* of the *Wealth of Nations* (1763) – a very clear and essential text which anticipates the main work – Smith develops his theory by starting from a comparison between savage society and civilized, or market, society.[22] He compares, as Locke did, "an Indian prince, the absolute master of the lives and liberties of a thousand naked savages" and "a common day labourer in Britain or in Holland" (Smith 1975 [1763]: 562), and maintains that the latter's luxury is "in much superior". Then Smith asks: how to explain this circumstance not "so easily understood"? How to explain the fact that in a civilized society a peasant or a labourer, that is, the poor in this society, "provide both for themselves and for the enormous luxury of their superiors" (ibid.: 563), despite the highly unequal distribution of wealth which characterises the "civilized and thriving" societies, or the existence of an "universal opulence" in these societies? This is, according to Smith, a paradox that must be explained.[23]

We might naturally expect, Smith writes, that among the savages, where "every individual enjoys the whole produce of his own industry" (ibid.), he "should have a much greater affluence of the necessaries and conveniencies of life than can be possessed by the inferior ranks of people in a civilized society" (ibid.). But experience, Smith continues, demonstrates the contrary. The explanation of this paradoxical fact lies in the division of labour:

> The division of labour, by which each individual confines himself to a particular branch of business, can alone account for that superior opulence which takes place in civilized societies, and which, notwithstanding the inequality of property, extends itself to the lowest member of the community.
>
> (Ibid.: 564)

The division of labour gives origin to an "immense multiplication of the productions" which "occasions in all civilized societies the universal opulence which extends itself to the lowest rank of the people" (ibid.: 566). It happens that:

> Each man performs so great a quantity of that work which peculiarly belongs to him that he can both offer something to those who do not labour at all, and at the same time have as much behind as will enable him, by exchanging it for the productions of other arts, to supply himself with all the necessaries and conveniencies which he stands in need of.
>
> (Ibid.: 566)

The origin of the opulence of civil societies lies in the division of labour. Three different circumstances, according to Smith, can explain "the immense increase of the quantity of work performed" (ibid.: 567): "the increase of dexterity in every particular workman", "the saving of the time which is lost passing from one species of work to another" and "the invention of innumerable machines, which facilitate labour and enable one workman to do the business of many" (ibid.). These factors are especially effective in the civilized societies, where the markets are extended – and consequently the division of labour is extended – as an effect of the individual interest operating in what Smith terms the "obvious and simple system of natural liberty" or the "liberal plan of equality, liberty and justice" in which, thanks to the existence of 'good' political and legal institutions, individuals are allowed to pursue their own interests.[24] In this context, the 'invisible hand' mechanism operates:

> As every individual, therefore, endeavours as much as he can both to employ his capital in the support of domestic industry, and so to direct that industry that its produce may be of the greatest value; every individual necessarily labours to render the annual revenue of the society as great as he can. He generally, indeed, neither intends to promote the public interest, nor knows how much he is promoting it . . . By directing that industry in such a manner as its produce may be of the greatest value, he intends only his own gain, and he is in this, as in many other cases, led by an invisible hand to promote an end which was no part of his intention.
>
> (Ibid.: 456)

Since this is the system of "natural liberty", it guarantees the realization of human nature. Therefore, the theoretical problem becomes that of connecting division of labour and market exchange to human nature. This connection allows Smith not only to confirm the superiority of civilized societies but also to explain the naturalness of such societies and the relationship between savage and civilized societies.

1.2.3 Market exchange, division of labour and human nature: The theoretical basis of Smith's interpretation of history

After establishing the crucial role of the division of labour in social development, Smith identifies its origin in "a certain principle in human nature"[25]:

> This division of labour from which so many advantages result is originally the effect of no human wisdom which forsees and intends that general opulence which it gives occasion. It is the necessary though very slow and gradual consequence of a certain principle or propensity in human nature, which has in view of no such extensive utility. This is a propensity, common to all men, and to be found in no other race of animals, *a propensity to truck, barter and exchange one thing for another.*
>
> (Ibid., 570–71; emphasis added)

Smith poses the question of the origin of this propensity to truck, barter and exchange. In the *Glasgow Lectures*, he derives it from some original principles, in opposition to Hobbes' view of human nature, and in harmony with the hypothesis of a natural human generosity formulated in the *Theory of Moral Sentiments*. These anthropological antecedents on which exchange is founded are reason and speech, connected with the human tendency to persuade. In his *Lecture on Jurisprudence*, Smith compares exchange to oratory[26]:

> If we should enquire into the principle in the human mind on which this disposition of trucking is founded, it is clearly the natural inclination every one has to persuade. The offering of a shilling . . . is in reality offering an argument to persuade one to do so and so as it is for his interest. Men always endeavour to persuade others to be of their opinion even when the matter is of no consequence to them . . . And in this manner every one is practising oratory on others through the whole of his life.
>
> (Smith 1975 [1762]: 352)

This disposition to barter is "by no means founded upon different genius and talents". In fact:

> It is doubtful if there be any such difference at all; at least it is far less than we are aware of . . . The difference between a porter and a philosopher in the first four or five years of their life is properly speaking none at all. When they come to be employed in different occupations, their views widen and differ by degrees. As every one has this natural disposition to truck and barter, by which he provides for himself, there is no need for such different endowments, and accordingly among savages there is always the greatest uniformity of character . . . We have shown that different genius is not the foundation of this disposition to barter, which is the cause of the division of labour.
>
> (Ibid.: 493)

The real foundation of this disposition, Smith reiterates, is "that principle to persuade which so much prevails in human nature":

> When any arguments are offered to persuade, it is always expected that they should have their proper effect. If a person asserts any thing about the moon, tho' it should not be true, he will feel a kind of uneasiness in being contradicted, and would be very glad that the person he is endeavouring to persuade should be of same way of thinking with himself. We ought then mainly to cultivate the power of persuasion, and indeed we do so without intending it. Since a whole life is spent in the exercise of it, a ready method of bargaining with each other must undoubtedly be attained.
>
> (Ibid.: 493–4)

Smith's reasoning was intended to persuade the reader of the natural origin of the division of labour and exchange, and therefore of the naturalness of civilized society. At the same time, he was able to show the historical continuity between savage and civilized societies.

The categories of exchange and the division of labour, considered as constitutive factors of human society, are the keys with which the stages of human society must be interpreted. Savage societies are, firstly, the reverse of civil society: they are societies of misery, without exchange and division of labour, and without a state, that is, the new triad which replaces the old one: they are societies without a king, law, or religion. Secondly, savage societies are the initial stage of human history. As a first stage of evolution, they contain what will be *in fieri*. This continuity is due to the immutability of human nature. Savage and civil society are therefore different but commensurable: human nature is always the same, Smith maintains, as Hume did; consequently, civilized man is naturally no different from the savage man. Simply, the savage man is not yet developed. This representation of the savage societies as being in a state of unavoidable backwardness entails the impossibility of recognizing positive features, primarily in the material sense; recognizing the existence of affluence and abundance is precluded in Smith's system. But also the recognition of 'noble savage' traits must be attenuated. Hence the capacity of the savage man compared with the ignorance and stupidity of a large part of the population in civilized societies is contrasted with the possibility of countering those negative features with an extensive system of education which can be implemented in the civilized societies.

1.2.4 The problem of the naturalness of market exchange, or the Smithian 'original sin'

According to Smith, man has a natural propensity "to truck, barter and exchange one thing for another" which differentiates man from the animals. Because it is natural, this propensity is possessed by both the savage and the civilized man, although only in civil societies can exchange find the conditions for its complete realization. This propensity is founded on the disposition to persuade: by exercising it, mankind attains "the method of bargaining with each other". Through it, Smith establishes the continuity of the category of exchange in the human history. He establishes the relationship between an immaterial exchange – to persuade others of our opinion (an exchange of opinions, therefore) – and a material exchange (to persuade others to exchange goods). The purpose of the former type of exchange is to intellectually satisfy oneself; the purpose of the latter type of exchange is to obtain a material gain, a profit. The former would give "method" to the latter, but this seems to stretch the meaning somewhat, because we face two radically different types of exchange. In fact, Smith emphasizes that the act is formally the same – an exchange of something, material or immaterial – but neglects the institutional context in which it happens. Put otherwise, he posits the market as the institutional context of both forms of exchange. Smith's deduction – from persuading someone of our own opinion to market exchange – whose purpose is to show the universal human disposition to exchange, does not seem acceptable.

This mechanism of generalizing market exchange, is used by Smith when he 'describes' the origin of exchange and division of labour in the savage societies, in order to show the continuity of that mechanism:

> Among a nation of hunters or shepherds a particular savage is observed to make bows and arrows with more readiness and dexterity than any other person. He sometimes exchanges them for venison or for cattle with his

> companions, and by degrees comes to find that he can in this manner procure more venison and more cattle than if he himself went to the field to hunt them. From a regard to his own interest and ease, therefore, it grows to be his chief business to make bows and arrows; and he becomes in this manner a kind of armourer. Another excels in making the frames and covers of their little huts or moveable houses. He is accustomed in this way to be of use to those of his own tribe, who reward him in the same manner with cattle and with venison, till at length he finds it for his interest to dedicate himself entirely to this employment, and he becomes a sort of house carpenter. In the same manner, a third becomes a smith; a fourth a tanner or dresser of hides and skins, the principal part of the clothing of savages; and thus the certainty of being able to exchange all that part of the produce of his own labour which he himself has no occasion for, for such parts of the produce of other men's labours as he has occasion for, enables every man to apply himself to a particular occupation and to cultivate and bring to perfection whatever natural genius or talent he may possess for that particular species of business.
>
> (Smith 1975 [1762]: 572)

This passage reveals an abuse by Smith of the conjectural method. He does not inquire into the exchange as it happens in the savage and archaic societies as, for example, partially described in his main ethnographic source, Lafitau. Smith avoids investigating the ethnologically known facts about exchange. On the contrary, he reconstructs a hypothetical exchange among savages which is simply a market exchange. His conjectural anthropology assumes the categories of civilized society and, in this way, maintains, but does not demonstrate, that exchange is natural. Thereafter, Smith deals with the problems of how this exchange happens and according to what rules. He does introduce the issue of value (of exchange). Hence the issue of value and the theory of value – the theoretical basis of economics – emerges from an unresolved issue, on the philosophical level. This can be called the 'original sin' of political economy.

Smith's conjectural anthropology was a-critically accepted by the classical economists after him, and the hidden issue was forgotten. The notion of the naturalness of the economic categories was later criticized by Marx.

1.3 In "the realm of necessity": Karl Marx's theory of pre-capitalist societies

1.3.1 Mode of production and conception of history

The key to Marx's analysis of the pre-capitalistic societies lies in the methodological hypothesis presented in the so-called *1857 Einleitung* [*Introduction*], chapter on "The method of political economy": "Human anatomy contains a key to the anatomy of the ape. The intimations of higher development among the subordinate animal species, however, can be understood only after the higher development is already known" (Marx 1973 [1857–58]: 46).

Bourgeois society is "the most developed and the most complex historic organization of production", Marx writes. Therefore "the categories which express its relations" (ibid.), and make its structure intelligible, also afford understanding of the structure and production relations of past societies. These represent the prehistory of capitalist society and their study is the study of the genealogy of capital.

Therefore, the categories of political economy must be used to examine past societies. But, Marx adds, "this is to be taken with a grain of salt", without, as the bourgeois economists do, glossing over all historical differences, and seeing "bourgeois relations in all forms of society" (ibid.). According to Marx, analysis of the historical emergence of the relations of production leads to "primary equations – like the empirical numbers e.g. in natural science – which point towards a past lying behind this system" (ibid.: 393). These indications, Marx continues, "together with a correct grasp of the present", "also offer the key to the understanding of the past". At the same time, this "correct view" leads to the points at which "the suspension of the present form of production relations gives signs of its becoming – foreshadowing of the future" (ibid).

The real basis of society is identified in its economic structure: that is, in those relations of production appropriate to a given stage in the development of the society's material forces of production. In the preface to *Zur Kritik der Politischen Okonomie* published in 1859, Marx, synthesized as follows the general conclusions of his studies until then:

> In the social production of their existence, men inevitably enter into particular relations, that are independent of their will; these relations of production correspond to a given stage in the development of their material forces of production. The totality of these relations of production constitutes the economic structure of society, the real foundation, on which rises a legal and political superstructure and to which correspond particular forms of social consciousness. The mode of production of material life determines the general process of social, political and intellectual life.
>
> (Marx 1951 [1859]: 8; our translation)

Although Marx gives exchange a strategic role in the development of the capitalistic mode of production, it no longer has the central role given to it by Smith. For Marx, as he writes in the *Grundrisse*, exchange is "merely a moment mediating between production with its production-determined distribution on one side and consumption on the other" (Marx 1973 [1857–-58]: 39–40); rather, it appears "as a moment of production". In fact:

> It is clear, firstly, that the exchange of activities and abilities which takes place within production itself belongs directly to production and essentially constitutes it. The same hold, secondly, for the exchange of products, in so far as the exchange is the means of finishing the product and making it fit for direct consumption. To that extent, exchange is an act comprised within production itself. Thirdly, the so-called exchange between dealers and dealers is

> by its very organization entirely determined by production, as well as being itself a production activity.
>
> (Ibid.: 40)

Production, distribution, exchange and consumption are, according to Marx, "members of a totality, distinction within a unity", that is production. A definite production thus determines definite consumption, distribution and exchange as well as "definite relations between these different moments" (ibid.). A "mutual interaction takes place" between the different moments: "this is the case with every organic whole" (ibid.: 41).

Material production is the object of Marx's analysis, the point of departure of which is not the individual and isolated hunter and fisherman with whom Smith and Ricardo began – he "belongs among the unimaginative conceits of the eighteenth-century Robinsonades" (ibid.: 25) – but "individuals producing in society, hence socially determined individual production" (ibid.). Condemnation of the abstraction of the isolated individual does not mean condemnation of any abstraction, but rather its reformulation. In fact, even if "whenever we speak of production, then, what is meant is always production at a definite stage of social development" (ibid.: 26), "all epochs of production have certain common traits". "Production in general" is an abstraction, but "a rational abstraction in so far as it really brings out and fixes the common element" (ibid.). This general category "is itself segmented many times over and splits into different determinations" (ibid.: 27).

In summary, Marx identifies in the economic structure – that is, the material production by associated individuals – the key to explanation of human history. This economic structure establishes the real relations – the production relations – which correspond to a determined level of development of material productive forces. Hence, the analysis of history becomes the analysis of different modes of production. The tools used in this analysis are general determinations, the general conditions common to every production, and the particular concrete determinations.

1.3.2 The periodization of pre-bourgeois history in Marx's Deutsche **Ideologie** *and in the* **Formen**

The materialistic conception of history takes shape in the *Deutsche Ideologie*, written by Marx (and Engels), and published in 1845. Here the periodization of pre-bourgeois history is outlined for the first time.

Marx maintains that the various stages of development in the division of labour correspond to different forms of property: tribal, ancient, feudal, bourgeois. The first form of ownership is tribal property. This corresponds to the undeveloped stage of production where a people sustains itself by hunting, fishing, cattle-raising, or at most, farming. At this stage, the division of labour is still very elementary and is merely an extension of the natural division of labour existing in the family (the kinship group). The social structure is therefore limited to an extension of the family. Population increase, the growth of wants, and the extension of external relations, of both war and barter, lead to the separation of industrial and commercial labour from agricultural labour, and hence to the separation of town and country. This gives rise to the second form of property: the communal and state property in antiquity. It springs especially from the union of several tribes into a city by agreement or by conquest, and which is accompanied by slavery. Communal city property is the main form of ownership, but movable and immovable private property already emerges, although it is at first subordinate to communal property. The rise of this private property makes the communal property decay. The division of labour is already rather developed. There is already antagonism between town and country, which will be followed by the antagonism between states which represent town interests and those which represent country interests, within the towns themselves, and between free men and slaves. Roman society was the ultimate development of this phase. The third form of ownership is feudal or rank property, which Marx presents as an alternative evolution of primitive communalism, due to low population density on a wide territory, and where the countryside (not the city) is the centre of social organization. The basis of social organization is the collective ownership by the feudal lords, supported by their military organization. The class opposition is between feudal nobility and serfs, and in the towns between the guilds of master craftsmen or merchants and the journeymen and apprentices. Both landed property and small-scale craft work are the main form of property under the feudalism. The division of labour is underdeveloped. The feudal monarchies represent the political units. The evolution of feudalism determines the transition to capitalism, the fourth form of property. The process begins in the cities: here the emergence of a bourgeois class is accompanied by a division of labour between production and trade, a development which provides the basis for long-distance trade and the division of labour among different cities. As a consequence, manufacturers independent of the guilds rise. The formation of the world market represents the complete development of this phase.

Marx's analysis in the *Deutsche Ideologie* is clearly indebted to Smith's theory and more in general to the four-stage theory, given the importance attributed to factors like population, division of labour and exchange. It must be regarded, as the Marxist historian Eric Hobsbawm wrote, "as a very rough and provisional hypothesis of historical development" (Hobsbawm 1965: 32), owing to the small amount of historical data examined by Marx. It is, in any case, the foundation of the historical sections of the *Manifest der Kommunistischen Partei.* The next stage of Marx's thought, more than a decade later, is represented by the *Formen, die der kapitalistichen Production vorhergehen.* This is "considerably more sophisticated" (Hobsbawn 1965: 32), being based on more varied historical studies than in the *Deutsche Ideologie. Formen* is a section of the bulky manuscript composed by Marx in 1857–58 in preparation for his *Kapital.* Never published during Marx's lifetime, it later came out under the title *Grundrisse der Kritik der Politischen Okonomie.* Here, Marx examines some alternative routes out of the tribal community: the Oriental, the Ancient, the Germanic, the Slavonic (a form which is not further discussed and has affinities with the Oriental form).

The distinctive characteristic of the Oriental system is the absence of property in land due to special conditions, that is, public works and irrigation schemes requiring centralization, and – this is considered the fundamental characteristic of this system – the self-sustaining unity of manufacture and agriculture within the village commune, which thus contains within itself, Marx writes, all the conditions for reproduction and surplus production. Herein lies a resistance to disintegration and economic evolution more stubborn than that of any other system. The basis of what Marx calls "Oriental Despotism" is the tribal or communal property.

The other two systems, the Ancient and the Germanic ones, are more structured forms of evolution of the tribal community. The ancient world is a dynamic system founded on the city and characterized by slavery. The economic limitations of chattel-slavery could be able to explain its replacement with more flexible and productive forms of exploitation represented by feudalism and capitalism. The basic unit of the Germanic system is neither the village community nor the city but each separate household, which forms an independent centre of production. These are separate households, more or less loosely linked with each another, which occasionally unite for war, religious ceremonies, the settlement of disputes, etc. They are different forms of the evolution of private property, but also a step forward in the evolution from the "realm of necessity" to the "realm of freedom". Marx did not abandon the idea of progress elaborated by the eighteenth-century theoreticians of history; rather, he reformulated it. This is clearly apparent in the famous passage on the subject of utopia in the third volume of Marx's *Das Kapital*:

> In fact, the realm of freedom does not commence until the point is passed where labour under the compulsion of necessity and of external utility is required. In the very nature of things it lies beyond the sphere of material production in the strict meaning of the term. Just as the savage must wrestle with nature, in order to satisfy his wants, in order to maintain his life and reproduce it, so civilized man has to do it, and he must do it in all forms of society and under all possible modes of production. With his development the realm of natural necessity expands, because his wants increase; but at the same time the forces of production increase, by which these wants are satisfied. The freedom in this field cannot consist of anything else but of the fact that socialized man, the associated producers, regulate their interchange with nature rationally, bring it under their common control, instead of being ruled by it as by some blind power; that they accomplish their task with the least expenditure of energy and under conditions most adequate to their human nature and most worthy of it. But it always remains a realm of necessity. Beyond it begins that development of human power, which is its own end, the true realm of freedom, which, however, can flourish only upon that realm of necessity as its basis. The shortening of the working day is its fundamental premise.
>
> (Marx 1894: 571)

1.3.3 The primitive mode of production in the Grundrisse *and* Das Kapital: *A dualistic conception*

Marx's ethnological interest in the primitive societies became significant at the beginning of the 1880s when he compiled the *Ethnological Notebooks*.[27] His interest had previously been rather limited, substantially until the end of the 1860s; that is, until publication of the first volume of *Das Kapital*. The marginality of the role of primitive societies in the construction of Marx's historical model, as shown in the great works of his maturity, made the primitive man of the *Grundrisse* and *Das Kapital*, what the American anthropologist Lawrence Krader described as a simple "abstraction of the primitive condition as a means and in opposition to the concretion of the capitalist economy, without reference to particular primitive peoples" (Krader 1974: 5).

Like Smith, Marx identified the primitive societies in opposition to capitalistic society. The fundamental difference between pre-capitalist and capitalist societies consists in their different forms of social reproduction.

In pre-capitalist societies, the individual "directly and naturally reproduces himself" (Marx 1973: 95) and "his productive activity and his share in production are bound to a specific form of labour and of product, which determine his relation to others in just that specific way". This condition is "very different" from the capitalist one, where "Activity, regardless of its individual manifestation, and the product of activity, regardless of its particular make-up, are always exchange value, and exchange value is a generality, in which all individuality and peculiarity are negated and extinguished" (ibid.).

Exchange value expresses the social bond between "individuals who are indifferent to one another" (ibid.). In fact, in capitalism there is a reversal of social relations: "the social character of the activity", "the social form of the product", "the share of individuals in production", appear in capitalism as things "alien and objective, confronting the individuals, not as their relation to one another", but "as their subordination to relations which subsist independently of them and which arise out of collisions between mutually indifferent individuals" (ibid.). General exchange becomes "a vital condition for each individual" (ibid.: 96). In exchange value, "the social connection between persons is transformed into a social relation between things" (ibid.). By contrast, in the pre-capitalist societies "the ties of personal dependence, of distinctions of blood, education, etc." (ibid.: 101) determine the relations between individuals, "individuals imprisoned within a certain definition, as feudal lord and vassal, landlord and serf, etc., or as a member of a caste etc. or as member of an estate etc.": "personal ties all appear as personal relations" (ibid.).

The "first form of the mode of existence", Marx writes in the *Formen*, is hunting, pastoralism and nomadism. Herein exists the "clan community", the communality of "blood, language, customs": it represents "the first presupposition . . . for the appropriation of the objective conditions of their life, and of their life's reproducing and objectifying activity (activity as herdsmen, hunters, tillers, etc.)" (ibid.: 404). Here, as in all pre-capitalist societies, the earth is the natural "workshop" of the individual. The relationship with the earth is a condition of existence for primitive societies as well: they appropriate the earth for a residence, or for roaming, or for animal pasture, etc.:

> Property is, it is true, originally mobile, for mankind first seizes hold of the ready-made fruits of the earth, among whom belong e.g. the animals, and for him especially the ones that can be tamed. Nevertheless even this situation – hunting, fishing, herding, gathering fruits from trees etc. – always presupposes appropriation of the earth, whether for a fixed residence, or for roaming, or for animal pasture, etc.
>
> (Ibid.: 429)

Earth is the "great workshop", "the arsenal which furnishes both means and material of labour" (ibid.: 404), and "the seat, the base of the community". Individuals "relate naively to it as the property of the community" and each of them "conducts himself only as a link, as a member of this community as proprietor or possessor" (ibid.). The individual appears originally "as a species-being, clan being, herd animal – although in no way whatever as a *zoon politikon* in the political sense" (ibid.: 433). Simply, "an isolated individual could no more have property in land and soil than he could speak" (ibid.: 423).

The relationship between the individual and the others is therefore that of proprietor and member of the community. At the same time, the individual works; but the individuals in this society are not in a relationship of workers because they do not distinguish their activities in the sphere in which they work: the earth, in fact, is not external to them because they are proprietors of their objective labour conditions:

> Property thus originally means no more than a human being's relation to his natural conditions of production as belonging to him, as his, as presupposed along with his own being; relations to them as natural presuppositions of his self, which only form, so to speak, his extended body.
>
> (Ibid.: 429)

The real appropriation through the labour process, Marx writes, "happens under these presuppositions, which are not themselves the product of labour, but appear as its natural or divine presuppositions" (ibid.: 404). Property, considered as the relationship between man and his natural conditions, is the presupposition of labour, not vice versa. What we call labour and labourer, Marx maintains, is far away in the future: the individual 'labourer' is "a product of the history".

At the dawn of ancient communities, Marx writes, "there springs up naturally a division of labour, caused by differences of sex and age" (Marx 1867: 244), a division that is consequently based on a "purely physiological foundation", which enlarges with the expansion of the community. The different kinds of labour appear as "the particular organs of a compact whole" (ibid.: 245). Primitive and ancient communities belong, we may say, to the natural order.[28] They are stationary productive organisms.

Marx considers an enlightening example to understand the reason for such a stationary character: "those small and extremely ancient Indian communities, some of which have continued down to this day" (ibid.: 247), "based on possession in common of the land, on the blending of agriculture and handicrafts, and on an unalterable division of labour". They represent "a compact whole producing all it requires"; that is, a self-sufficient simple productive form that occupies small areas, whose production "is chiefly destined for direct use by the community itself", and the surplus alone takes becomes a commodity. The law that regulates the division of labour in these communities that constantly reproduce themselves in the same form "acts with the irresistible authority of a law of Nature" (ibid.).

According to Marx, this was still the situation at the time of the guilds, when "the labourer and his means of production remained closely united, like the snail with its shell" (ibid.: 248). And no different, from the point of view of material production, was the situation in the ancient society. Referring to Greek society, Marx notes that the ideal of Athenians remained "even with regard to material production, the αυταρκεια [self-sufficiency], as opposed to division of labour" (ibid.: 258, n. 56). He quotes Thucydides: "παρων γαρ το, ευ, παρα τουτων χαι το αυταρεσς" – with the latter there is well-being, but with the former there is independence.

A sort of homeostasis exists in all pre-capitalistic societies; but primitive societies are distinctive because in them the internal social dynamics between productive forces and production relationship are totally absent. These simple productive organisms are outside history and remain untouched "by the storm-clouds of the political sky" (ibid.: 248).

The impetus to enter history in these societies originates from outside the community: it is the exchange, during a long historical process, to dissolve the primitive and pre-capitalistic community. This happens when, at a certain degree of the division of labour, the exchange of products begins, because, according to Marx, different communities have different ways of life and products. This 'natural' difference determines the exchange of products which gradually become commodities. Marx writes:

> the exchange of products springs up at the points where different families, tribes, communities, come in contact; for, in the beginning of civilisation, it is not private individuals but families, tribes, &c., that meet on an independent footing. Different communities find different means of production, and different means of subsistence in their natural environment. Hence, their modes of production, and of living, and their products are different. It is this spontaneously developed difference which, when different communities come in contact, calls forth the mutual exchange of products, and the consequent gradual conversion of those products into commodities.
>
> (Ibid.: 244)

Exchange initially emerges as a natural and gradual event, Marx writes. However, at a certain point, its development determines a break, when the connection between the various kinds of work becomes the exchange of the products as commodities: "where the physiological division of labour is the starting-point, the particular organs of a compact whole grow loose, and break off" (ibid.: 245). This is principally due to the exchange of commodities with foreign communities, Marx writes. It is a process in which "the sole bond, still connecting the various kinds of work, is the exchange of the products as commodities" (ibid.).

In the *Grundrisse*, when discussing the transition from capitalist circulation to capitalist production, Marx explains the "civilizing influence of external trade" thus:

> With semi-barbarian or completely barbarian peoples, there is at first interposition by trading peoples, or else tribes whose production is different by nature enter into contact and exchange superfluous products. The former case is a more classical form. Let us therefore dwell on it. The exchange of the overflow is a traffic which posits exchange and exchange value. But it extends only to the overflow and plays an accessory role to production itself. But if the trading peoples who solicit exchange appear repeatedly (the Lombards, Normans, etc. play this role towards nearly all European peoples), and if an ongoing commerce develops, although the producing people still engages only in so-called passive trade, since the impulse for the activity of positing exchange values comes from the outside and not from the inner structure of its production, then the surplus of production must no longer be something accidental, occasionally present, but must be constantly repeated; and in this way domestic production itself takes on a tendency towards circulation, towards the positing of exchange values. At first the effect is of more physical kind. The sphere of needs is expanded; the aim is the satisfaction of the new needs, and hence greater regularity and an increase of production. The organization of domestic production itself is already modified by circulation and exchange value; but it has not yet been completely invaded by them, either over the surface or in depth. This is what is called the civilizing influence of external trade. The degree to which the movement towards the establishment of exchange value then attacks the whole of production depends partly on the intensity of this external influence, and partly on the degree of development attained by the elements of domestic production – division of labour etc.
>
> (Marx 1973: 193–4)

Therefore, according to Marx, there are three steps in the passage from the primitive society to the society based on the production of commodities. First, the exchange of commodities begins on the boundaries of primitive communities, "at their points of contact with other similar communities, or with members of the latter" (ibid.: 61). However, "as products once become commodities in the external relations of a community, they also, by reaction, become so in its internal intercourse". Marx assumes that the proportions in which they are exchangeable are at first a matter of chance: "What makes them exchangeable is the mutual desire of their owners to alienate them" (ibid.). In the meantime, the need for foreign objects of utility gradually establishes itself:

> The constant repetition of exchange makes it a normal social act. In the course of time, therefore, some portion at least of the products of labour must be produced with a special view to exchange. From that moment the distinction becomes firmly established between the utility of an object for the purposes of consumption, and its utility for the purposes of exchange. Its use-value becomes distinguished from its exchange-value. On the other hand, the quantitative proportion in which the articles are exchangeable, becomes dependent on their production itself. Custom stamps them as values with definite magnitudes.
>
> (Ibid.: 62)

The definitive break occurs when the articles exchanged acquire "a value-form independent of their own use-value, or of the individual needs of the exchangers". The necessity for a value-form grows "with the increasing number and variety of the commodities exchanged" (ibid.). Hence the general equivalent arises, namely money:

> The problem and the means of solution arise simultaneously. Commodity-owners never equate their own commodities to those of others, and exchange them on a large scale, without different kinds of commodities belonging to different owners being exchangeable for, and equated as values to, one and the same special article. Such last-mentioned article, by becoming the equivalent of various other commodities, acquires at once, though within narrow limits, the character of a general social equivalent. This character comes and goes with the momentary social acts that called it into life. In turns and transiently it attaches itself first to this and then to that commodity. But with the development of exchange it fixes itself firmly and exclusively to particular sorts of commodities, and becomes crystallised by assuming the money-form.
>
> (Ibid.)

The emergence of the money-form, and its development, entails the break-up of pre-capitalistic societies. The generalization of exchange is the factor determining the passage from the primitive community to a (market) society based on the production of commodities. Assuming the fortuitousness of the origin of exchange excludes, as in Smith, consideration by Marx of the logic of exchange in the primitive society. In fact, exchange connects primitive societies to history through a process which is initially accidental and fortuitous and which recalls Smith's conjectural anthropology. In fact, the analysis of primitive societies in Marx seems to show a fundamental difficulty of interpretation. On the one hand, primitive societies are conceived as the first stage of historical evolution, the first stage of what Marx called the "realm of necessity" and the first stage of the evolution of property. Its main characteristic is economic backwardness, caused by the limited development of the productive forces – like the absence of the division of labour and simple technology in the classical economists. And the consequences of this state are, again as in the classics, the limitedness of needs, the absence of surplus, and the incapacity of development – in short, the absolute dominance of necessity. Only the development of productive forces could allow a society to reduce its backwardness. On the other hand, in Marx's analysis in the *Formen*, these societies appear radically different from the others that follow: they exhibit a sort of continuity between nature and society, because absent in them are the forces able to activate the historical dynamics and because they have a direct relationship with nature. In this sense, they are prehistorical, outside of history, unable endogenously to overcome their primitive state, and therefore difficult to treat within the materialistic conception of history. This dualistic conception recurs in Marx's last discussion of primitives, that of the *Ethnological Notebooks*.

1.3.4 The **Ethnological Notebooks***: Marx, Morgan and the noble Iroquois*

Marx developed his theoretical reflections on human history and pre-capitalistic societies from a limited factual basis. But in the last years of his life, he felt the need to pay systematic attention to the anthropological studies in a systematic way. In the period 1880–82, he read and critically reviewed in his *Ethnological Notebooks* the ethnological writings of Lewis Henry Morgan, John Budd Phear, Henry Sumner Maine and John Lubbock (Lord Avebury). Marx was particularly interested in (and influenced by) the work of the American anthropologist Lewis Henry Morgan, on whose *Ancient Society* (1877) he took copious notes: in fact, they fill more than a half of the *Notebooks*, and the majority of them are on the Iroquois.[29]

Two years later, Friedrich Engels made use of Marx's notes on Morgan in his own book, *Der Ursprung der Familie, des Privateigentums und des Staats* [The Origin of the Family, Private Property and the State] – subtitled *In the light of the researches of Lewis H. Morgan.* Engels found in Morgan's book confirmation of the materialist conception of history. In the preface to his book, he wrote:

> The following chapters are, in a sense, the execution of a bequest. No less a man than Karl Marx had made it one of his future tasks to present the results of Morgan's researches in the light of the conclusions of his own – within certain limits, I may say our – materialist examination of history, and thus to make clear their full significance. For Morgan in his own way had discovered afresh in America the materialistic conception of history discovered by Marx forty years ago, and in his comparison of barbarism and civilization it had led him, in the main points, to the same conclusions as Marx . . . My work can only provide a slight substitute for what my departed friend no longer had the time to do. But I have the critical notes which he made to his extensive extracts from Morgan, and as far as possible I reproduce them here.
>
> (Engels 1990 [1884]: preface)

The analogy between the conception of Marx and Engels and Morgan's can be found mainly in the first part of *Ancient Society*, entitled "Growth and Intelligence through Inventions and Discoveries", where Morgan outlines his version of the theory of stages: "Mankind commenced their career at the bottom of the scale and worked their way up from savagery to civilization through the slow accumulations of experimental knowledge" (Morgan 1877: 3).

Morgan identifies three different conditions of existence – a state of savagery, barbarism, and a state of civilization: "these three distinct conditions are connected with each other in a natural as well as necessary sequence of progress" (ibid.). The pathway of human progress is characterized on the one hand, by a sequence of inventions and discoveries, and on the other, by a series of institutions which express the growth of certain ideas and passions, principally the ideas of government, family and property.

Marx was not only interested in comparing the results of his historical inquiry with Morgan's. He was also interested in the second part of Morgan's book, where the author treats the subject of the growth of the idea of government. Chapters 2 through 5 are devoted to the structure and evolution of Iroquois society.[30] In Morgan's schema, the Iroquois are representative of the lower status of barbarism. Their government deals with persons and personal relationships: in fact, the social organization is based on the *gens* and its development: phratry, tribe and confederacy, this last being an aggregation of tribes for mutual defence. Two elements of Morgan's analysis are emphasized by Marx: the democratic character of the *gens*, and the existence of principles of liberty, equality and fraternity as its cardinal principles. On the first point Morgan writes, summarizing a long description of the exercise of democracy in Iroquois society, that the principle of democracy was apparent in three aspects:

> The principle of democracy, which was born of the gentes, manifested itself in the retention by the gentiles of the right to elect their sachem and chiefs, in the safeguards thrown around the office to prevent usurpation, and in the check upon the election held by the remaining gentes.
>
> (Ibid.: 72)

Moreover, the right to depose sachem and chiefs, in the event of "unworthy behaviour, followed by a loss of confidence" (ibid.: 73) revealed the democratic constitution of the *gens*.

On the second point Morgan writes:

> All the members of an Iroquois gens were personally free, and they were bound to defend each other's freedom; they were equal in privileges and in personal rights, the sachem and chiefs claiming no superiority; and they were a brotherhood bound together by the ties of kin. Liberty, equality, and fraternity, though never formulated, were cardinal principles of the gens. These facts are material, because the gens was the unit of a social and governmental system, the foundation upon which Indian society was organized. A structure composed of such units would of necessity bear the impress of their character, for as the unit so the compound. It serves to explain

> that sense of independence and personal dignity universally an attribute of Indian character.
>
> (Ibid.: 86)

The Iroquois Confederation was, according to Morgan, "a masterpiece of Indian wisdom. Such in truth it was; and it will remain in history as a monument of their genius in developing gentile institutions" (ibid.: 129). It was "essentially democratic; because it was composed of gentes each of which was organized upon the common principles of democracy, not of the highest but of the primitive type, and because the tribes reserved the right of local self-government" (ibid.: 152). The qualities of the Iroquois people manifested themselves in this democratic organization:

> The Iroquois were a vigorous and intelligent people, with a brain approaching in volume the Aryan average. Eloquent in oratory, vindictive in war, and indomitable in perseverance, they have gained a place in history. If their military achievements are dreary with the atrocities of savage warfare, they have illustrated some of the highest virtues of mankind in their relations with each other. The confederacy which they organized must be regarded as a remarkable production of wisdom and sagacity. One of its avowed objects was peace; to remove the cause of strife by uniting their tribes under one government, and then extending it by incorporating other tribes of the same name and lineage.
>
> (Ibid.: 152–3)

Marx (and above all, Engels) searched for and found support for Morgan's materialistic approach. In fact, Morgan described the history of mankind as a process – necessary, slow and gradual – from the savage state to civil society. However, Marx was also attracted by the parts of the book in which Morgan glorified the Confederation's liberty, equality and democracy, the active participation of women in tribal life, the sense of independence and the personal dignity of the Iroquois – in short, the radical difference of savage society. In Morgan's description of the Iroquois forms of government – which showed the functioning of a democratic society of free and equal individuals[31] – and in the imagining of the American savage's nobleness, Marx found the complexity and fascination of that figure of the noble savage which had struck Western thinkers from Montaigne to Diderot and Ferguson and (partly) Smith, making them conscious of what had been lost with the material progress of civil society.

Notes

1 Daniel Defoe's *The Adventures of Robinson Crusoe* (1719) played an important role in this regard. The book, a mixture of fact and fiction, was the most famous description of savages in English literature at the beginning of the eighteenth century. James Joyce (1964: 24–25) wrote that Crusoe is "the true symbol of the British conquest . . . who, cast away on a desert island, in his pocket a knife and a pipe, becomes an architect, a

carpenter, a knife grinder, an astronomer, a backer, a shipwright, a potter, a saddler, a farmer, a tailor, an umbrella-maker, and a clergyman. He is the true prototype of the British colonist, as Friday (the trusty savage who arrives on an unlucky day) is the symbol of the subject races."

2 America plays an important role in Locke's philosophical and political reflection, and he was also practically involved in colonial administration (see Arnell 1996).

3 After being widely read and discussed in the eighteenth century, Lafitau's work was largely forgotten in the nineteenth; twentieth-century anthropologists of Iroquois society rediscovered him, first as an ethnographic source, then as a methodological predecessor. See Fenton (1969) and Feest (2001). Lafitau is considered the father of comparative ethnology by Alfred Metraux (1963): he describes him as a precursor of French ethnology and his book a bridge between the simple travel accounts and the classical ethnological works published at the end of the nineteenth century.

4 This similarity enabled Lafitau to sustain the biblical monogenetic thesis of the original unity of humankind, that is, he sought to demonstrate that all of the peoples of the world stemmed from a common origin as described in Genesis. Similarities were explained by migration processes in ancient times, so that the new peoples were descendants of Eurasians, while the differences were considered to result from processes of decline and degeneration, essentially religious and moral. See Harvey (2008).

5 Lahontan's work influenced some of the greatest thinkers of his day: not only Rousseau, but also Voltaire, Diderot, Chateaubriand, and, last but not least, the great German philosopher Gottfried Wilhelm Leibniz. In a letter to his friend Friedrich Wilhelm Bierling – who in a previous exchange with Leibniz himself had wondered whether Adario and his author were invented characters and how the indigenous peoples of Canada could live "in peace since they had neither laws nor public courts" – Leibniz wrote that Lahontan was "a very real man" and, concerning the Indian political life: "It is completely true . . . that the Americans in these regions live together without government but in peace; they know no struggle, nor hate, nor battles, or very few, except against men of different nations and languages. It would almost say that it is a *political miracle*, unknown by Aristotle and passed over by Hobbes" (letter of 10 November 1710, quoted in Ouellet 1983: 99–100).

6 According to Meek (1976), Lafitau's book had a strong impact on Smith and the other members of the Scottish Enlightenment, because it seemed to show convincingly that the contemporary Amerindian societies could be considered living models of human society in its first stage of development. See also Pagden (1982) and Blaney and Inayatillah (2010).

7 This was a point already made by Montaigne in his *essai* on cannibals.

8 Skinner (1975), used the term "philosophical history", referring to the use by Smith of more general theories to provide general explanations.

9 The conjectural method was adopted in different ways by the Scottish thinkers – strong conjectural history being not approved by some of them, Adam Ferguson above all (see Garrett 2003).

10 Recent research has challenged Meek's thesis in the case of Turgot (see Pauchant 2015).

11 This claim by the stage theory's proponents that Montesquieu was a precursor of the theory of stages seems to be only partially correct. In the *Esprit des loix*, the use of the concept of the "manner of procuring subsistence" is substantially limited to Book XVIII: it is one of the social factors considered by Montesquieu in relation to laws. In this analysis, there is no trace of determinism, with the partial exception of

the discussion of savage peoples. Rather, as Cassirer emphasized in his *Philosophy of Enlightment* (1932), material causes are generally, in Montesquieu's work, subordinate to spiritual ones. Above all, as Groethuysen (1956) wrote, Montesquieu grasped the true nature of laws distinguishing the circumstances using the "*esprit de finesse*". Similarly, in his *Défence de l'Esprit des lois* (1750), Montesquieu wrote that "good sense" (*bon sens*) consists essentially in knowledge of the "nuances of things" ("*les nuances des choses*"). It is probably not incorrect to say that the *esprit de finesse* and the good sense to which Montesquieu referred were often forgotten by the theoreticians of stages. It is worth mentioning, here, that in the preface to the French edition of the *General Theory*, Keynes referred to Montesquieu in a laudatory way: "Montesquieu was the real French equivalent of Adam Smith. The greatest of your economists, head and shoulders above the physiocrats in penetration, clear-headedness and *good sense (which are the qualities an economist should have)*" (Keynes 1973c [1936]: xxxiv; emphasis added).

12 "When de Pauw revived and exacerbated the argument of the inferiority of the American it contained already, although he himself was largely unaware of it, a strange assortment of elements – strains of political theory and racial prejudice, humanitarian axioms and geogenic hypotheses, zoological laws and fragments of history: the dregs, in short, of three centuries of debate, all jumbled together with the leftovers of even older speculations picked up and swept along by this murky current to be finally deposited on the threshold of the new era" (Gerbi 1973: 79).

13 We do not, to the contrary, refer to the famous *Supplément au Voyage de Bougainville* (1772), a set of philosophical dialogues inspired by Louis Antoine de Bougainville's *Voyage autour du monde*, the usual reference in the literature when the issue of savages in Diderot is addressed. On Diderot's *Supplément*, see Muthu 2003.

14 See M. Duchet, 1971 and 1978. Duchet 1978 has identified all the parts of the *Histoire* that can be credited to Diderot with a reasonable degree of certainty.

15 The subject of Montaigne's reflection in his *essai* "Des Cannibales" is "the New World, discovered in these latter days, and in that part of it where Villegaignon [the French vice-admiral Nicolas de Villegaignon] landed, which he called Antarctic France" (Montaigne 1877 [1580–88]: 249). A French colony existed between 1555 and 1567 in Brazil on a small island in front of present-day Rio de Janeiro, and in an extensive region then inhabited by Tupinanbà indians. Their usages and habits were described in the *Cosmographie universelle* (1572) of André Thévet and in *Histoire d'un voyage faict en la terre du Brésil* (1578) by Jean de Léry, the sources of Montaigne's *essai* "Des cannibales".

16 The peoples inhabiting these lands are described thus: "Every thing is great in these peoples who are not enslaved. This is the sublime of nature, in all its horror and its beauties" (ibid.: 147).

17 For Montaigne, a natural life consisted in the most simple physical and psychological needs, not corrupted by an attachment to luxurious material goods, as he wrote "They [the Amerindians] are still in that happy state of desiring only as much as their natural needs demand; anything beyond this is superfluous to them" (Montaigne 1877: 260), thus maintaining a relatively egalitarian society in which hierarchies are absent.

18 Montaigne emphasizes this point.

19 In general terms, this opposition is recognized by Blaney and Inayatullah (2010) who emphasize that in *Wealth of Nations* primitive societies are understood essentially in contraposition to civilized societies. They write that, "the Indians do not speak in their own terms; their histories are submerged in the historical reconstructions of the Enlightenment scientist. Indeed, the Indians do not speak at all. Their views of their

own societies or of other, including European, societies are silenced" (Blaney and Inayatullah 2010: 44).

20 A second, traditional, opposition is considered by Smith: the opposition between societies without a state and societies with a state. Among the savages, Smith writes, "there is properly neither sovereign nor commonwealth", "there is seldom any established magistrate or any regular administration of justice" (Smith 1976 [1776]: 690, 709). Age is the sole foundation of authority: it is "among nations of hunters, such as the native tribes of North America . . . the sole foundation of rank and precedency. Among them, father is the appellation of a superior: brother, of an equal; and son, of a inferior" (ibid.: 711). Smith explains the absence of an authority by poverty as well as by the absence of private property: "Universal poverty establishes there universal equality, and the superiority, either of age, or of personal qualities, are the feeble, but the sole foundations of authority and subordination" (ibid.: 712).

21 On the other hand, there exist in Smith's works, but not in the *Wealth of Nations*, passages which refer to the abundance of free time in the primitive societies: free time which savages devoted to music and dancing. In one of his *Essays on Philosophical Subjects*, written in the mid-1700s, Smith writes: "Among savage nations, the great body of the people have frequently great intervals of leisure, and they have scarce any other amusement; they naturally, therefore, spend a great part of their time in almost the only one they have" (Smith 1982: 187).

22 For our purposes here, the *Draft* is more useful than the corresponding pages of the *Wealth of Nations* because in the 1763 text Adam Smith focuses on the comparison between savage and civil societies.

23 It is interesting to note that this was not a paradox according to Locke. In the chapter entitled "Of property" in the *Second Treatise of Government*, he described the "nations of the Americans", as "rich in land and poor in all the comforts of life": "nature having furnished as liberally as any other people, with the materials of plenty, i.e. a fruitful soil, apt to produce in abundance, what might serve for food, raiment, and delight; yet for want of improving it by labour, have not one hundredth part of the conveniencies we enjoy: and a king of a large and fruitful territory there, feeds, lodges, and is clad worse than a day-labourer in England" (Locke 1824 [1689]: 122).

24 In Smith, self-interest is not to be confused with selfishness, just as sympathy is not to be identified with a principle of benevolence. As it is well known, an old but enduring interpretation of Smith's thought claimed the existence of an 'Adam Smith Problem'. The reference was to an alleged inconsistency between the *Wealth of Nations*, where individuals are considered self-interested, and *The Theory of Moral Sentiments*, which is based on the principle of sympathy. This charge of inconsistency stems from a misunderstanding, that is, the attribution of incorrect meanings to the concepts of self-interest and sympathy. Many studies have shown this misunderstanding (see, for example, Griswold 2006 and Metha 2006).

25 It is not necessary to emphasize the importance of the concepts of "nature" and "laws of nature" in Smith's system. The philosophy of the seventeenth and eighteenth centuries elaborated the category of nature and the laws of nature on which physics was already founded. Order, harmony, equilibrium and the stability of the physical world result from a theoretical process of systematization of the events through this category. Enlightenment moral philosophy performed the same intellectual experiment for the moral world. See Cassirer 1932 and Preti 1977.

26 This connections is emphasized in Rothschild and Sen 2006, who provide an excellent synthesis of Smith's writings on economic subjects.

27 In 1882–83, Marx compiled some ethnological excerpts and commentaries, published by Lawrence Krader in 1974.
28 Marx's writings on primitive communities lack Smithian remarks on the extreme poverty of savages. However, there is no doubt that also for Marx these societies were, from the material point of view, at the lowest stage of evolution.
29 On Marx and Morgan, see Krader 1974 and Shaw 1984.
30 Morgan was at that time the leading scholar of Iroquois society. Twenty years before the *Ancient Society*, in 1851, he had published *The League of Iroquois*. On the Iroquois in the *Ancient Society*, see Fenton 1965.
31 On the influence of Iroquois institutions in the formation of American democracy, see Grinde and Johansen 1991.

2 Economics imperialism revealed

Neoclassical economists and primitive man

2.1 Occupy anthropology: Lionel Robbins, Raymond Firth and the formalist school

2.1.1 The source of the formalist interpretation: Lionel Robbins's Essay

In 1932, the English economist Lionel Robbins, professor at the London School of Economics, published "An Essay on the Nature and Significance of Economic Science", a fundamental contribution to methodology in the history of modern economics. It is the work in which the conception of economics, developed in the period of the marginalist or neoclassical revolution and then reorganized along non-utilitarian lines essentially by Vilfredo Pareto, "is defined with the maximum of awareness about the nature of the scientific work earlier conducted" (Napoleoni 1973: 104).

The main purpose of Robbins's essay is "to arrive at precise notions concerning the subject-matter of Economic Science and the nature of the generalisations of which Economic Science consists" (Robbins 1932: xiv). Robbins rejects the definitions of economics which "relate it to the study of the causes of material welfare", because, he maintains, there still remains an economic problem, for both for society and the individual, "of deciding between the 'economic' and the 'non-economic'"; that is, the problem of choosing between these two kinds of activity. Solving this problem requires an analytical definition of economics: "It does not attempt to pick out certain *kinds* of behaviour but focuses attention on a particular *aspect* of behaviour, the form imposed by the influence of scarcity" (ibid.: 16–17). The fundamental implication is the following:

> in so far as it presents this aspect, any kind of human behaviour falls within the scope of economic generalisations. We do not say that the production of potatoes is economic activity and the production of philosophy is not. We say rather that, in so far as either kind of activity involves the relinquishment of other desired alternatives, it has its economic aspect. There are no limitations on the subject-matter of Economic Science save this.
>
> (Ibid.: 17)

From the point of view of the economist, Robbins writes, the conditions of human existence exhibit four fundamental characteristics:

1 "The ends are various. The time and the means for achieving these ends are limited and capable of alternative application. At the same time the ends have different importance" (ibid.: 12).
2 The context in which the economic action of the individual occurs. Robbins presents it in a succinct and effective manner:

> Here we are, sentient creatures with bundles of desires and aspirations, with masses of instinctive tendencies all urging us in different ways to action. But the time in which these tendencies can be expressed is limited. The external world does not offer full opportunities for their complete achievement. Life is short. Nature is niggardly. Our fellows have other objectives. Yet we can use our lives for doing different things, our materials and the services of others for achieving different objectives.
> (Ibid.: 13)

3 Human action assumes the form of choice only when these conditions – multiplicity of objectives, limited means capable of alternative application – all exist at the same time.
4 Scarcity is the fundamental principle: "Scarcity of means to satisfy ends of varying importance is an almost ubiquitous condition of human behaviour. Here, then, is the unity of subject of Economic Science, the forms assumed by human behaviour in disposing of scarce means" (ibid.: 15).

It follows that "economics is the science which studies human behaviour as a relationship between ends and scarce means which have alternative uses" (ibid.: 16). In Robbins's approach, economics is essentially a deductive science: "the propositions of economic theory, like all scientific theory, are . . . deductions from a series of postulates" (ibid.: 78), some universal, other of a more limited nature. The main postulates are of general applicability, Robbins maintains, because they are "assumptions involving in some way simple and indisputable facts of experience relating to the way in which scarcity of goods . . . actually shows itself in the world of reality" (ibid.). They establish the propositions of economic theory and make them universally applicable. There are three main postulates. They respectively regard the theory of value, the theory of production, and the theory of dynamics:

> The main postulate of the theory of value is the fact that individuals can arrange their preferences in an order, and in fact do so. The main postulate of the theory of production is the fact that there are more than one factor of production. The main postulate of the theory of dynamics is the fact that we are not certain regarding future scarcities.
> (Ibid.: 78–9)

On the basis of these foundations, pure economics examines "the implications of the existence of scarce means with alternative uses" (ibid.: 83), as in pure mechanics the existence of certain given properties of bodies is explored. However, applying economic analysis to modern market society "involves the use of a great multitude of subsidiary postulates regarding the condition of markets, the number of parties to the exchange, the state of the law" (ibid.: 79): drawn from the examination of historical material, they are designated "historico-relative" (ibid.: 80). The main assumptions, too, are based upon experience and refer to reality, but "it is experience of so wide a degree of generality as to place them in quite a different class from the more properly designated historico-relative assumptions" (ibid.: 80–81). Therefore, the laws of economics are not limited to some particular conditions of space and time; rather, they have universal validity. They, we can say, are 'natural', as for Smith; but whilst in Smith economic categories are conceived as 'natural' because they refer to a society which, through a slow and gradual historical process, has completely achieved its natural essence, in Robbins's approach economic categories are universally applicable, independently from any reference to a certain historical phase, precisely because they refer to the man as such, primitive or developed. Robbins writes: "The generalisations of the theory of value are as applicable to the behaviour of isolated man or the executive authority of a communist society, as to the behaviour of man in an exchange economy" (ibid.: 20).

Of course, economic analysis "has *most interest and utility* in an exchange economy" (ibid.: 19), but its subject-matter is not limited to such phenomena. In fact "the exchange relationship is a technical incident", but a technical incident "which gives rise to nearly all the interesting complications, but still . . . subsidiary to the main fact of scarcity" (ibid.). The laws of choice in conditions of scarcity are, for Robbins, the key to explaining both the workings of the exchange economy and the behaviour of the isolated man.

It follows that the purpose of economic science is to furnish awareness of the consequences of individuals' actions without making any value judgements – "economic analysis is *wertfrei* in the Weber sense", Robbins writes (ibid.: 91). Economic analysis makes judgements on how an individual reaches certain ends given certain scarce means; that is, it judges the *consistency* of behaviour and the *adequacy* of means to ends, or, we may say, about the economic rationality of behaviour. The concept of 'rational', as synonymous with 'consistent and adequate', is central to Robbins's argument. It is a fundamental postulate, but not in the sense that economic science is applicable only when the action is completely consistent: it is not true, Robbins writes, that "the generalisations of economics are limited to the explanation of situations in which action is perfectly consistent. Means may be scarce in relation to ends, even though the ends be inconsistent" (ibid.: 92). In other words, it is the (neoclassical) economic analysis which represent the point of view of rationality. It is used to explain real situations where the economic action may be inconsistent. Robbins adds that we may nevertheless argue that human behaviour always has some degree of rationality in order to acquire an economic aspect. In this sense, it is "purposive". He writes:

> There is a sense in which the word rationality can be used which renders it legitimate to argue that at least some rationality is assumed before human behaviour has an economic aspect—the sense, namely, in which it is equivalent to "purposive". As we have seen already, it is arguable that if behaviour is not conceived of as purposive, then the conception of the means-end relationships which economics studies has no meaning. So if there were no purposive action, it could be argued that there were no economic phenomena.
>
> (Ibid.: 93)

Economic rationality essentially corresponds to consistency, that is, the ability to choose the means adequate to the ends. Economic science, Robbins writes, does not requires human action to be always perfectly rational. The hypothesis of "perfect rationality in the sense of complete consistency" (ibid.: 94) – which corresponds in economic analysis to the mathematical concept of maximization – is simply "one of a number of assumptions of a psychological nature which are introduced into economic analysis at various stages of approximation to reality", in order "to study, in isolation, tendencies which, in the world of reality, operate only in conjunction with many others" (ibid.). Economic Man is only

> an expository device—a first approximation used very cautiously at one stage in the development of arguments which, in their full development, neither employ any such assumption nor demand it in any way for a justification of their procedure—it is improbable that he would be such a universal bogey.
>
> (Ibid.: 97)

. . . that is, a Weberian ideal-type construct.

In Robbins's perspective, economic science is the rational point of view on a world which is only partially rational; it finds its "practical *raison d'être*" in the assumption that it is desirable for men to act rationally, the opposite being irrationally:

> This, then, is a further sense in which Economics can be truly said to assume rationality in human society. It makes no pretence, as has been alleged so often, that action is necessarily rational in the sense that the ends pursued are not mutually inconsistent. There is nothing in its generalisations which necessarily implies reflective deliberation in ultimate valuation. It relies upon no assumption that individuals will always act rationally. But it does depend for its practical *raison d'être* upon the assumption that it is desirable that they should do so. It does assume that, within the bounds of necessity, it is desirable to choose ends which can be achieved harmoniously. And thus in the last analysis Economics does depend, if not for its existence, at least for its significance, on an ultimate valuation—the affirmation that rationality and ability to choose with knowledge is desirable. If irrationality, if the surrender to the blind force of external stimuli and unco-ordinated impulse at every

> moment is a good to be preferred above all others, then it is true that the *raison d'être* of Economics disappears.
>
> (Ibid.: 157)

Hence economics can analyse different societies and examine the relative rationality of behaviours in them, and classify them on this basis. Market societies – where the economic mode of action is most developed and finds its 'natural' environment – are superior, from the economics point of view, to other preceding societies. They have reached the most developed "stage", and therefore the one most permeated with rational behaviour.

The universal character of economic analysis in Robbins's methodological approach derives from the fact that wherever scarcity exists – and according to Robbins "scarcity of means to satisfy ends of varying importance is an almost ubiquitous condition of human behaviour" (ibid.: 15), because "we have been turned out of Paradise" (ibid.)[1] – man must choose. And he can choose in a more or less economic way, where 'economic' means rational and consistent. Economic action requires conditions of scarcity: if they are general – and for Robbins's economics they are so – economics is applicable to every type of society. This is the key idea that formalist anthropologists drew from Robbins's essay.

2.1.2 Raymond Firth's primitive economy

Raymond Firth, a pupil of Bronislaw Malinowski at the London School of Economics in the 1920s, was a leading figure in British anthropology. In 1928, he began a long relationship with a Polynesian people living in Tikopia, one of the Solomon Islands in the western South Pacific Ocean. This relationship and Firth's field research resulted in many books and articles, some of them focused on the economic life of the Tikopia. In 1939, he published *Primitive Polynesian Economy*, a second edition of which came out in 1965.

This book is considered by Firth himself as "a contribution to a general theory of economic anthropology" (Firth 1965: x). The fundamental problem considered by Firth is this: can a society like that of the Tikopia be analysed using the tools of neoclassical economics? Does the fact that in this primitive society there do not exist institutional forms such as business firms, banks, developed means of communication, markets, the calculation in price terms, and so on "invalidate the use of economic analysis in a primitive, non-monetary field?" (ibid.: 25). "I do not think so", Firth answers. The main problems relating to the functioning of an economic system recognized by economists – "the determination of what goods and services are to be produced and in what quantities relative to one another; the determination of the relative proportions of the various factors of production required; the determination of how the total output of goods and services thus obtained shall be distributed among the participants in the economy" (ibid.) – also exist in primitive societies.

On outlining "a general theory of economic anthropology" in *Primitive Polynesian Economy*, Firth assumes the validity and usefulness of applying neoclassical economic science to the study of primitive economic systems. The work already done in the field of economic anthropology demonstrated the validity of this economic approach, Firth maintains. He adds that "some different arrangements of the concrete data than that conventionally adopted by economists may be needed and some broader supplementary assumptions", but "no radically different mode of thinking about the problems is required" (ibid.: 26). Nevertheless, Firth recognizes, two difficulties obstruct the use of economic theory in anthropology: the high degree of abstraction and the nature of the premises which constitute the starting point of the economic analysis. This latter is considered the more serious difficulty. The very general assumptions of economists may be recognized by the anthropologist "as being plausible for the analysis of primitive societies" (ibid.: 8). But the anthropologist cannot introduce the modern economist's subsidiary assumptions "of a technical, institutional order, such as the assumption of the existence of market and money prices, of banks and of joint stock companies, obviously directed by the conditions of modern industrial society" (ibid.), as well as the assumption concerning the degree of competition in an economic relationship. The anthropologist must substitute many of the assumptions which economists employ with other assumptions "more in accord with the conditions of these non-Western societies" (ibid.: 11), and founded on the empirical examination of each society. Such empirical investigation "must include a study not only of economic behaviour in the narrow sense, but also of the social institutions of the people as a whole" (ibid.: 12): "without it, one may be unable to account for many changes, to explain their relative magnitude, or to predict their possibility" (ibid.).

The task of economic anthropology, Firth emphasizes, is above all comparative. Firth makes a plea for a comparative economics "the categories of which will transcend those of the Occidental industrial system" (ibid.: 14, note). This means that what is required from economic anthropology is the analysis of "material from non-industrialized, often exotic communities" in such a way that it is directly comparable with the material of modern economics, "matching assumption with assumption and so allowing generalizations to be ultimately framed which will subsume the phenomena of both price and non-price communities into a body of principles about human behaviour which will be truly universal" (ibid.: 14). The anthropologist's contribution to economics is of analytical and comparative type, not theoretical and technical:

> The formal analysis and techniques of economics need no help from the anthropologist. Nor can there be any other systematic set of formal proposition of an economic order differing of necessity from the accepted economic ones just because they relate to a different social universe. In my view an analysis of a primitive economic system . . . can be made without sacrifice of the basic approach of modern economics. Most assumptions about resources, wants and choices made by an economist in his formal analysis are so general that they can apply to any human society. Even the oft-challenged maximization principle can be regarded as universally valid provided that it can be

> understood to include reference to such elements as status and prestige, and not only to material wealth, where the inclusion of these other elements in the maximand are necessary for improving the explanatory and predictive powers of theory.
>
> (Ibid.: 13)

"A main theme of modern economics" (ibid.: 15), Firth writes, is the study of "the disposal of scarce means in relation to alternative ends". Therefore, first of all:

> we have to consider how far means are scarce in the Tikopia community, and what means are scarcer than others, to what extent ends are really alternative, and what is the scale of preferences when choice is made between them . . . what these ends and means are, and the manner in which they are socially conditioned.
>
> (Ibid.)

Secondly, "the problem of the existence of market conditions in the economist's sense must also be faced" (ibid.: 15–16): the absence of a price system, which regulates market conditions in the Western societies, in a primitive economy, raises the question of whether these concepts can be extended to provide a basis for generalization:

> it is relevant to inquire what processes of exchange exist, what notion of value there are, what part they play in the economic system, and whether there are any objects the function of which approximate to those of money. If there are not, how is production organized and how are the wants of consumers met, since the rationale of an economic system is to satisfy wants by the production of consumers' goods?
>
> (Ibid.: 16)

Thirdly, there is the question of maximization of individual satisfactions on the basis of consistent choice, "an assumption justified by appeal to everyday experience": "how far in a primitive society is choice guided by rational considerations, and what are the satisfactions which are aimed at to the maximum extent?"; "what is the system of distribution of resources . . . and are these resources directed into production in a manner calculated to secure the most adequate satisfaction of wants?" (ibid.).

Firth's economic anthropology seeks to answer these questions by examining Tikopia society and at the same time to cast light on the social institutions governing the satisfaction of wants. The features which characterize a primitive society are:

- "simple non-mechanical technology, with little or no innovation" (ibid.: 17);
- "relatively low differentiation of economic roles of the people in production, entrepreneurial and management functions" (ibid.);
- absence of market institutions or "generally acceptable media of exchange" (ibid.), that is, a non-monetary economy.

A primitive economy does not derive resources by exchange from outside. In this sense that of the Tikopia can be termed a 'subsistence economy'. But, according to Firth, this term is liable to generate "some misconception". In a primitive economic system, the ordinary everyday interest of the people may be directed primarily to food production; but, Firth writes:

> it is by no means focused completely upon acquiring only enough food to support them at a minimal or relatively low level of living . . . The economy is geared towards the production of a range of items with recreational and status significance which cannot be comprised under any narrow definition of 'subsistence'.
>
> (Ibid.: 18)

In fact, by the term 'subsistence economy' is sometimes meant a system in which there is production by individuals or households, entirely for their own needs, and no system of exchange is therefore necessary: "In this sense no such economy, even of the most primitive society, exists. In every economic system studied by anthropologists some forms of exchange occur". According to Firth, "the characteristic feature of a subsistence economy is not its lack of exchange but the fact that such exchange remains internal to the particular economic system" (ibid.). Hence a more adequate expression is "internal subsistence economy". Firth consequently criticizes the traditional conception of primitive man. Modern work in economic anthropology, he maintains, has corrected some popular fallacies:

> It has been shown that primitive man in even the simplest types of society is not concerned solely with the food quest, that he has not a simple individual or household economy alone, that his organization of production involves forms of specialization, and that his system of exchange covers a wide area . . . Moreover, it is clear that he does not live by a day-to-day satisfaction of his needs but shows foresight and engages in forms of economic abstinence.
>
> (Ibid.: 6)

So the conception of primitive society, even if it maintains the meaning of 'economically backward' in comparison with other more developed societies, has been modified and enriched by fieldwork.

The basic aspects of this primitive economic system, Firth writes, "do correspond to the data of ordinary economic analysis, and can be covered by the same general propositions" (ibid.: 353). First of all, there is a scarcity of the means available for satisfying wants. A twofold explanation of this is put forward, although it is unpersuasive because it refers to non-ordinary events in an primitive economy. Firstly, Firth writes:

> In times when crops have been affected by hurricane or drought, this interest in sheer subsistence does become very marked indeed. At such times notions

> of scarcity become very obvious, and anxieties about the allocation of labour resources to produce foods and the distribution of foods are expressed in very acute form.
>
> (Ibid.: 18)

Secondly, the existence of scarcity is explained with dependence on the outside for certain goods:

> The economy of Tikopia, non monetary as it was in 1929 [1928–29 was Firth's first period of field research in Tikopia] . . . has depended to a very significant degree for about a century upon vessels from the outside world for iron tools and fish hooks, as well as some tobacco and cloth. Even earlier the people had sporadic economic relations with those of other islands, whereby commodities of external origin were obtained by barter or by reciprocal gifts.
>
> (Ibid.: 19)

Moreover, Firth adds, "problems of scarcity were recognized by the Tikopia" (ibid.: 26). It was "a concept familiar to them": "their leading men in particular commonly envisaged the economic situation of the island community as a whole, as was often demonstrated in their discussions with anthropologists and government officials" (ibid.).

Wants are arranged on a broad scale of preference, Firth maintains, and choice is exercised in a rational manner. Despite the fact that choices are often largely socially conditioned by social and ritualistic considerations, individuals constantly make choices "where they realize the implications of alternative mode of action and where their attempts to find the best solution gives them much thought and even anxiety" (ibid.: 29). Firth emphasizes four points:

- "[T]he employment of the factors of production is governed by some recognition of the advantages of the division of labour and specialization in employments according to differential skill" (ibid.: 353), although Firth recognizes that individuals easily change from one occupation to another, except in ritually defined cases.
- "[O]ne may speak of the employment of capital, though it does not fulfil all the functions of this factoring a modern industrial system" (ibid.). According to the three main senses in which the term 'capital' is liable to be used, as summarized by Fraser (1937) – productive equipment, use of purchasing power and control over resources, and claims to or expectation of interest – the first is certainly usable in a primitive economy: "in the Tikopia economy certain classes of goods obviously fall into the category of productive equipment" (Firth 1965: 272). As regards the second, "to some extent such goods may be regarded as giving control of purchasing power (if this term is reinterpreted for such a non-price economy)" (ibid.). As far as claims to future income are concerned, "Tikopia capital fulfils this function only in a very broad sense" (ibid.: 273).

- "[A]n implicit concept of margin in the use of various factor of production" exists, "as in the transference of labour from one area of land to another according to variations in its productive capacity" (ibid.: 353); therefore "in certain fields of the Tikopia economy there is . . . some realization of the operation of the law of diminishing returns" (ibid).
- [V]alue notions exist. Firth agrees with anthropologists like Thurnwald, Malinowski and Mauss that exchange rates fluctuate according to specific conditions and "their efficacy is linked essentially with the concept of reciprocity" (ibid.: 348); however he thinks that it does not depend on the existence of "an intrinsic type of primitive mind per se". He argues this claim as follows:

> That a primitive economic system . . . is not the outgrowth of an intrinsic type of primitive mind per se, is seen by the behaviour of the people when they come under the influence of a European economic system. Given an external market to regulate the conditions of supply and demand . . . these tend to become more impersonal; there is more insistence on immediate and exact indemnification of services; the transfer of goods by gift is replaced by barter and sale; exchange can no longer be enforced by appeal to weakened social sanctions; a price mechanism is introduced.
>
> (Ibid.: 351)

Certainly, Firth notes, many behavioural characteristics of a capitalist economy are absent in a primitive economy, thus questioning the applicability of economic science to primitive societies. In fact:

- The Tikopia may be said to lack technical ambition" (ibid.: 88); "the idea that it is a duty laid upon man to utilize to the full the resources of nature would be incomprehensible to the Tikopia" (ibid.: 108). The society is thus characterized by "an absence of interest in invention" and "by an absence of the potentialities for invention" (ibid.).
- Social cooperation is common; it is greater than that required by technical level and complexity:

> the codes which govern the behaviour of individuals in this society are such that a great deal of economic cooperation is based upon a primary interest in the social aspects of cooperation for its own sake rather than in its economic advantage.
>
> (Ibid.)

- The goods most important for the community, like land and canoes, are not privately owned.
- The distributive concept is: "all participants in a productive activity should receive a share of the product" (ibid.: 312), but "social considerations do not make it necessary for this share to be exactly proportionate to the contribution in time, labour or skill that each individual has made" (ibid.: 313).

- In individual transactions "the Tikopia work on what are in effect conventional exchange rates" (ibid.: 348), whose efficacy is linked not to the economic value of goods but to the concept of reciprocity: this is "one of the foundations of Tikopia social relationships" (ibid.), as in every primitive community, which make "the estimation of ultimate social advantage as more important than immediate material gain" (ibid.: 350). Moreover, there are some spheres of exchange in which goods "are not completely convertible into those of other series" (ibid.: 340): for example, food cannot buy a canoe, which can be exchanged only with certain types of goods. In other words, social conventions interpenetrate and overlay the economic organization.

On this basis, Firth writes, "we might even be tempted to deny the existence of Tikopia economics in the sense in which the term is ordinarily employed" (ibid.: 352). However, this doubt is removed on observing that "the fact remains that problems involving the provision of material goods and questions of human material welfare do exist in Tikopia, and they are solved by an organized and intelligible system of activity" (ibid.: 352–3).

This "organized and intelligible system" makes it possible to use (neoclassical) economics for its analysis even if economic rationality is restricted by the cultural and institutional environment. Economics can be applied because the assumptions of neoclassical economic analysis may be found – this is Firth's belief – in the fundamental aspects of the primitive economy. The differences between a primitive economy and a civilized one have to be emphasized, but they are "quantitative rather than qualitative" (ibid.: 355): "to some degree, the elements characteristic of Tikopia can be paralleled in modern industrial life" (ibid.).

In conclusion, according to Firth, economic analysis can be applied to primitive economies because there is a common and universal concept of rationality. Therefore, economics can make intelligible the essence of primitive behaviour behind the appearance of anti-economic behaviour.

2.1.3 The methodological controversy between Frank Knight and Melville Herskovits

In 1940, Melville Herskovits (1895–1963), a leading American anthropologist and a pupil of Franz Boas at Columbia University, published a textbook in economic anthropology, *Economic Life of Primitive Peoples*, which was long considered a basic text in the field. Its methodological objective was to foster closer collaboration between anthropology and economics in the comparative study of economic systems. In the words of Herskovits, the purpose of the book was:

> to provide information concerning the economic life of nonliterate peoples, to consider some of the questions in economic science that can be examined by the use of these data, and to suggest lines of attack which may be profitably defined for future use.
>
> (Herskovits 1940: preface)

Herskovits added that he had tried "to follow the conventional categories of economics and to indicate the points at which the economies with which we are concerned diverge so sharply from our own that it is not possible to follow these conventions" (ibid.).

Herskovits, like Firth, maintained that a unitary treatment of all the different economies in history is justifiable on the basis of the fact that characteristics common to all economies exist, differentiating them in degree rather than in kind. As a consequence, it is possible to conceive the totality of economic systems as lying on a kind of continuum:

> At one pole we find the societies living closest to the subsistence level, with the exploitation of natural resources slight, a slender endowment of technical knowledge, and implements few and simple. At the other end we place the great literate population aggregates, with their machine technologies, producing vast stores of goods and supporting a great variety of specialists to satisfy the wants of the people. Between these extremes lie the many societies having intermediate degrees of economic complexity and technical resource. As we move from the less to the more complex, the choices that are afforded between alternative possibilities become greater, the range of wants to be satisfied wider. But in every case choices must be made.
>
> (Ibid.: 11–12)

Herskovits's work is essentially descriptive and taxonomic; a sort of census of the great variety of allocative, productive and distributive systems in the primitive economies. However, the feature shared by all societies is identified in the principle of maximizing satisfactions by the conscious exercise of choice among scarce means. But, Herskovits emphasizes, the *homo oeconomicus* of economic theory – the rational isolated individual à la Robinson Crusoe as the "point from which all development of theoretical principles must begin" (ibid.: 7) – never exists in primitive societies, and "social interaction in terms of cultural tradition dictates reconsideration of the earlier starting-point" (ibid.): it must be "the individual operating as a member of his society, in terms of the culture of his group" (ibid.: 8).

The perspective adopted by Herskovits induces him to use the concept of rationality in a highly flexible way: "The question of rationality . . . poses itself: rational in terms of what system of thought and behavior?" (ibid.: 22):

> The cross-cultural perspective . . . gives us pause when defining 'rationality'. We are tempted to consider as rational the behavior that represents only the typical reactions to be expected of those who order their lives in terms of the economic systems of Europe and America, where it is rational to defer the gratification of wants, to accumulate resources, to produce more goods and multiply services. Yet, as we shall abundantly see, there are many cultures, if not a majority of them, where the deferment of wants is held to be disadvantageous, where best judgment dictates that resources be expended, where there is no tradition of expanding production and increasing services. None the

> less, in societies having traditions of this sort, choices are not only made, but debated. It will be our task . . . to discern the economic universals in human society by sampling the many forms in which they are manifest.
>
> (Ibid.: 24)

Frank Knight, a prominent Chicago economist of that time, one of the founders of modern anti-Marshallian microeconomics,[2] and methodologically close to Robbins, wrote a lengthy and critical review of Herskovits's book. It was published in 1941, together with a rejoinder by Herskovits himself, in the prestigious *Journal of Political Economy* of which Knight was editor (with Jacob Viner).[3]

Knight begins his review of Herskovits by stating that

> [The book is] an able pioneer effort in a field which has long been crying for cultivation. That field . . . is the interrelations of the different social science disciplines, and the objectives clearly in mind of the author are more effective collaboration, and less mutual misunderstanding and criticism, between the workers in the different branches of social science.
>
> (Knight 1941: 247)

The purpose of Knight's critique of Herskovits (1940) is "to contribute something to the promotion of the cause in the interest of which the book . . . was written" (ibid.).

Knight's starting point is criticism of the Marshallian definition of economics to which Herskovits refers: "Economics is the study of mankind in the ordinary business of life." According to Knight, this does not correctly represent the modern conception of economics, as outlined by himself and Robbins. Herskovits thought that Marshall's definition was reductive because it de facto applied to market societies: on the contrary, Knight considered it obsolete and the reference to market societies incorrect, opposing to it the conception of economics as a deductive science. For Knight, economic science is the only non-empirical social science using inference from abstract principles that are knowable intuitively and not verifiable, that is, grounded in intuition, as a method, while the other social sciences are empirical:

> The principles of economy are known intuitively; it is not possible to discriminate the economic character of behavior by sense observation; and the anthropologist, sociologist, or historian seeking to discover or validate economic laws by inductive investigation has embarked on a 'wild goose chase'.
>
> (Ibid.: 254)

Knight adds:

> This relationship between observation, induction from observations, and inference from "a priori" principles forms the very pivot of the problem of collaboration between the social sciences, and especially of the collaboration between economic theory and the 'quasi-empirical' sciences of

> history, sociology, and anthropology, including institutional – one might say anthropological – economics.
>
> (Ibid.)

In the Knight-Robbins perspective, sciences are distinguished from each other not by a different subject of inquiry, but because they inquire into different aspects of the same phenomenon. Economics focuses on economic rationality – defined by Knight as "the deliberate, problem-solving, planned use of means to given ends". In this methodological context, the concept of *homo oeconomicus* "is merely an analytical, essentially terminological, device for referring to the economic aspect of behavior, an aspect universal to all behavior in so far as it is purpositive" (ibid.). At the same time, it is a concept and also a normative ideal, "that men in general . . . wish to behave economically, to make their activities and their organization 'efficient' rather than wasteful" (ibid.: 252). Therefore economics is a "science of principles" and not a descriptive empirical science. According to Knight, Herskovits correctly recognizes that there are "universal economic principles" – first of all, the general principle of maximizing satisfaction. But he then argues incorrectly on the limits of application of these principles; in fact, Knight maintains: "the most general principles are not different in different culture situations – exactly as the principles of mathematics are not different" (ibid.). Herskovits introduces, Knight writes, an emotional bias which he brands "political romanticism" (ibid.: 257).

In Knight's discussion, the dialogue between economists and anthropologists advocated by Herskovits is asymmetric – that is, the need of anthropologists for economic theory is supposed to be greater than the need of economists for anthropology. He writes:

> The chief requisite for better mutual understanding between economists and anthropologists is that the latter should have some grasp of the categorical difference emphasized above between economics as an exposition of principles which have little more relation to empirical data of any sort than do those of elementary mathematics – and as a descriptive exposition of facts. From the opposite point of view, there is this important difference – that any intelligent or useful exposition of facts imperatively requires an understanding of principles, while the need for facts in connection with the exposition of principles is far more tenuous.
>
> (Ibid.: 260)

In his rejoinder, Herskovits writes that

> what Professor Knight has to say is to be regarded as an important step toward establishing the study of comparative economics, to which both anthropology and economics must make their contributions if work in such a field is to constitute a significant development in our search for knowledge.
>
> (Ibid.: 269)

But Herskovits strongly rejects the strict deductivism, implicit in Knight's conception of economics as a non-empirical science:

> I am convinced . . . that it is going to be extremely difficult to attain this objective if the deductive point of view stressed by Professor Knight comes to be the accepted approach. For no social science, it seems to me, can accomplish its ends if it disregards the first commandment of science in general – that only through constant and continuing cross-reference between hypothesis and fact can any understanding of problems and valid interpretations of data be had.
>
> (Ibid.)

Herskovits reaffirms the uselessness of the concept of *homo oeconomicus* employed by economic science: "a concept that has been more largely responsible than any other for that complacent intellectual provincialism to which I refer in my book, manifested by so many of those who profess a discipline of the vast importance of economics" (ibid.: 270). He asks: "can its continued use be defended when investigators of human societies all over the world are unanimous in testifying that no such creature exists or, as far as the data indicate, ever did exist?" (ibid.: 271).

He therefore rejects "the world of logical irreality" in which economists live. The universal principles of economics, if they exist, Herskovits concludes, must be verified by study of the actual facts concerning the economic life of as many different societies as can be reached.

The controversy between Knight and Herskovits was essentially methodological in nature: Knight's conception of economics and its deductivist method versus a positivist approach and its inductivist method, also in verification of theoretical postulates (see Hammond 1991 and Binembaum 2008). The most important aspect, from the point of view adopted in this book, is the agreement between the two scholars that there are general principles of neoclassical economic theory applicable to the analysis of any economic system. For Herskovits, as for Firth, those principles constitute a theoretical framework in which the anthropological description of primitive economies can make them 'understandable', or 'intelligible', in their universal essence.

2.2 Beyond the formalist approach: Clifford Geertz's and Richard Posner's informational approach for peasant and primitive societies

2.2.1 The New Institutionalism and Gary Becker's microeconomics of non-market behaviour

Since the 1970s, amid the increasing theoretical difficulties of traditional neoclassical economics in explaining empirical facts, major changes have taken place in microeconomics with the introduction of the assumptions of incomplete and asymmetrical information and bounded rationality. New theories have enhanced the interpretative capacity of economics while at the same time renouncing the traditional preference of economists for simple, but heuristically weak, models. On the other hand, a generalization of the rational choice model has come about, in part taking the above-mentioned conceptual novelties into account. In this context, the emergence of a new-institutionalist perspective constitutes an important part of this theoretical change. In the set of new-institutionalist currents, two are relevant to our discussion here: those represented respectively by Douglass North and Gary Becker, with their attempts to employ economic theory in contexts not traditionally of interest to economists.

The economic historian Douglass North (1920–2015), Nobel Prize winner in economics in 1993, renewed research in economic history by applying economic theory and quantitative methods in order to explain economic and institutional change. He furnished a general framework for historical research which integrates information costs, uncertainty and transaction costs in the neoclassical theory in order to analyse the changing structure of economies and institutional change over time. The central idea is that institutions – that is, the rules of the game in a society and how they evolve – shape economic performance. Together with the technology employed, they determine the cost of transacting and producing. In other words, how successfully an economy develops depends on how well it can create institutions that minimize transaction costs.

The Chicago economist Gary Becker (1930–2014), Nobel Prize winner in economics in 1992, is the father of modern economics imperialism. He extended the domain of microeconomic analysis to encompass a wide range of human behaviour and interaction, including non-market behaviour. He applied the principle of rational, optimizing behaviour to areas where researchers formerly assumed that behaviour is habitual and often irrational; areas traditionally belonging in the domain of sociology, psychology, law, and other fields like organization of the family, crime, racial discrimination, and drug addiction. Gary Becker's research programme was founded on the idea that an individual's behaviour adheres to the same fundamental principles in a number of different areas. The same explanatory model – the economic approach of rational choice – should thus, according to Becker, be applicable in analysing highly diverse aspects of human behaviour. It is assumed that individual agents behave rationally, and that their behaviour can be described as if they are maximizing a specific objective function, such as utility.

The increasing attention paid to the study of non-market institutions by economists from the 1970s onwards made a new form of application of economic theory to primitive social institutions possible. Among the works produced from this perspective (for example, Grossbard 1978, Ault and Rutman 1980, North 1977), the most significant and ambitious was Richard Posner's essay "A Theory of Primitive Society" (1980), which presented a general economic theory of primitive society influenced in particular by Geertz (1978) and by conversations with Gary Becker. In these conversations, the American Nobel Prize winner argued that many of the distinctive institutions of primitive society can be explained as adaptations to uncertainty or high information costs. Unlike the formalist approach, this one considered rationality to be a characteristic of primitive man manifest in all areas of society; this idea was certainly included in Robbins' methodological perspective, but explicitly and fully applied only by Becker and his followers. This approach was considered able to apply economic theory to primitive society in an unapologetic way beyond what had hitherto been considered the sterile debate between formalists and substantivists.[4]

2.2.2 Geertz's bazaar economics

The American anthropologist Clifford Geertz (1926–2006) applied the economics of information to the study of the exchange in African bazaars in an article published in 1978 in the *American Economic Journal*, his purpose being to develop a model of how the market works in a peasant economy. He tried to show that the conditions of information in peasant market systems, or what he called "bazaar economies", can explain the differences between primitive and modern markets.

Geertz maintained that the developments in economic theory that have to do with the role of information, communication and knowledge in exchange processes provide an analytical framework useful for understanding how a bazaar works and how they allow the incorporation of sociocultural factors into the interpretative model.

Geertz examined the bazaar of Sefrou, a town in the foothills of the Middle Atlas Mountains in Morocco. This was an important caravan stop on the route south from Fez to the Sahara and a thriving market centre. There were two sorts of bazaar in Sefrou: a permanent one, consisting of the trading quarters of the old town; and a periodic one, which met at various locations – one for rugs, another for grain outside the town walls on Thursdays, as part of a very complex regional cycle involving various other marketplaces and the other days of the week. The two sorts of bazaar were distinct but their boundaries were quite permeable, so that individuals moved freely between them, and they operated on broadly the same principles. Geertz writes: "The empirical situation is extremely complex – there are more than 600 shops representing about forty distinct commercial trades and nearly 300 workshops representing about thirty crafts – and on Thursdays the town population probably doubles" (Geertz 1978: 29).

The importance of this local institution is beyond doubt; in fact, two-thirds of the town's labour force was employed there:

> the bazaar is more than another demonstration of the truth that, under whatever skies, men prefer to buy cheap and sell dear. It is a distinctive system of social relationships centering around the production and consumption of goods and services – that is, a particular kind of economy, and it deserves analysis as such.
>
> (Ibid.)

'Bazaar' is "as much an analytic idea as the name of an institution", Geertz writes, and its study is, like that of the market, "as much a theoretical as a descriptive enterprise" (ibid.).

Geertz first analyses the distinctive characteristics of the bazaar. He thinks that applicable "here as elsewhere", are the economic assumptions that sellers seek maximum profit, consumers seek maximum utility, price relates supply and demand, factor proportions reflect factor costs. However, he adds, "the principles governing the organization of commercial life are less derivative from such truisms than one might imagine from reading standard economic textbooks". Transactions are matters "less of utility balance than of information flows". They give the bazaar "its particular character and general interest" (ibid.). Geertz therefore identifies the characteristics of information in this peculiar institution:

> in the bazaar information is poor, scarce, maldistributed, inefficiently communicated, and intensely valued. Neither the rich concreteness or reliable knowledge that the ritualized character of nonmarket economies makes possible, nor the elaborate mechanisms for information generation and transfer upon which industrial ones depend, are found in the bazaar: neither ceremonial distribution nor advertising; neither prescribed exchange partners nor product standardization. The level of ignorance about everything from product quality and going prices to market possibilities and production costs is very high, and much of the way in which the bazaar functions can be interpreted as an attempt to reduce such ignorance for someone, increase it for someone, or defend someone against it.
>
> (Ibid.)

Bazaar participants, Geertz writes, realize the difficulty of knowing if a certain good is sound or its price is right. Capital, skill, and industriousness play an important role in the bazaar, as well as luck and privilege. They secure for their possessor an advantage "in an enormously complicated, poorly articulated and extremely noisy communication network" (ibid.). The institutional peculiarities of the bazaar are "connected elements of a system":

> An extreme division of labor and localization of markets, heterogeneity of products and intensive price bargaining, fractionalization of transactions and stable clientship ties between buyers and sellers, itinerant trading and extensive traditionalization of occupation in ascriptive terms – these things do not just co-occur, they imply one another.
>
> (Ibid.: 29–30)

The search for information is laborious, uncertain, complex, and irregular: it is "the central experience of life in the bazaar" (ibid.: 30). Every aspect of the bazaar economy reflects the fact that "the primary problem facing its participants . . . is not balancing options but finding out what they are." Thus information search is the really advanced art in the bazaar, "a matter upon which everything turns" (ibid.).

The two most important search procedures in the bazaar are clientelization and bargaining. Clientelization is the tendency for repetitive purchasers of particular goods and services to establish continuing relationships with particular purveyors of them, rather than search widely through the market on each occasion of need. It takes the form of a flexible structure of informal personal connections. Clientship relations "are not dependency relations, but competitive ones". In fact, clientship is "symmetrical, egalitarian, and oppositional", and, whatever the relative power, wealth, knowledge, skill, or status of the participants, "clientship is a reciprocal matter" (ibid.):

> By partitioning the bazaar crowd into those who are genuine candidates for his attention and those who are merely theoretically such, clientelization reduces search to manageable proportions and transforms a diffuse mob into a stable collection of familiar antagonists. The use of repetitive exchange between acquainted partners to limit the costs of search is a practical consequence of the overall institutional structure of the bazaar.
>
> (Ibid.)

Clientalization represents an actor-level attempt to counteract, and profit from, the system-level deficiencies of the bazaar as a communication network – its structural intricacy and irregularity, the absence of certain sorts of signalling systems and the undeveloped state of others, and the imprecision, scattering, and uneven distribution of knowledge concerning economic matters of fact – by improving the richness and reliability of information carried over elementary links within it.

The other search procedure is bazaar bargaining. Geertz emphasizes two aspects of such bargaining: its "multidimensionality" and "intensive nature" (ibid.). As regards the former, Geertz stresses the spirit of bargaining which permeates the relation of exchange:

> Quantity and/or quality may be manipulated while money price is held constant, credit arrangements can be adjusted, bulking or bulk breaking may conceal adjustments, and so on, to an astonishing range and level of detail. In a system where little is packaged or regulated, and everything is approximative, the possibilities for bargaining along non-monetary dimensions are enormous.
>
> (Ibid.: 31)

The second aspect concerns intensiveness. This signifies "the exploration in depth of an offer already received, a search along the intensive margin, as contrasted to seeking additional offers, a search along the extensive" (ibid.).

The economics of information applied in a non-developed context proves, according to Geertz, to be a field of fruitful interchange between economics and anthropology. It was the American jurist and economist Richard Posner, a leading figure in the field of law and economics, who developed this analysis by constructing a model that he considered a generalization of Geertz's model.

2.2.3 Posner's general theory of primitive societies

In the first part of his long paper "A Theory of Primitive Society" (1980), Posner sketches a general economic theory of primitive society. He argues that many of the distinctive institutions of primitive society can be explained "as adaptations to uncertainty or high information costs" (Posner 1980: 4).

The starting point of his analysis is the concept of information costs. He argues that the costs of obtaining information are higher in primitive than in advanced societies, that is, more inputs of time or other resources are required to obtain the same amount of information. This statement follows from the assumption that primitive peoples are technically backward; they do not understand the laws of nature well, Posner writes. In fact, he maintains, belief in magic and sorcery must be considered a substitute for scientific knowledge. Primitive peoples have no system of writing and consequently no records, and they lack modern communications technology. On the basis of these assumptions concerning the technical–informational conditions of primitive society, Posner elaborates a general economic theory of primitive society in order to explain the distinctive institutions and values of that society:

> Weak government, ascription of rights and duties on the basis of family membership, gift-giving as a fundamental mode of exchange, strict liability for injuries, emphasis on generosity and honor as high ethical norms, collective guilt – these and other features of social organization recur with such frequency in accounts of primitive and archaic societies, as to suggest that a simple model of primitive society . . . may nonetheless explain much of the structure of primitive social institutions.
>
> (Ibid.: 8)

The basic assumptions of the model are the following:

- Absence of effective government, or a lack of government, due to illiteracy;
- Scarce technical knowledge, so that only a limited variety of consumption goods can be produced;
- Scarcity of commercial relationships with other societies due to the costs of transportation, plus (other) transaction costs created by language differences, a lack of currency, and a lack of contract-enforcement mechanisms;
- Impossibility of storing consumption goods due to the technical problem of food preservation;
- Negligibility of private gains from innovation "because such gains cannot be appropriated [the privacy problem] or because scarcity of natural resources or other exogenous conditions make cost reduction or product improvement unattainable goals at any feasible scale of investment" (ibid.: 10).

These characteristics imply the existence of a strong redistributive ethic without, Posner underlines, necessarily entailing the assumption of altruistic behaviour by primitive people. Insurance, specifically against hunger, is very important in such a society:

> The conditions of production, in particular the difficulty of storing food, create considerable uncertainty with regard to the future adequacy of an individual's food supply and hence considerable variance in his expected wealth. In these circumstances a transaction whereby A, who happens to produce a harvest that exceeds his consumption needs, gives part of his surplus to B in exchange for B's commitment to reciprocate should their roles some day be reversed will be attractive to both parties . . . The attractiveness to A of insurance is further enhanced by the assumed scarcity of alternative goods for which to exchange his surplus food.
>
> (Ibid.)

However, the absence of an effective government impedes the emergence of a formal insurance market, so that reciprocity may not be honoured. In this way, the family, as a mutual insurance company comes to rescue. However, a family may be too small to constitute an adequate risk pool for insurance purposes. This may be the reason why kinship relationships are so important in primitive societies. Another way to remedy the lack of formal insurance, Posner writes, is generosity toward other members of one's village or band as well as toward kinfolk, a substitute for formal insurance. Posner writes:

> Generosity – toward other members of one's village or band as well as toward kinsmen – is a more highly valued trait in primitive than in modern society and the reason appears to be that it is a substitute for formal insurance.
>
> (Ibid.: 14)

The fact that in primitive societies a man can obtain prestige by giving away what he has rather than by keeping it – the potlatch of the North-west Indians of Canada is the most striking example of this behaviour – should not be taken as evidence for the inapplicability of the economic model to primitive society, because, Posner maintains, utilitarian logic is not denied by such behaviour:

> Since, in a society where consumption goods are limited in variety and durability, giving away one's surplus may be the most useful thing to do with it, at least from society's standpoint, one is not surprised that it should earn the prestige that in a different kind of society is bestowed on a great inventor, scientist, captain of industry, or entertainer.
>
> (Ibid.: 10)

Therefore, Posner maintains, generosity and other "redistributive" mechanisms of primitive society like gifts, non-interest-bearing loans, feasts, "are not the product of altruism . . . They are insurance payments":

> The principle of reciprocity, which commands a man to repay a loan when he can or a gift when he can, or to feast his benefactors when he can, provides some protection against the free-riding or moral-hazard problems that so inclusive and informal a system of insurance as is found in primitive societies would otherwise create.
>
> (Ibid.: 16)

Posner notes that the absence of legal sanctions for failure to reciprocate may make the system of reciprocity fragile. He consequently adds a sixth assumption to the model: the state of immobility of the population, "in the sense that the member of one village, band, or tribe, cannot readily join another and distant unit" (Posner, 1980: 17). If this were possible, mobility would make the incentive to free ride and the reluctance to share without an enforceable promise to reciprocate very strong.

One effect of insurance is that it tends to equalize the ex-post distribution of wealth. But, Posner adds, equality of wealth is not only a by-product of insurance, it is also a precondition for the maintenance of a pre-governmental political equilibrium. In fact, a wealthy man who has accumulated a food surplus may acquire political power – "establish a state with himself as its head" (ibid.: 19) – but the absence of government means that "there are institutions that limit the ability of the abler or more energetic people to use their surplus food for political ends. The insurance institutions of primitive society have this effect by tending to dissipate surpluses" (ibid.).

Further characteristics of primitive society are interpreted by Posner as adaptations to high information costs. Thus, superstition appears to increase the society's economic well-being because it can be considered a rational response to the demand for insurance: a man who becomes too wealthy is likely to be considered a sorcerer. Analogously, the common practice in primitive societies of burying people with their personal possessions, or destroying those possessions upon their death, may be thought of as method to equalize wealth in the next generation. Also the assignment of tasks or roles on the basis of age (age grading) can be interpreted as a way to economize on information: age and sex are proxies for individual fitness for a particular job, by avoiding an assessment of individual strength, skill, and character. Gifts, besides being explained in terms of mutual insurance, also have a direct informational aspect: a gift is a way to communicate information about one's wealth, tastes and attitudes more credibly than by means of a statement, especially in circumstances where a statement would be difficult to verify and guarantees of its truth would not be enforceable.

Marginality of trade may be explained, Posner argues, by the fact that transaction costs are presumably high because of the high costs of information regarding the reliability of the seller, the quality of the product, and trading alternatives (that is, the market price). Institutions which reduce these transaction costs are:

- Gift-exchange is viewed as a means to communicate information about one's character and intentions.

- "[C]ustomary" prices – given the high costs of markets in primitive societies, such prices may be less inefficient, on balance, than freely bargained prices.
- The transformation of an arm's-length contract relationship into an intimate status relationship: repeated exchanges with the same man may turn the individuals who exchange into blood brothers: "It is a way of bringing reciprocity into the exchange process and thereby increasing the likelihood that promises will be honored despite the absence of a public enforcement authority" (ibid.: 26).
- The sense of honour "may be related to the importance of the threat to retaliate as a device for keeping order in a society lacking (for reasons based on information costs) formal institutions of law enforcement" (ibid.: 27): the sense of honour increases the probability that a man will retaliate for a wrong to him or to his kin and "it thereby increases the credibility of threatened retaliation as a deterrent to antisocial behavior" (ibid.).
- Also the art of rhetoric can be considered a response to high information costs, because in an environment where privacy is lacking, people must learn to express themselves very precisely, with decorum and formality, to avoid recriminations and misunderstandings, and they must be credible.

In this generalization of the rational choice approach, economic science goes beyond a simple representation of the material backwardness of primitives. Using the contemporary development of microeconomics, Richard Posner pursues an extremely ambitious goal: to elaborate a general theory of primitive society. He presents a model of primitive society where the primitive man is a rational optimizing individual, and social behaviours and institutions result from high transaction and information costs in conditions of high uncertainty due to the knowledge limitations of primitives, which make the possibilities of exploitation of resources limited and material wealth scarce.

2.3 Beyond the formalist approach: Jack Hirshleifer's bioeconomics and the human behavioural ecology of primitive economies

2.3.1 Chicago economics and the relationship between economics and biology

At various times, Gary Becker, as well as Richard Posner (see, for example, Becker 1976b and Posner 1973), contemplated the role that biology could play in economics and they emphasized the benefits of combining economics and sociobiology. In an influential article, Becker (1976b) wrote:

> Both economics and sociobiology would gain from combining the analytical techniques of economists with the techniques in population genetics, entomology, and other biological foundations of sociobiology. The preferences taken as given by economists and vaguely attributed to 'human nature'

> or something similar – the emphasis on self-interest, altruism towards kin, social distinction, and other enduring aspects of preferences – may be largely explained by the selection over time of traits having greater genetic fitness and survival value.
>
> (Becker 1976b: 826)

This attitude favourable to cooperation between the two disciplines was not new among the members of the Chicago School of economics. Armian Alchian and Milton Friedman, two leaders of the school, had already advanced 'selection arguments' in some path-breaking articles in the 1950s (Alchian 1950, Friedman 1953). The following generation of Chicago's economists, represented, in addition to Becker and Posner, by economists like Gordon Tullock and Jack Hirshleifer, developed the topic of the relationship between economics and biology, maintaining the mutually beneficial transfer of concepts and ideas between the two disciplines. Among them, Hirshleifer is considered to be the economist who displayed the most serious interest in the field (see Vromen 2011).[5]

Jack Hirshleifer (1925–2005), was an economist with multi-disciplinary interests, and one of the advocates of using evolutionary biology in economics who, in the second part of the 1970s, contributed greatly to the emergence of the new field of bioeconomics with some seminal contributions on the subject (1977, 1978a, 1978b), symbols of "the naturalistic ambitions of economics" (Fontaine 2012).

2.3.2 Hirshleifer's bioeconomics

Hirshleifer's theoretical non-economic sources come from the adaptionist and sociobiological field in evolutionary biology; that is, from the work of scientists like William D. Hamilton, George C. Williams, Robert L. Trivers, Richard D. Alexander, Michael T. Ghiselin, Richard Dawkins and, last but not least, Edward O. Wilson, the founder of sociobiology. In fact, in the 1960s and 1970s, these authors made fundamental (though highly controversial) theoretical contributions in the field of evolutionary biology, mainly on the evolutionary biological basis of behaviour.

Hamilton (1964) pointed out that because related individuals share some of the same genes because they have common ancestors, selection may sometimes favour genes that induce their bearers to do things that harm their own reproductive interests if, in so doing, they substantially increase the reproductive success of relatives. This argument became the centrepiece of the "selfish gene theory" (Dawkins 1976). According to Richard Dawkins's theory, the base unit of evolution is the individual gene. Since evolutionary fitness is measured in terms of passing on one's genes to the next generation, Dawkins theorized that each gene acted in a way that would afford it the best opportunity to be replicated and passed on to the next generation. Williams (1966) clarified the question concerning the level in the hierarchy of life at which adaptations are most likely to evolve and he outlined, in his *Adaptation and Natural Selection*, a gene-centred view of evolution then considered a classic analysis. In the

1970s, Robert L. Trivers (in particular, Trivers 1971) extended the selfish gene theory to reciprocity, as well as to other topics such as parental behaviour and sexual selection. He demonstrated how reciprocal altruism can evolve between unrelated individuals: repeated social interactions between individuals might provide a route to the evolution of stable prosocial behaviour.[6] Edward O. Wilson's *Sociobiology. The New Synthesis* and the above quoted Dawkins's *The Selfish Gene* were published in 1975 and 1976 respectively, just a few years after Trivers's seminal papers. These theoretical ideas formed a coherent perspective sometimes labelled 'adaptationism' and 'selectionist thinking', that viewed organisms as products of natural selection favouring phenotypes that enhance the representation in future generations of the genes that coded for them. In the final chapter of *Sociobiology*, Wilson, as well as Dawkins in *The Selfish Gene*, suggested that this perspective could shed light on human social behaviour.

As Hirshleifer (1977) emphasized, the biologists adopting the adaptionist perspective made significant use of tools and approaches of neoclassical economics: for example, Trivers (1972) demonstrated that several aspects of parental behaviour can be explained in terms of differences in the selectional return on investment to the male and female parents; Ghiselin (1974) invited biologists to adopt the methodological individualism of economics, and Wilson (1975) employed linear programming models to determine the optimal number and proportion of castes in the division of labour among social insects. But, Hirshleifer notes, "the more significant intellectual influence has been in the other direction, from biology to social science" (Hirshleifer 1977: 6): social Darwinism is the body of thought which has attempted to explain patterns of social stratification as the consequence of the selection of superior human types and forms of organization through social competition. According to Hirshleifer the "too-total" rejection of social Darwinism has meant a lack of appreciation of its valid core of scientific insights, that is:

> (1) that individuals, groups, races, and even social arrangements . . . are in never ending competition with one another, and . . . the competition itself is a fact with explanatory power for social phenomena; (2) that the behavior of mankind is strongly influenced by the biological heritage of the species, and that the forces tending towards either cooperation or conflict among men are in large part identical with phenomena observable in the biological realm.
>
> (Hirshleifer 1977: 6–7)

Hirshleifer's articles of 1977 and 1978 furnish an in-depth biological interpretation of economic theorizing. Hirshleifer's interest is essentially to clarify "what message sociobiology has for economics" (1977: 4). His starting point is the thesis that "the various social sciences devoted to the study of man, economics among them, constitute but a subdivision of the all-encompassing field of sociobiology" (1978a: 238). But, he stresses, the link between economics and sociobiology is special:

> The fundamental organizing concepts of the dominant analytical structures employed in economics and in sociobiology are strikingly parallel . . . Fundamental concepts like scarcity, competition, equilibrium, and specialisation play similar roles in both spheres of inquiry. And terminological pairs such as species/industry, mutation/innovation, evolution/progress, mutualism/exchange have more or less analogous denotations.
>
> (Hirshleifer 1977: 2; see also 1978: 239)

More systematically, Hirshleifer writes, the isomorphism between economics and sociobiology "involves the intertwining of two level of analysis" – that of optimizing and that of equilibrium:

> On the first level, acting units or entities choose strategies or develop techniques that promote success in the struggle or competition for advantage in given environments. The economist usually calls this process 'optimizing', the biologist, 'adapting'. The formalizations involved are equations of constrained maximization.
>
> The second, higher level of analysis examines the social or aggregate resultant of the interaction of the striving units or agents. The formalizations here take the form of equations of equilibrium . . . The solutions on the two levels are of course interdependent.
>
> (1977: 2; see also 1978a: 239)

If economics is regarded as essentially coextensive with the sociobiology of human behaviour, what role is left for the other social sciences? Hirshleifer answers that he adopts "a unified social-science viewpoint" in which economics and other social sciences are regarded "as interpenetrating rather than compartmentalized" (1977: 3). However, according to him, economics has a peculiarity. By breaking through the traditional analytical constraints – rational self-interested behaviour and individual interactions taking the form of market exchanges – thanks to the work of economists like Becker, Tullock and Buchanan, economics has taken all human activity as its subject matter. Therefore, because economics employs its tools of analysis across a wider range of social issues – that is, because economics behaves 'imperialistically' – , "it will *become* sociology, and anthropology and political science" (Hirshleifer 1977: 4). Correspondingly, as these other disciplines grow "increasingly rigorous", "they will not merely resemble but will *be* economics": "It is in this sense", Hirshleifer concludes, "that 'economics' is taken here as broadly synonymous with 'social science'" (ibid.).

In his *American Economic Review* paper (1978a), Hirshleifer emphasizes that the idea of a relationship between economics and biology is not new in the history of economics: he recalls above all Marshall's work,[7] but maintains that an interpretation of the relation between the two fields of study, different from Marshall's – and which he considers "exciting" and, we may say, functional to his programme – is the one proposed by the biologist Michael Ghiselin, that biology should be regarded as 'natural economy' to be coordinated with 'political economy' or 'economics', "together forming a branch of knowledge which we may call 'general economy'" (Ghiselin 1978: 233). The step from natural economy to political economy, Hirshleifer writes, is not as sharply discontinuous as considered in the traditional political philosophy. On the contrary, as comparative sociobiology teaches, political economy institutions *emerge* from some emotional dispositions serving to control internal strife in a social group: law and government deter or limit the internal fighting characterizing the natural economy – the *Hobbesian state of nature* – that would be dysfunctional for the group as a whole: "with property recognized, exchange becomes a possibility – and, ultimately, the more sophisticated dealing in deferred reciprocations that constitute the essence of contract" (Hirshleifer 1978a: 238). Yet institutions cannot be so perfect as to entirely displace the underlying realities of natural economy: "every living organism remains to some degree in a Hobbesian state of nature." This implies that, even under law and government a rational self-interested individual "will strike a balance between lawful and unlawful mean of acquiring resources – between production and exchange on the one hand and theft, fraud, and extortion from the other" (ibid.).

Competition, Hirshleifer writes, is the all-pervasive law of natural economy interactions. And the source of competition is scarcity: "the limited resource base of the globe in face of the universal Malthusian tendency to multiply" (ibid.: 239). This biological competition works through natural selection: "By natural selection the biosphere has come to be filled by life forms successful at multiplying and pressing upon one another for command over resources" (ibid.). Here Hirshleifer raises the issue of altruistic behaviour. He asks, "if competition is the basic law of life, how is that organisms sometimes confer benefits on others? . . . Or, where conflict exists, how and why is it that the battle is often limited rather than all out?" (ibid.: 240).

It is the economist's approach that provide us with assistance in answering this question: in fact, the economist approaches problems of optimal action by distinguishing between preferences and opportunities. Traditionally, s/he takes the preferences of a self-interested person as arbitrary or inexplicable brute facts – neoclassical economics regards itself as the logic of choice under conditions of given tastes – and emphasizes the importance of opportunities: "the mutual advantages that entirely self-interested persons can gain through social cooperation, to wit, increased production through specialization and the division of labour and improved allocations of products through exchange" (ibid.). But, Hirshleifer continues, sociobiology tells us that preferences are not arbitrary but are themselves adaptive to environmental conditions.[8] The biological approach to preferences, to what economists call the 'utility function', postulates that "all such motives or drives or tastes represent proximate aspects of a single underlying goal – fitness. Preferences are governed by the all-encompassing drive for reproductive survival" (Hirshleifer 1977: 19):

> The fundamental brute fact is the selfishness of the gene . . . The gene is an economic gene. It has been selected to survive on the basis of successful selfishness. However, depending on opportunities, the interests of the gene may sometimes be served if the organism housing it is programmed to help or to hurt other organisms. Biologists have examined the problem of social cooperation . . . under the heading of altruism followed by some economists.
>
> (Hirshleifer 1978a: 240)

Therefore the problem of altruism is solved by taking into account that, from the evolutionary point of view, altruistic behaviour must be profitable in fitness terms in order to survive the selectional process: "It must somehow be the case that being generous (at least sometimes, to some beneficiaries) is selectively more advantageous than being selfish!" (ibid.: 20), Hirshleifer comments. The mechanism identified by biologists falls into two categories: that of selfish altruism – it does not require compensation or reciprocity to be viable – and that of reciprocal altruism (Trivers, 1971), and what economists call 'exchange'. The key question for the selectional advantage of such reciprocal aid is the control of cheating. This is a prisoner's dilemma problem (Axelrod and Hamilton (2010 [1981]: 356). The market cheater may be punished by law; that is, Hirshleifer comments, "the shift from natural economy to political economy solves the Prisoner's Dilemma problem via third-party enforcement of contract" (Hirshleifer 1978a: 241). In biological context, altruistic motivations can provide a better guarantee of reciprocity, as contended by Trivers: in economic terms, altruism economizes on costs of policing and enforcing agreements. Trivers's arguments are taken up by Hirshleifer:

> Trivers argues that human evolution has developed a balance between the abilities to engage in and to detect and suppress subtle cheating while participating in reciprocal interactions. The sense of justice, what Trivers calls 'moralistic aggression', is an emotion that involves third parties as additional enforcers to punish cheaters. Finally, the selectional advantage of these emotions has led to the ability to simulate or mimic them – to hypocrisy. Note . . . how these emotional qualities, absent from the make up of 'economic man', turn out to have an important place in the biological economy of human relationships.
>
> (Hirshleifer 1977: 28)

Becker's aim of reciprocally useful cooperation between economics and sociobiology which strengthens the imperialistic approach of economics finds an important accomplishment in Hirshleifer's work. This cooperation makes it possible, according to Hirshleifer, to re-launch the imperialistic role of economics among the social sciences. His idea that bioeconomics 'becomes' the other social sciences is well shown by the changes that have taken place in anthropology with the emergence of human behaviour ecology, in which the primitive societies are re-examined in the 'neo-Darwinian' context.

2.3.3 Human behavioural ecology and the 'rational savage'

Human behavioural ecology (HBE) is a relatively recent discipline – it began in the mid-1970s – which is practised for the most part by anthropologists. It applies evolutionary ecology models and concepts – which study evolution and adaptive design in ecological contexts – to the study of human behavioural diversity. In the anthropological field, behavioural ecology is distinguished from traditional theory by its idea that much of the content of culture is a consequence of decisions by individuals to enhance their inclusive fitness.[9] Bruce Winterhalder and Eric Alder Smith, two eminent exponents of this discipline to whom we will principally refer here, write (Winterhalder and Smith, 2000) that HBE's early goals were to set the cultural ecology of Julian H. Steward (1955), particularly as developed in his hunter-gatherer work and as represented in later studies such as those by Richard Lee (1979), on a sounder theoretical footing "by allying it to emerging, neo-Darwinian approaches to behavior" (Winterhalder and Smith 2000: 51). Smith and Winterhalder (1992) argue that explaining what a behaviour does is not fully to account for how that behaviour became common in a society. Commenting on this statement, Kelly (2004) writes that functional explanations depend on causal explanations, and "causal explanations in evolution require showing how a behaviour becomes prevalent through natural selection" (Kelly 2004: 32). HBE, Kelly argues, following Smith and Winterhalder (1992), makes "cultural ecology more complete by adding the process through which variation is channeled in one direction or another: natural selection" (ibid.).

To these neo-Darwinian theoretical sources HBE adds a hypothetico-deductive research strategy: it derives testable hypotheses from mathematical models anchored in basic principles of evolution by natural selection. As advocates of a strictly scientific paradigm, human behavioural ecologists, like the formalist anthropologists of some decade ago, are methodological individualists, meaning that they analyse social phenomena as products of the actions of individuals. They seek to capture the essential features of an adaptive problem; as Winterhalder and Smith write: "HBE assumes that complex socioecological phenomenon are most fruitfully studied in a reductionist rather than wholistic fashion" (2000: 52).

The research on resource selection and harvesting behaviour – production in economic terms – which has formed the largest part of the HBE literature in the past decades, draws from the 'optimal foraging theory' (OFT), a theory developed by biologists. In 1966, Robert H. MacArthur and Eric Pianka laid the foundations for the development of this theory, by presenting a model that helped predict how an animal behaves when it is searching for food: OFT consists of a family of models addressing resource selection, time allocation, and habitat movement, or patch choice. In order to illustrate the logic of the HBE approach in general, Winterhalder and Smith (2000) focus on a particular foraging model, "by far the most popular": the diet breadth or prey-choice model. As with all HBE models, the prey-choice model incorporates:

- a goal (optimize net acquisition rate),
- a currency (usually the net acquisition rate of energy – but also another rate measure like protein capture, material need, monetary return, prestige – for measuring the costs and benefits),
- a set of constraints (characterizing the social and environmental context) and
- a decision or alternative set (the range of behavioural options to be examined).

It is, of course, a model treating the economic problem à la Robbins. The model specifies which resource types can be harvested most efficiently from among those available in a given locale. It tests the assumption that foragers have the goal of responding to changing environmental constraints with choices that optimize net yield. The constraints include those endogenous to the forager, such as the information available, cognitive processing capacities, and technology, as well as exogenous factors such as distribution, density and the nutritional content of the available resources. The alternative set is the diet combinations achieved by step-wise addition of resources which have been ranked by their pursuit and handling profitability. It is assumed that foraging strategies that maximize the net acquisition rate of energy while foraging have higher fitness: "we should expect selection to favor cognitive mechanisms and culturally inherited rules of thumb to produce behaviors keyed to this goal" (Winterhalder and Smith 2000: 54).

Foraging models concern the production decisions of individuals; however, for humans, the harvesting and consumption of resources occurs in a group. Paying attention to the social interaction and the dynamics of resource distribution, Winterhalder and Smith stress the fact that group-based subsistence efforts may offer several advantages: "1) increased per capita encounter rates with resources, 2) reduced variation in encounter rates, 3) reduced losses to competitors and 4) increased vigilance and predator detection" (2000: 59).

Whilst hand-to-mouth feeding provides no incentives for food transfers beyond the provisioning of related infants or juveniles until they are competent as independent foragers, the situation is different if group members harvest one or more of their resources as a divisible packet, a unit too large for it to be consumed immediately by the individual holding it:

> The technical equivalent of this condition is that the value of the packet is subject to short-term, diminishing marginal returns to the individual possessing it. This virtually guarantees that portions of the packet will be valued differently by different group members.
>
> (Ibid.)

Consequently, a variety of evolutionary mechanisms may come into play:

> The models differ in the evolutionary mechanism they apply . . . Simple individual-level selection will generate transfer by *scrounging* (tolerate theft) when those not possessing a resource packet benefit more by taking portions than the holder can benefit by defending them. Resource sharing eliminates the involuntary element of coercion, replacing it with the delayed cost benefit

> calculus of reciprocal altruism. In *by product mutualism* the individual discovering or possessing a resource obtains a net gain as a result of others participating in its capture, defence or consumption . . . [marginalist logic] . . . If individuals produce significant parts of their diet unpredictably, risk minimization is among the important benefits of resource transfers.
>
> (Ibid.: 59; original emphasis)

Since the mid-1970s, hunter-gatherer decisions concerning resource selection and land use have been the subject of many works by anthropologists like James O'Connell, Kristen Hawkes, Bruce Winterhalder and Eric Alden Smith who have applied optimal foraging models.[10] They make the assumption that hunter-gatherers are proficient and skilled, and they apply that assumption through the methodology of constrained optimization. Resource selection models analyse the selection of resources and how this is affected by factors such as the value, density and predictability of those resources, as well as their local and regional patterns of spatial distribution.

The models focus on resource selection and the location and movement of foragers with respect to resources, and intra-group transfer of resources. Researchers have recognized a wide variability among hunter-gatherers. Nevertheless they have also recognized the existence of some generalizations about these societies (see Winterhalder 2001), two of which are particularly interesting in our context: apparent under-production and routine food sharing. How does HBE explain these ethnological facts?

Under-production is explained as dependent on residential mobility. Residential mobility is a result of resource distribution patterns, including localized depletion. Mobility may suppress the desire for property, and transfer behaviour can discourage excess production. Therefore, foraging economies typically discourage ambitious production. As regards sharing, this is explained as a response to a mix of ecological and social factors (intermediate-sized resources, subsistence risk) and social factors (social prestige, signalling).[11]

In the HBE framework, hunter-gatherers appear as rational actors in obtaining subsistence efficiency. This efficiency is explained, first of all, with evolutionary reasons:

> Neo-Darwinian selection eliminates variants that do not efficiently acquire resources for survival and reproduction. A tendency towards optimization is built into the evolutionary process, even if optimality as such is rarely achieved . . . The lengthy duration of this mode of livelihood itself is an indication of its effectiveness.
>
> (Winterhalder 2001: 32)

Secondly, rational choice is considered part of the explanation:

> Some hunting and gathering behaviour is carefully calculated. On discovering moose tracks, Cree hunters carefully study their age and conditions for what they reveal about the animal's size, movements, and intentions. They survey

> surrounding forage for evidence that the animal would be tempted to linger nearby for browse. Thy evaluate the temperature, wind, and snow conditions to appraise the likelihood it was in an especially wary frame of mind. These and other factors are carefully appraised in reaching a decision . . . pursue the trail of this moose, or continue searching for a better pursuit opportunity. (Ibid.)[12]

Third, it is emphasized that many foraging decisions are probably guided by rules of thumb "arrived at through various selective mechanism acting on cultural heritage" (ibid.).

Therefore, efficient behaviour in the acquisition and distribution of natural resources, given technological and informational knowledge, is explained with a combination of economic rational behaviour (rational choice plus rules of thumb) and neo-Darwinian selection – a theoretical context coherent with Hirshleifer's bioeconomics and the 'subordination' of the other social sciences to economics. On the economic thesis of the inherent backwardness of primitive societies, HBE is agnostic, confining itself to acknowledgement, due to the ethnographic data, that hunter-gatherer societies are not 'simple'. This combination of elements – the acknowledgement of the efficient behaviour of primitives using an economic-biological approach and the agnosticism about backwardness – substantially strengthens Posner's rational-choice model of primitive behaviour.[13]

Notes

1 In an important article devoted to the analysis of certain major anthropological themes of the long term in the Judeo-Christian cosmology, such as the pleasure-pain principle of human action and the idea of an egoistical human nature underlying social behaviour, anthropologist Marshall Sahlins refers to Robbins's famous determination of what economics is all about. He correctly notes that "the economic man of modern times [is] still Adam. Indeed, the same scarcity-driven creature of need survived long enough to become the main protagonist of all human sciences" (Sahlins 1996: 397). On this revisitation of the Western cultural edifice and its theory of needs, see also Sahlins 1993 and 1994. On Sahlins' contribution to economic anthropology, see Part II of the present volume.

2 On Knight's role in the foundation of modern microeconomics, see Marchionatti 2003.

3 The controversy aroused a great deal of interest, also recently. See Polakoff 1953, Binembaum 2005.

4 Substantivist criticisms, Polanyi's above all (see Part II, Chapter 5), constitute a straightforward challenge for these new economists. This was clearly recognized by the economic historian Douglass North (1977). What gives Karl Polanyi's challenge a force not found in other scholars' criticism of the economist's tools, North wrote, was that he offered "an alternative analytical framework to account for past and present institutional organization" (North 1977: 707). The only way to meet his challenge, North maintains, was to develop "an analytical framework that can explain past and present institutional structure" (ibid.). North thinks that "transaction costs analysis is a promising analytical framework to explore non-market forms of economic organization" (ibid., 709).

5 In fact, Becker's role in the new field is considered marginal in the recent literature. Robson (2001: 11, note 1) writes that "Gary Becker (1976b) . . . considered the relationship between biology and economics, to some extent taking economics to be more basic."

6 The vision bears evident similarities with the "Iterated prisoner's dilemma" of game theory. In his *The Evolution of Cooperation*, political scientist Robert Axelrod (1984) formally developed Trivers's ideas. Axelrod identified a possible mechanism for the evolution of cooperation, which would emerge from the adoption of a simple strategy called 'tit-for-tat' (according to which individuals should cooperate on the first move, and then reciprocate the other player's previous move). In an earlier article, Axelrod and William Hamilton (1981: 211) concluded that "Darwin's emphasis on individual advantage has been formalized in terms of game theory. This establishes conditions under which cooperation based on reciprocity can evolve."

7 On Marshall about economics and biology, see Marchionatti and Cassata and 2011.

8 Hirshleifer writes: "The refusal of modern economics to examine the biological functions of preferences has meant that the bridge between human physiology and social expressions of desires has been studied by no one" (1977: 17–18). On the other hand, Becker's view of a generalized utility function "in which selfishness is only the midpoint of a spectrum ranging from benevolence at one extreme to malevolence to the other" is considered by Hirshleifer "really an empty generalization" (ibid.: 19–20).

9 In an important book, the American anthropologist Robert L. Kelly recognizes that the ecological perspective "cannot explain the particulars of Australian Dreamtime theology, Bushmen kinship, or Kwkwak'awakw mythology", but concludes that "we have to start someplace" (Kelly 2004: 23).

10 For reviews of the discipline, see Winterhalder and Smith 2000, and the more recent Nettle et al. 2013.

11 See Winterhalder 2001 and Kelly 2004 for extensive reviews of the anthropological literature of the lifeways of hunter-gatherers.

12 Winterhalder's 1981 article on prey choice and patch choice among the sub-Arctic Cree is one of the best-known early examples of ethnographic application of optimal foraging models.

13 HBE scholars argue that if observations are inconsistent with the goal of maximizing nutrient return rates, this is due to hunter-gatherers being likely to maximize their social position. This would be the case, for instance, of the Hadza of north-central Tanzania: their hunters bypass items they can easily take at relatively low but consistent rates in favour of other resources (for example, big game), that yield higher but much less reliable daily returns (see Hawkes et al., 1991). Hawkes and co-authors argue that big-game hunting is often a form of costly signalling, by means of which men establish and maintain social positions relative to their peers and competitors. Still, the concept of maximization seems to have here relatively scarce explanatory value: it can rather be said to configure a case of indeterminacy of the criterion of economic rationality. On this point, see Part II, Ch. 5.1.3.

3 Primitive societies in the interpretation of classical and neoclassical economics

A common model

The accounts of primitive societies offered across two hundred years, from Adam Smith to Richard Posner, by economic theory in its different characterizations of the subject may be referred to a common model. This can be summarized as follow:

1 Primitive societies are at the early phase of a substantially linear historical evolution. The stage theory of eighteenth-century sociology was superseded in its naive formulation and then partially abandoned, but the evolutionary core of the theory has been preserved. According to Smith, primitive society was the "rudest" stage of human society; according to formalist economics and anthropology, primitive society was the society in which rational behaviours were strongly limited by the institutional structure; according to the contemporary economics of non-market institutions, primitive society is the place where high transaction and information costs together with high uncertainty about future events determine the emergence of institutions. These are the result of a rational behaviour – in particular, in the field of acquisition and distribution of natural resources, as the behavioural ecology has shown – but they are insufficient and inadequate because they do not give rise to the property rights necessary to make development and wealth accumulation possible.

2 The fundamental characteristic shared by the various models of primitive society is economic backwardness: Smith's judgement on that society as being one of misery and high scarcity of resources, where the search for food is the main daily activity, is confirmed; although it is attenuated by formalist economists and then by contemporary economists, according to whom primitive societies are backward, or underdeveloped, from the technological, informational and institutional points of view. In economic theory, the concept of backwardness is the general concept able to define primitive, and pre-capitalist in general, societies.

3 Two necessary consequences derive from this picture: limited needs and the absence of certain surplus. The limitation of needs, considered 'unnatural' by economic science because needs are supposed to be 'naturally' unlimited, implies that the state of general poverty and insecurity is not eliminable;

this fact generates an imposed, not chosen, strong redistributive ethic and equality; the usual absence of surplus makes economic development and a statual organization impossible. In the rare cases in which surplus potentially exists, institutional conditions prevent the transformation of 'saving' into 'investment' and the development of a market system. Self-sufficiency, though often uncertain, is a necessary consequence of this situation.

4 The absence, or very limited existence, of market exchange is the necessary result of the absence of stable surpluses and limited needs.

5 In this representative picture, primitive society is subjected to an iron logic mechanism of necessary material dependence. A system of connections, a virtuous circle, among exchange, increasing division of labour, technological change and the creation of property rights, may make it possible to overcome under-development, but this system cannot be generated endogenously in a primitive society.

Part II

Economics and the challenge of primitive societies

Anthropological non-formalist approaches

Part II is devoted to analysis of the anthropological (non-formalist) approaches to primitive societies, which offer a substantially different interpretation of primitive economies.

Chapter 4 presents Marcel Mauss's *Essai sur le don* (1923–24), a systematization of previous works on the phenomenon of exchange in primitive and pre-capitalistic worlds, essentially offered in Boas's and Malinowski's classic ethnological works, which contributed crucially to deeper understanding of primitive societies: their accounts of, respectively, the *potlatch* and the *kula*, two primitive systems of gifts-exchange, are the main pillars of Mauss's work. It is in gift exchange, not in market, proto-capitalist relationships governed by economic rationality, that Mauss identifies both the foundations and the manifestation of society itself.

Chapter 5 centres upon the theoretical results of anthropologists and economists of the substantivist school established by Karl Polanyi in the 1950s. Substantivists argued that conventional economic categories were largely inapplicable to primitive societies; rather, they came to consider (non-market) reciprocity as the rule ensuring social organization. In the attempt to resolve the dispute between formalists and substantivists, anthropologist Marshall Sahlins argued, at the beginning of the 1970s, that an anthropological turn should reshape economics. Sahlins advocated a culturalist approach that "does honour to different societies for what they are". Building on several quantitatively informed ethnographic studies conducted on hunter-gatherers, Sahlins introduced the "original affluent society" model, which rapidly became a widely discussed topic in the anthropological literature.

Chapter 6 presents Mauss's *Essai* as interpreted by the political anthropology literature. In other words, it illustrates the political philosophy of the gift, as popularized by Marshall Sahlins along lines drawn by Claude Lévi-Strauss. Pierre Clastres's notes on the relationship between gift exchange and war in primitive societies, strengthening the political reading of Mauss's *Essai*, are also considered. The discussion is intended to make primitive economic organization fully intelligible from a perspective of, as Sahlins would say, "anthropological economics".

4 The primitive system of gift exchange discovered

Marcel Mauss's *Essai sur le don*

4.1 Anthropologists and 'real' primitive economies

Until the end of the nineteenth century, primitive economies remained a largely unknown subject for the community of social scientists. The rediscovery of the real primitive economies was made possible by the works of some anthropologists between the end of the nineteenth century and the first twenty years of the twentieth century: the English Charles Seligman (1873–1940) and Alfred Reginald Radcliffe-Brown (1881–1955), the Austrian Richard Thurnwald (1869–1954); and, above all, Franz Boas and Bronislaw Malinowski.[1]

Franz Boas (1858–1942), born in Germany, emigrant to the United States in 1887, professor at Columbia University after 1899, was one of the most influential American anthropologist of the twentieth century and founder of the cultural relativism school of American anthropology. In a methodologically important essay on the limitations of the comparative method in anthropology written in 1896, he provided a critique of nineteenth-century evolutionary anthropology (that is, that of Edward B. Tylor and Lewis H. Morgan) according to which human society had developed everywhere in the same ways, governed by general laws of development applicable to all societies. Boas considered this theory to lack a historical basis: in fact, he stressed, field research observations did not support the thesis of a uniform development, but rather one characterized by variously different cultural processes. He contrasted the evolutionary method with the historical method and argued that cultures could be understood only within their specific historical and ethnographic contexts: in this way, it could be possible to reconstruct the cultural processes generating differences between societies.

Boas was a specialist in North American Indian cultures. His field research from 1885 onwards gave risen to the 1897 monograph *The Social Organization and the Secret Societies of the Kwakiutl Indians*, which was followed by other books on the subject in the following thirty years (Boas 1921 and 1966).

Bronislaw Malinowski (1884–1942) was a Polish anthropologist, recognized as a founder of social anthropology. From 1910, he was at the London School of Economics and Political Science (LSE) – initially as a pupil of Seligman – until the end of the 1930s, when he moved to Yale University in the United States. His main work, *Argonauts of the Western Pacific: An account of native enterprise and adventure in the Archipelagoes of Melanesian New Guinea* (1922), about the Trobriand people living on the Kiriwana Island chain, dismantled the view of savage peoples typical among economists at that time. Arguing against "the scholastic deductions of abstract economics" (Malinowski 2002 [1922]: 47) and its construction of the imagine of the "shadowy Primitive Economic Man" which differed entirely from "the real native in flesh and bones", he writes: "The economic nature of man is a rule illustrated on imaginary savages for didactic purposes only, and the conclusions of the authors are in reality based on their study of the facts of developed economics"(ibid.: 48n).

In a functionalist perspective based on fieldwork and "participant observation"[2] Malinowski was able to criticize the representation of the primitive as a man "prompted in all his actions by a rationalistic conception of self interest, and achieving his aims directly and with the minimum of effort" (ibid.: 46). In his field research, "the primitive Trobriander furnishes us with such an instance, contradicting this fallacious theory". In fact: "He works prompted by motives of a highly complex, social and traditional nature, and towards aims which are certainly not directed towards . . . the direct achievements of utilitarian purposes" (ibid.).

Already in an article published in 1921 in the *Economic Journal*, based on the lectures given at the LSE, where he presented some of the first data on the Trobriand Islanders' economic life, Malinowski emphasized that primitive economies "are not by any means the simple matter we are generally led to suppose" (Malinowski 1921: 15):

> In savage societies national economy certainly does not exist, if we mean by the term a system of free competitive exchange of goods and services, with the interplay of supply and demand determining value and regulating all economic life . . . We find a state of affairs where production, exchange and consumption are socially organized and regulated by custom, and where a special system of traditional economic values governs their activities and spurs them on to efforts.
>
> (Ibid.)

Malinowski called this state of affairs "Tribal Economy", a new term required by his new conception. In order to obtain deep understanding of a primitive community, Malinowski wrote, "the analysis of the natives' own conceptions of value, ownership, equivalence, commercial honour and morals opens a new vista of economic research" (ibid.): the study of interrelations between the economic and the other aspects of tribal life – social, customary, legal and magico-religious – is the core component of the analysis. *Argonauts of the Western Pacific* is the result of the field research conducted by Malinowski in the period 1914–18. The book can be considered the first systematic analysis of economic activities considered as social phenomena.

In fact, Malinowski and Boas (although the latter was scarcely interested in economic subjects), made fundamental contributions to knowledge on primitive social mechanisms, particularly with their analyses of two typical systems of gift-giving – called *potlatch* and *kula* – practised respectively by indigenous peoples of the Pacific Northwestern coast of Canada and the United States and by Trobriand islanders. Boas's studies on the *potlatch* of the American Indians of the Pacific Northwest Coast of Canada and Malinowski's studies on the Melanesian *kula*, were the basis of the fundamental *Essai sur le don. Forme et raison de l'échange dans les sociétés archaïques* written by the French sociologist Marcel Mauss and published in 1923–24 in the *Année Sociologique*.

Marcel Mauss (1872–1950)[3] was the nephew and disciple of Emile Durkheim, architect of modern social science, and he was professor of 'history of religion and uncivilized peoples' at the *Ecole Pratique des Hautes Etudes* from 1901, leader of the group centred on the journal *Année sociologique*, founder of the *Institut d'ethnologie de Paris*, and an outstanding figure in the French field of human sciences – among his disciples were Michel Leiris, Alfred Metraux and Claude Lévi-Strauss. His work, as Valeri (2013 [1966]) has highlighted, is closer to the humanism of the Renaissance, in particular to that of Montaigne and with reference to this volume's earlier discussion on savages in philosophers' reflections, it took the Montaigne-Diderot line.

The *Essai* has been an enormously influential work which has never lost interest among social scientists and philosophers; still today it is a source of continuing reflection. The great importance of this essay and its originality has been emphasized by the great French anthropologist Lévi-Strauss as follows:

> Like language, the social is an autonomous reality (the same one, moreover); symbols are more real than what they symbolize, the signifier precedes and determines the signified . . . The revolutionary character of the *Essai sur le don* is that it sets us on that path . . . For the first time in the history of ethnological thinking . . . an effort was made to transcend empirical observation and to reach deeper realities. For the first time, the social . . . becomes a system, among whose parts connections, equivalences and interdependent aspects can be discovered.
>
> (Lévi-Strauss, 1987 [1950]: 37–8)

4.2 Mauss's *Essai sur le don*

4.2.1 Gift exchange as a "total social phenomenon"

In the *Essai*, Mauss synthesized and systematized the many studies devoted to the phenomenon of exchange published in the first twenty years of the twentieth century; in particular, as noted, Boas's and Malinowski's works.

Mauss established a relation among "social phenomena" observed in the Northwest of Canada, in Polynesia, in Melanesia, as well as in many archaic societies. This inquiry was the product of a long intellectual journey. When he was writing his *Essai sur le variations saisonnières des societés Eskimos* (1904–05), Mauss had discovered Boas's writings on Kwakiutl *potlatch*, which became the subject of Mauss's lectures at the *Ecole del Hautes Etudes* in 1905.

Moreover, his reading of the American anthropologist John Reed Swanton's studies on the Northwest tribes of Haida and Tlinglit showed him the widespread existence of the *potlatch* in that area. At that time – the early years of the new century – Mauss thought that the *potlatch* was a unique phenomenon in the history of mankind, confined to the Northwest coast of America. However, his reading, some years later, of Seligman's and Thurnwald's works on certain Melanesian peoples (Seligman 1910, Thurnwald 1912) showed him that the *potlatch* existed in Melanesia as well, and also, as he himself proved (Mauss 1921), in the Indo-European world. This intellectual journey in search of *potlatch*-type systems was completed with the reading and deep analysis of Malinowski's 1922 book. The Trobrianders' *kula* – the exchange carried on by communities inhabiting a wide ring of islands forming a closed circuit – was, according to Mauss, a further fundamental example of the general existence of forms of exchange of that type. The nexus between *Argonauts of the Western Pacific* and the *Essai* was clearly understood by Lévi-Strauss:

> the whole of the *Essai sur le don* emerges, in the most direct way, out of Malinowski's *Argonauts of the Western Pacific*, also published in 1922, which was to lead Malinowski himself, independently, to conclusions very close to those of Mauss.
>
> (Lévi-Strauss 1987 [1950]: 37).[4]

The fundamental theoretical idea introduced in Mauss's analysis is that of "total social phenomena" (*phénomènes sociaux totaux*). When examining primitive and archaic societies, Mauss writes, we face "an enormous complex of facts" in themselves "very complicated": "Everything intermingles in them, everything constituting the strictly social life of societies that have preceded our own, even those going back to protohistory" (Mauss 1990 [1923–24]: 3).

In these total social phenomena, "all kinds of institutions are given expression at one and the same time – religious, juridical, and moral, which relate to both politics and the family; likewise economic ones" (ibid.). Among all these complex facts, Mauss studies one characteristic: "the so to speak voluntary character of these total services, apparently free and disinterested but nevertheless constrained and self-interested", which have taken "the form of the gift" (ibid.: 4).

The primitive and archaic societies are not devoid of economic markets, Mauss notes, but we find the phenomena of exchange of goods and contract; what is called 'a natural economy' "has never existed". It is the "system of exchange" that is different from that of modern capitalist societies. There is not a simple exchange of goods among individuals, as supposed in the Smithian fiction of the bartering savage, but rather a complex phenomenon that Mauss called the "system of total services" (*prestation totale*):

> In the economic and legal systems that have preceded our own, one hardly ever finds a simple exchange of goods, wealth, and products in transactions concluded by individuals. First, it is not individuals but collectivities that

> impose obligations of exchange and contract upon each other. The contracting parties are legal entities: clans, tribes, and families who confront and oppose one another either in groups who meet face to face in one spot, or through their chiefs, or in both these ways at once. Moreover, what they exchange is not solely property and wealth, movable and immovable goods, and things economically useful. In particular, such exchanges are acts of politeness: banquets, rituals, military services, women, children, dances, festivals, and fairs, in which economic transaction is only one element, and in which the passing on of wealth is only one feature of a much more general and enduring contract. Finally, these total services and counter-services are committed to in a somewhat voluntary form by presents and gifts, although in the final analysis they are strictly compulsory, on pain of private or public warfare. We propose to call all this the *system of total services*.
>
> (ibid.: 6–7; original emphasis)

There are three characteristics of gift exchange, Mauss writes: the obligation to give, the obligation to receive, and the obligation to reciprocate. They occur in multifaceted forms. Mauss analyses two of these "total services": the *potlatch* and the *kula*.

As for the *potlatch*, as already said, the main sources of Mauss's analysis are Boas's (and also Swanton's) field researches on some tribes of the American Northwest: Haida, Tlingit, Tsimshian, Salish, Nuu-chah-nulth and Kwakiutl. Within these tribes, Mauss writes:

> there appears what is certainly a type of these 'total services', rare but highly developed. We propose to call this form *potlatch*, as moreover, do American authors using the Chinook term, which has become part of the everyday language of Whites and Indians from Vancouver to Alaska. The word potlatch essentially means 'to feed', 'to consume'.
>
> (Ibid.: 7)

Mauss writes that these tribes, which are "very rich", have a dual structure: from the end of spring they disperse to go hunting, to gather roots and the juicy mountain berries, and to fish for salmon in the rivers; at the onset of winter they concentrate once more in what are called 'towns'. They spend the winter in a continual festival of feasts, fairs and markets, which also constitute the solemn assembly of the tribe. It is then, during the period when they are gathered together in this way, that they live in a state of perpetual excitement.

The tribe is organized by hierarchical confraternities and secret societies. Everything – marriages, initiations, shamanic seances and meetings for the worship of the great gods, and so on – is woven "into an inextricable network of rites, of total legal and economic services, of assignment to political ranks in the society of men, in the tribe, and in the confederations of tribes, and even internationally" (ibid.). Yet what is noteworthy about these tribes, Mauss emphasizes following Boas, are the principle of rivalry and hostility that prevails in all these practices and the purely sumptuary destruction of wealth that has been accumulated in order to outdo the rival chief as well as his associate (normally a grandfather, father-in-law, or son-in-law). There is total service, Mauss writes, in the sense that

> it is indeed the whole clan that contracts on behalf of all, for all that it possesses and for all that it does, through the person of its chief..But this act of 'service' on the part of the chief takes on an extremely marked agonistic character. It is essentially usurious and sumptuary. It is a struggle between nobles to establish a hierarchy amongst themselves from which their clan will benefit at a later date.
>
> (Ibid.: 8)

The term *potlatch* is reserved by Mauss for this kind of institution, which, he says, can also be called, at greater length, "*total services of an agonistic type*" (ibid.; original emphasis). In the winter season, "there are potlatches everywhere, in response to other potlatches" (ibid.: 45). Commenting on Boas's description of the *potlatch*, Mauss emphasizes that in the *potlatch* giving, receiving and reciprocating are obligations: "The obligation to give is the essence of the *potlatch*" (ibid.: 50). He stresses that:

> A chief must give potlatches for himself, his son, his son-in-law, or his daughter, and for his dead. He can only preserve his authority over his tribe and village, and even over his family, he can only maintain his rank among the chiefs – both nationally and internationally – if he can prove he is haunted and favoured both by the spirits and by good fortune, that he is possessed, and also possesses it. And he can only prove this good fortune by spending it and sharing it out, humiliating others by placing them 'in the shadow of his name'.
>
> (Ibid.)

If the chief does not give, he loses face: "to lose one's prestige is indeed to lose one's soul." On the other hand, "the obligation to accept is no less constraining" (ibid.: 52):

> One has no right to refuse a gift, or to refuse to attend the potlatch. To act in this way is to show that one is afraid of having to reciprocate, to fear being 'flattened' [that is, losing one's name] until one has reciprocated . . . One does more than derive benefit from a thing or a festival: one has accepted a challenge, and has been able to do so because of being certain to be able to reciprocate, to prove one is not unequal . . . The obligation to reciprocate constitutes the essence of the potlatch, in so far as it does not consist of pure destruction.
>
> (Ibid.: 52–3)

According to Mauss, the main characteristics of this constant giving and returning are the following: the collective nature of the contract; the notion of credit – "it is in the nature of a gift to impose an obligatory time limit" (ibid.: 45), and the notion of honour:

> Nowhere is the individual prestige of a chief and that of his clan so closely linked to what is spent and to the meticulous repayment with interest of gifts that have been accepted, so as to transform into persons having an obligation those that have placed you yourself under a similar obligation. Consumption and destruction of goods really go beyond all bounds. In certain kinds of potlatch one must expend all that one has, keeping nothing back. It is a competition to see who is the richest and also the most madly extravagant. Everything is based upon the principles of antagonism and rivalry. The political status of individuals in the brotherhoods and clans, and ranks of all kinds, are gained in a 'war of property', just as they are in real war, or through chance, inheritance, alliance, and marriage. Yet everything is conceived of as if it were a 'struggle of wealth'.
>
> (Ibid.: 47)

Examples of this institution, Mauss writes, are found in Melanesia and Papua, but also elsewhere:

> a quite considerable number of intermediate forms between those exchanges comprising very acute rivalry and the destruction of wealth, such as those of the American Northwest and Melanesia, and others, where emulation is more moderate but where those entering into contracts seek to outdo one another in their gifts.
>
> (ibid.: 8)

The Melanesian *kula* studied by Malinowski "is a sort of grand *potlatch*" (ibid.: 27), Mauss maintains, and he considers it "typical" (ibid.: 34): "it would be difficult to come across a custom of gift-through-exchange more clear-cut, complete, and consciously performed, and, moreover, better understood by the observer recording it than the one Malinowski found among the Trobriand people" (ibid.).

Like the *potlatch*, the *kula* is part of a vast system of services and counter-services, "services rendered and reciprocated" (ibid.), "a constant give and take" (ibid.: 37).

Malinowski had defined the *kula* as "a novel type of ethnological fact" (Malinowski 2002 [1922]: 402). This novelty had three aspects:

1. the size of its sociological and geographical extent – "a big, inter-tribal relationship, uniting with definite social bonds a vast area and great numbers of people, binding them with definite ties of reciprocal obligations" (ibid.);
2. "the character of the transaction itself, which is the proper substance of the kula" – "a half commercial, half ceremonial exchange, it is carried out for its own sake, in fulfilment of a deep desire to possess", but it is no ordinary possession, but rather "a special type, in which a man owns for a short time,

and in alternating manner, individual specimens of two classes of objects" (ibid.), and

3 "the natives' mental attitude towards the tokens of wealth", "neither used nor regarded as money or currency" (ibid.).

The *kula* is a form of gift exchange of two objects – bracelets of white shell (called *mwali*), and necklaces of red shell discs (called *soulava*) – carried on by communities inhabiting a wide ring of islands which form a closed circuit; it is a vast, intertribal web of relationships. Along this circuit, these articles constantly travel in opposite directions: the *soulava* moves in a clockwise direction, while the *mwali* moves in a counter-clockwise direction. Every movement of the *kula* articles, every detail of the transactions, is fixed and regulated by a set of traditional rules and conventions; some acts of the *kula* are accompanied by an elaborate magical ritual and public ceremonies. On every island and in every village, a more or less limited number of men take part in the *kula* – that is to say, receive the goods, hold them for a short while, and then pass them on. Therefore one transaction does not conclude the *kula* relationship, "the rule being 'once in the kula, always in the kula' and partnership between two men is a permanent and lifelong affair" (ibid.: 62). The ceremonial exchange of the two articles is the main aspect of the *kula*, but, associated with it there is a great number of secondary activities and features. Thus, side by side with the ritual exchange, the native carry on ordinary trade. The natives distinguish the *kula* (gift followed by a counter-gift) from barter, which they practise extensively, and for which they have a term, *gimwali*: in this, the articles are exchanged from hand to hand, and the equivalence between the two objects is discussed and bargained. On the contrary, there is no bargaining in the *kula*.

4.2.2 The spirit of "the thing given"

According to Mauss, the exchange of gifts characterizes the primitive and archaic society; it is a phenomenon typical of societies prior to the emergence of the state. Mauss writes that, on the one hand "to refuse to give, to fail to invite, just as to refuse to accept, is tantamount to declaring war; it is to reject the bond of alliance and commonality" (Mauss 1990 [1923–24]: 17); on the other hand, the obligation to reciprocate the gifts is "imperative" (ibid.: 54). How can this fact be explained? Mauss refers to a native concept, the *hau* in Maori dialect, a force embedded in the gifts. This concept is used by Mauss in order to pose the central question of the *Essai*: "What rule of legality and self-interest, in societies of a backward or archaic type, compels the gift that has been received to be obligatorily reciprocated? What power resides in the object given that causes its recipient to pay it back?" (ibid.: 4).

Hau is this power. Mauss found this concept in a Maori text – "of capital importance" (ibid.: 14), he writes – gathered in 1909 by Elsdon Best, a New Zealander ethnologist, on the basis of information provided by an old native informant called Tamati Ranaipiri. According to Mauss, he gives us "the key of the problem":

> I will speak to you about the *hau* . . . The *hau* is not the wind that blows – not at all. Let us suppose that you possess a certain article (*taonga*) and that you give me this article. You give it to me without setting a price on it. We strike no bargain about it. Now, I give this article to a third person who, after a certain lapse of time, decides to give me something as payment in return (*utu*). He makes a present to me of something (*taonga*). Now, this *taonga* that he gives me is the spirit (*hau*) of the *taonga* that I had received from you and that I had given to him. The *taonga* that I received for these *taonga* (which came from you) must be returned to you. It would not be fair (*tika*) on my part to keep these *taonga* for myself, whether they were desirable (*rawe*) or undesirable (*kino*). I must give them to you because they are a *hau* of the *taonga* that you gave me. If I kept this other *taonga* for myself, serious harm might befall me, even death. This is the nature of the *hau*, the *hau* of personal property, the *hau* of the *taonga*, the *hau* of the forest. *Kati ena*.
>
> (Ibid.)

Mauss observes that the essential elements of the *potlatch* can be traced in Samoa: the search for honour and prestige, *mana* (a word that symbolizes the magical force in every creature), and "the absolute obligation to reciprocate these gifts under pain of losing that *mana,* that authority – the talisman and source of wealth that is authority itself" (ibid.: 11). Mauss notes that the *taonga*, articles strongly linked to the person, the clan, and the earth, at least in the theory of Maori law and religion "are the vehicle for its *mana*, its magical, religious, and spiritual force" (ibid.: 13). Mauss examines the Maori text in order fully to understand what the "Maori juridical expert" says. One need only say, Mauss writes:

> The *taonga* and all goods termed strictly personal possess a *hau*, a spiritual power. You give me one of them, and I pass it on to a third party; he gives another to me in turn, because he is impelled to do so by the *hau* my present possesses. I, for my part, am obliged to give you that thing because I must return to you what is in reality the effect of the *hau* of your *taonga*.
>
> (Ibid.: 15)

Herein lies, according to Mauss, the key idea that seems to dominate "the obligatory circulation of wealth, tribute, and gifts" (ibid.):

> it is clear that in Maori law, the legal tie, a tie occurring through things, is one between souls, because the thing itself possesses a soul, is of the soul. Hence it follows that to make a gift of something to someone is to make a present of some part of oneself.
>
> (Ibid.: 16)

In these societies (Melanesia, Polynesia, the American Northwest, ancient India, and so on), "everything passes to and fro as if there were a constant exchange of a spiritual matter, including things and men, between clans and individuals" (ibid.: 18), because of the principle of reciprocity represented by the *hau*. This is Mauss's interpretation of the Maori text.

Many criticisms were made of this interpretation, and they will be discussed below. Here we simply emphasize, with Lévi-Strauss, that *hau* is not necessary to connect the different phases of the exchange. Mauss himself, Lévi-Strauss writes, offers the key to the problem, by noting *en passant* that in Papua and Melanesia there is "only one word to designate buying and selling, lending and borrowing". Mauss infers that "antithetical operations are expressed by the same word"; but Lévi-Strauss maintains that there is ample proof that the operations in question are far from 'antithetical'; that they are just two modes of the selfsame reality. We do not need *hau* to make the synthesis, because the antithesis does not exist: "The antithesis is a subjective illusion of ethnographers, and some times also of indigenous people" (Lévi-Strauss 1987 [1950]: 49). The problem is not what makes reciprocity compulsory, but why the primitive society is founded on reciprocity. In Mauss's text, Lévi-Strauss writes, there is a possible answer. Mauss writes that "everything passes to and fro"; therefore the exchange is the internal, deep structure of the society. The "total service" is in fact a "social contract", or, better, a political contract.

4.3 Mauss's critique of the *homo oeconomicus*

The fourth chapter of the *Essai* is devoted to the conclusions, moral, sociological and economic. We focus on these last. First, Mauss emphasizes that this economy of the exchange-through-gift falls outside the schemes normally put forward by economists:

> the notion of value functions in these societies. Very large surpluses, speaking in absolute terms, are amassed. They are often expended to no avail, with comparatively enormous luxury, which is in no way commercial. These are the signs of wealth, and kinds of money are exchanged. Yet the whole of this very rich economy is still filled with religious elements. Money still possesses its magical power and is still linked to the clan or to the individual. The various economic activities, for example the market, are suffused with rituals and myths. They retain a ceremonial character that is obligatory and effective. They are full of rituals and rights.
>
> (Ibid.: 91)

Malinowski had made an attempt to classify from the point of view of motives of self-interest and disinterestedness, all the transactions that he noted among the Trobriand Islanders. He graded them from the pure gift to pure barter after bargaining has taken place. But Mauss thinks that this classification is inapplicable:

> just as these gifts are not freely given, they are also not really disinterested. They already represent for the most part total counter-services, not only

> made with a view to paying for services or things, but also to maintaining a profitable alliance, one that cannot be rejected . . . This is a general fact.
>
> (Ibid.: 94)

Even pure destruction of wealth, Mauss adds, does not signify the complete detachment that one might believe is found in it:

> The purely sumptuary form of consumption (which is almost always exaggerated and often purely destructive), in which considerable amounts of goods that have taken a long time to amass are suddenly given away or even destroyed, particularly in the case of the potlatch, give such institutions the appearance of representing purely lavish expenditure and childish prodigality. In effect, and in reality, not only are useful things given away and rich foods consumed to excess, but one even destroys for the pleasure of destroying. For example, the Tsimshian, Tlingit, and Haïda chiefs throw these copper objects and money into the water. The Kwakiutl chiefs smash them, as do those of the tribes allied to them. But the reason for these gifts and frenetic acts of wealth consumption is in no way disinterested, particularly in societies that practise the potlatch. Between chiefs and their vassals, between vassals and their tenants, through such gifts a hierarchy is established. To give is to show one's superiority, to be more, to be higher in rank, *magister*. To accept without giving in return, or without giving more back, is to become client and servant, to become small, to fall lower.
>
> (Ibid.: 95)

Then Mauss considers the notion of interest, of the individual search for what is useful. In those civilizations, Mauss writes, individuals "are concerned with their own interest, but in a different way from our own age" (ibid.: 96):

> They hoard, but in order to spend, to place under an obligation, to have their own 'liege men'. On the other hand, they carry on exchange, but it is above all in luxury articles, ornaments or clothes, or things that are consumed immediately, as at feasts. They repay with interest, but this is in order to humiliate the person. initially making the gift or exchange, and not only to recompense him for loss caused to him by 'deferred consumption'.
>
> (Ibid.: 97)

This series of economic events is not governed by the economic rationalism "whose theory we are so willing to propound". Mauss emphasizes that the word 'interest' is itself recent, being originally an accounting technique, whereas "in ancient systems of morality of the most epicurean kind it is the good and pleasurable that is sought after, and not material utility" (ibid.):

> It is our western societies which have recently made man an 'economic animal' . . . *Homo oeconomicus* is not behind us, but lies ahead . . . For a

> very long time man was something different, and he has not been a machine for very long, made complicated by a calculating machine.
>
> (Ibid.: 98)

The economic science criticized by Mauss (and Malinowski) was essentially the old classical economics of the nineteenth century and the utilitarianism that characterized most of it; also, the value of his criticism went further than its specific object. However, ongoing in those decades were criticism of utilitarianism and the construction of a new economics searching for more general and abstract theoretical structures. On the methodological level, this transformation was characterized by the essay written by the English economist Lionel Robbins, one of the most influential thinkers of the new century, also outside economics – as the interest in his thought of anthropologists like Firth and Herskovitz showed (see Part I, Ch. 2.1.). The task of criticizing Robbins' economics was taken up, some decades after Mauss's *Essai*, by Karl Polanyi with his substantivist approach.

Notes

1 Pearson (2000) enlarges the perspective by including references to German economic thought around the turn of the century.

2 Malinowski, like Boas, criticized the evolutionary approach and considered the "participant observation", that is, the idea that the anthropologist must live in the community being studied, participate with individuals, observe and talk with them and interpret the situations observed, in order "to grasp the native's point of view, his relation to life, to realize *his* vision of *his* world" (Malinowski 2002 [1922]: 25, emphasis in original), to be the fundamental method of the anthropologist.

3 For an intellectual and political biography of Marcel Mauss, see Fournier 1994.

4 Malinowski and Mauss initially expressed different ideas about free and unfree gifts. Mauss criticized Malinowski's earlier interpretation of the "pure gift" among the Trobriands. In the context of social solidarity, Mauss maintained, an entirely free gift does not exist: exchange always requires reciprocity. Malinowski (1926) admitted his earlier mistakes as presented in *Argonauts*. He acknowledged his "distinguished friend M. Mauss" and his criticism of pure gifts, but stated that he had realized his mistakes before reading Mauss's strictures.

5 The substantivist perspective on the role of the economy in societies

Karl Polanyi's and Marshall Sahlins's contributions

5.1 Karl Polanyi's substantivism

5.1.1 Market societies as a particular case

Karl Polanyi (1886–1964), a representative of the great central European culture between the two world wars, emigrated in 1933 to England and then to the United States in 1940. He is well known above all for his book, *The Great Transformation. The political and economic origins of our time*, published in 1944. The book is an extensive original analysis of classic bourgeois market society, its internal conflicts and the transformation undergone by the liberal economic institutions in the 1930s. The thesis of the book is that the market society of the nineteenth century was not the natural evolutionary point of arrival of human history, but rather an extraordinary historical case whose basis consisted of "extraordinary assumptions":

> A market economy is an economic system controlled, regulated, and directed by markets alone; order in the production and distribution of goods is entrusted to this self-regulating mechanism. An economy of this kind derives from the expectation that human beings behave in such a way as to achieve maximum money gains. It assumes markets in which the supply of goods (including services) available at a definite price will equal the demand at that price. It assumes the presence of money, which functions as purchasing power in the hands of its owners. Production will then be controlled by prices, for the profits of those who direct production will depend upon them; the distribution of the goods also will depend upon prices, for prices form incomes, and it is with the help of these incomes that the goods produced are distributed amongst the members of society. Under these assumptions order in the production and distribution of goods is ensured by prices alone. Self-regulation implies that all production is for sale on the market and that all incomes derive from such sales . . . [Moreover] no measure or policy must be countenanced that would influence the action of these markets.
>
> (Polanyi 2001 [1944]: 71–2)

An economic system based on self-regulating markets, Polanyi maintains, is a relatively recent phenomenon: "never before our own time were markets more than accessories of economic life" (ibid.: 71). According to Polanyi's historical reconstruction, this autonomization of the economic sphere happened at the end of the eighteenth century in England at the time of Industrial Revolution. Thereafter, this phenomenon extended across the globe and a new society arose. The crucial step was the transformation of labour and land into commodities, because they were produced for sale. Before then, the human world had never experienced anything similar.

In Chapter 4 of *The Great Transformation*, entitled "Societies and Economic Systems", on the basis of impressive anthropological documentary research – from the already quoted Boas, Thurnwald, Malinowski, Radcliffe-Brown, Firth and Herskovitz, to Karl Bucher, Edwin Meyer Loeb and Ruth Benedict (Boas's pupil) – Polanyi refuted some anthropological or sociological assumptions contained in the philosophy of economic liberalism and in classical and neoclassical political economy; first of all, the motive of gain as natural to man. He then identified in the mechanisms of reciprocity and redistribution, respectively, the bases of primitive societies' social behaviour and the great pre-capitalist empires, where the economy was embedded in other institutions like kinship and religion.

5.1.2 The theoretical principles of substantivism

After *The Great Transformation*, Polanyi's research increasingly focused on "patterns of integration" different from those of market societies. Appointed visiting professor in economics at Columbia University, New York, in 1947, he undertook, together with the anthropologist Conrad Arensberg and his former student Harry Pearson, interdisciplinary research on economic aspects of institutional growth which involved a group of brilliant younger scholars. The result was a book published ten years later, in 1957, entitled *Trade and Markets in the Early Empires*, and in which three different lines of inquiry converged: criticism of neoclassical economic theory, construction of a typology of economic systems, and analysis of the origin and history of economic institutions. The book developed the principles of the substantivist school to oppose the formalist or neoclassical methodological approach. Polanyi's later works, in particular *The Livelihood of Man*, posthumously published in 1977, were essentially developments of the 1957 work.

The subtitle of *Trade and Markets* is *Economies in history and theory*, which was the theoretical subject of the interdisciplinary research. In his introductory note, Polanyi writes that the aim of the book is not to reject economic analysis but "to set its historical and institutional limitations, namely, to the economies where price-making markets have sway, and to transcend these limitations in a general theory of economic organization" (Polanyi 1957: xviii).

Therefore, its main task is to provide tools with which to analyse non-market economies; that is, those economies "where there is no 'economizing', that is, no institutional framework to compel the individual to 'rational' and 'efficient' economic activity, or 'optimum' allocation of his resources" (ibid.: xvii).

The first conceptual tool with which Polanyi tackles the issue of the transition from nonmarket to market economies, "from a nameless to a separate existence" (ibid.: 68), "is the distinction between *the embedded and the disembedded condition of the economy in relation to society*" (ibid.; emphasis added). The origin of these concepts lies, Polanyi writes, in the works of three great social scientists: the British comparative jurist and historian Henry Sumner Maine, the German sociologist Ferdinand Tonnies, and the German sociologist and political economist Max Weber, without forgetting Aristotle's contribution. In non-market economies status and community (*Gemeinschaft*) prevail. The economy "is embedded in non economic institutions" (ibid.: 71), the economic process "being instituted through kinship, marriage, age-groups, secret societies, totemic associations, and public solemnities" (ibid.: 70). Polanyi writes: "The term 'economic life' would here have no obvious meaning" (ibid.); that is, in these situations an 'economy' obviously exists, but the concept of 'economic' does not exist, because it is embedded in non-economic institutions:

> To the individual his emotions fail to convey any experience that he could identify as 'economic'. He is simply not aware of any pervading interest in regard to his livelihood which he could recognize as such. Yet the lack of such a concept does not appear to hamper him in the performance of his everyday tasks . . . There exists, as a rule, no term to designate the concept of economic. Accordingly, as far as one can judge, this concept was absent . . . The prime reason for the absence of any concept of the economy is the difficulty of identifying the economic process under conditions where it is embedded in non economic institutions. Only the concept of the economy, not the economy itself, is in abeyance.
>
> (Ibid.: 71)

Moreover, Polanyi adds, "another broad reason for the absence in primitive society of an integrating effect of the economy is its lack of quantitativity" (ibid.: 73), because "reciprocity demands adequacy of response, not mathematical equality" (ibid.). Another concept which is inapplicable in primitive conditions is that of property "as a right of disposing of definite objects" (ibid.: 75), and "services, not goods make up wealth" (ibid.: 77). Finally, the ideology is anti-economical. As further proof of this anti-economical attitude, Polanyi refers to Aristotle's philosophy on the prizes of life, which express a dominant attitude in the ancient world. He notes that:

> In the philosophy of Aristotle the three prizes of fortune were: honor and prestige; security of life and limb; wealth . . . wealth is the bliss of proprietorship, mainly of heirlooms or famed treasure . . . The *agatha* are the highest prizes of life, that which is most desirable and also rarest.
>
> (Ibid.)

According to Polanyi, these are some of the major reasons that so long impeded in the way of the birth of a distinctively economic field of interest: "Even to the professional thinker the fact that man must eat did not appear worthy of elaboration" (ibid.: 78).

If economics is unable to deal with primitive and pre-capitalistic societies, Polanyi writes, then we need a concept of economy adequate to those societies, because an economic process of course exists in all societies. A substantive view of economy takes shape. First of all, Polanyi clarifies the semantic confusion implicit in the term 'economic'. In fact, "the term economic is a compound of two meanings that have independent roots", which he calls "the substantive and the formal meaning":

> The substantive meaning of economic derives from man's dependence for his living upon nature and his fellows. It refers to the interchange with his natural and social environment, in so far as this results in supplying him with the means of material want satisfaction.
>
> The formal meaning of 'economic' derives from the logical character of the means-ends relationship, so apparent in such words as 'economical' or 'economizing'. It refers to a definite situation of choice, namely, that between the different uses of means induced by an insufficiency of those means. If we call the rules governing choice of means the logic of rational actions, then we may denote this variant of logic, with an improvised term, as formal economics.
>
> The two root meanings of 'economic', the substantive and the formal, have nothing in common. The latter derives from logic, the former from fact. The formal meaning implies a set of rules referring to choice between the alternative uses of insufficient means. The substantive meaning implies neither choice nor insufficiency of means; man's livelihood may or may not involve the necessity of choice and, if choice there be, it need not be induced by the limiting effect of a 'scarcity' of the means.
>
> (Ibid.: 243–4)

Polanyi's proposition is that only the substantive meaning of 'economic' is "capable of yielding the concepts that are required by the social sciences for an investigation of all the empirical economies of the past and present" (ibid.: 244). The substantive concept of economic has at its basis the empirical economy. It can be defined, Polanyi writes, "as an instituted process of interaction between man and his environment, which results in a continuous supply of want satisfying material means" (ibid.: 248). The economy, then, is an instituted process, in the sense that the human economy "is embedded and enmeshed in institutions, economic and noneconomic" (ibid.: 250). Instituting gives the economic process its unity and stability. From this, it follows that study of the change of the place of economies in societies is inquiry into the different ways in which the economic process has been instituted in space and time.

Necessary for this purpose are new tools of inquiry identified by Polanyi in the "forms of integration" or patterns of integration: they are *reciprocity*, *redistribution* and *exchange*. These are elementary structures of the circulation of products to which different models of social organization correspond, that is "definite institutional supports" (ibid.: 251). Reciprocity, the oldest form, which "denotes movements between correlative points of symmetrical groupings", (ibid.: 250) integrates the economy only if "symmetrically organized structures, such as a symmetrical system of kinship groups, are given" (ibid.: 251). Redistribution presupposes "the presence of an allocative center – examples of redistributive economies are the empires of ancient Mesopotamia, Egypt and Peru. Exchange requires the presence of 'a system of price-making markets'" (ibid.). These forms of integration, Polanyi emphasizes, "do not represent 'stages' of development" (ibid.: 256).

The substantive point of view makes it possible to re-examine the marketing approach, typical of neoclassical economics, to the interpretation of trade and money institutions. In this 'restrictive' interpretation:

> the market appears as the locus of exchange, trade as the actual exchange, and money as the means of exchange. Since trade is directed by prices and prices are a function of the market, all trade is market trade, just as all money is exchange money. The market is the generating institution of which trade and money are the functions.
>
> (Ibid.: 257)

According to Polanyi, this approach conflicts with "the facts of anthropology and history" (ibid.): trade, as well as some money uses, are as old as mankind, "while markets . . . did not gain importance until comparatively late in history". "Price-making markets, which alone are constitutive of a market system", Polanyi stresses, "were to all accounts non-existent before the first millennium of antiquity, and then only to be eclipsed by other form of integration". In other words, trade, money and market can exist separately, and only in the market form of integration do they "form an indivisible whole".

5.1.3 Against Robbins's approach and formalist anthropology

Formalist economists and anthropologists founded the universality of their approach to the study of societies on the hypotheses of the generality of the state of scarcity and of rational behaviour, in the sense of optimizing behaviour. These are the two cornerstones of their theoretical construction: if there is scarcity of means, multiplicity of ends and possibility of choice, rational action is defined as that action which maximizes the aim of the economic agent, whatever that aim is. This simple relationship assumed by the formalist approach seems to have an irrefutable logic, Polanyi writes. However, according to him, it has problematic aspects.

Firstly, Polanyi and his followers criticize the formalist way of arguing. The formalist approach assumes hypotheses concerning scarcity and rational behaviour of universal effectiveness; and the opposite is defined as an extreme case or a case due to particular conditions, that is, not general ones. Scarcity is taken to be the normal case of the human condition because the opposite case – opulence – is considered to be the particular and extreme case of the generous and prodigal nature which spontaneously provides for all the necessaries.

The second puzzling point of the formalist approach, the substantivists maintain, is the independence between the concept of scarcity and the concept of exchange. According to Robbins, scarcity expresses itself in value; hence value is an indicator of scarcity. Scarcity conditions establish the existence of value: there is equivalence between scarcity and value. In this sense, Robbins maintains that value exists independently of the existence of exchange. This reasoning is certainly correct from the logical point of view, but from the cultural and historical one it is undeniable that the concepts of value, measurability and scarcity are associated with a market society. Not considering this, the substantivists maintain, is equivalent to absolutizing these two concepts. It is to absolutize a historical fact, that is, to remove history. It thus becomes possible to attribute categories elaborated in a specific cultural context to all contexts independently of their cultural and historical characterization. The words used by Moses I. Finley, a great historian of ancient Greece, to explain the absence of the concept of 'economic' among the ancients can be conveniently used here in relation to primitive societies:

> The ancients were like Molière's M. Jourdain, who spoke prose without knowing it, but . . . they in fact lacked the concept of an 'economy', and, *a fortiori*, they lacked the conceptual elements which together constitute what we call 'economy'. Of course they farmed, traded, manufactured, mined, taxed, coined, deposited and loaned money, made profits or failed in their enterprises. And they discussed these activities in their talk and their writing. What they did not do, however, was to combine these particular activities conceptually into a unit, in Parsonian terms into a 'differentiated sub-system of society'. Hence Aristotle, whose programme was to codify the branches of knowledge, wrote no *Economics*. Hence, too, the perennial complaints about the paucity and mediocrity of ancient 'economic' writing rest on a fundamental misconception of what these writings were about.
>
> (Finley 1973: 21)

This absence of a concept of an economy is not the result of an intellectual inability, Finley writes: "A society that produced the work of Apollonius of Perge on conic sections had more than enough mathematics for what the seventeenth-century English and Dutch called 'political arithmetic' and we call 'statistics'" (ibid.: 25).

In the formalist approach, therefore, categories born in a determined society are considered universal, abstracting from their culturally determined nature. Scarcity is considered the normal case of human history. On the contrary, according the substantivist point of view, in primitive societies the idea of scarcity is absent because it is not applicable to them. Harry W. Pearson, one of the editors of *Trade and Markets*, wrote:

> The concept of scarcity will be fruitful only if the natural fact of limited means leads to a sequence of choices regarding the use of these means,

> and this situation is possible only if there is alternativity to the uses of means and there are preferentially graded ends. But these latter conditions are socially determined; they do not depend in any simple way upon the facts of nature. To postulate scarcity as an absolute condition from which all economic institutions derive is therefore to employ an abstraction which serves only to obscure the question of how economic activity is organized.
>
> (Ibid.: 320)

The concept of scarcity, as well as that of surplus, Pearson concludes, is fully applicable only when the institutional conditions which create scarcity are defined.

The third criticism concerns the universal applicability of the economic rationality criterion. In particular, its explanatory value is called into question and its indeterminacy is emphasized. As regards the former aspect, the South African anthropologist Percy S. Cohen maintains that the principle may turn out to be a simple tautology:

> Any action can be said to maximize someone's gain: if a man fails to obtain the highest possible price for his goods because of his impatience to quit the market, then he could be said to have maximized his gain, since the prospect of additional monetary gain is inadequate to outweigh some other advantage, such as attending a ceremony. But if the same man remains in the market and forgoes some other pleasure, thereby obtaining a higher price, it could be said that he has maximized his gain. If a man feeds his kinsmen, regardless of whether they contribute efficient labour or not, he is investing in social solidarity; if he refuses to feed them, then he is placing his material gain above that of solidarity. Since he is maximizing his gain *whatever* he does, the concept can hardly have explanatory value.
>
> (Cohen 1967: 106)

As regards the latter point, it was Polanyi himself who noted the indeterminacy of the criterion of economic rationality. He pointed out that not explicitly stated assumptions are involved in some cases of choice. Is it better to prefer bread and butter to heroic ideals? Is it better for a sick man to consult a doctor or crystal-ball gazer? Faced with the problems of choice, Polanyi writes, "two further meanings of rational were brought in" (Polanyi 1977: 13): "with regard to the ends, a utilitarian value scale was postulated as rational; and with regard to the means, the testing scale for efficacy was applied by science" (ibid.). In this way,

> The first scale made rationality the antithesis of the aesthetical, the ethical, or the philosophical; the second made it the antithesis of magic, superstition, or plain ignorance. In the first case it is rational to prefer bread and butter to heroic ideals; in the second, it appears rational for a sick man to consult his doctor in preference of a crystal-ball gazer.
>
> (Ibid.)

In conclusion, Polanyi maintains that "so long as rational is used, not as a fashionable term of praise but in the strict sense of pertaining to reason", "the validation of the scientific test of means as rational is no less arbitrary than the attempted justification of utilitarian ends" (ibid.).

5.2 Marshall Sahlins's neo-substantivism

5.2.1 The substantivist school after Polanyi

During the 1960s, Polanyi's and the substantivist school's writings had a favourable resonance and wide influence in the community of social scientists and historians.

This provoked a strongly critical response by the formalist school – the anthropologists in particular (Harold Schneider, Edward LeClair, Frank Cancian, Robbins Burling and Scott Cook, the principal proponents of the formalist approach). Scott Cook defended the formalists' point of view in an influential article (Cook 1966, see also Cook 1969), arguing above all with George Dalton and Paul Bohannan, the leaders of the substantivist school after Polanyi's death in 1964. In his article, he defined the term of the debate between formalists and substantivists as follows. He maintained that "the substantivists' intransigency concerning the cross-cultural applicability of formal economic theory is a by-product of a romantic ideology rooted in an antipathy toward the 'market economy' and an idealization of the 'primitive'" (Cook 1966: 322–3). The difference between Western-type market and primitive-subsistence economies, he argued, is one of degree:

> The Formalists may be characterized as those who focus on abstractions unlimited by time and place, and who are prone to introspection or are synchronically oriented; they are scientific in outlook and mathematical in inclination, favor the deductive mode of inquiry, and are basically analytic in methodology (i.e., lean toward the belief that parts determine the whole). The Romanticists, on the other hand, may be characterized as those who focus on situations limited in time and space, and who are prone to retrospection or are diachronically oriented; they are humanistic in outlook and non-mathematical in inclination, favor the inductive mode of inquiry, and are basically synthetic in methodology (i.e., lean toward the belief that the whole determines its parts).
>
> (Ibid.: 327)

According to Cook, implicit in Polanyi's writings is "a utopian model of primitive society" (ibid.) which minimizes the role of conflict, and is founded on a model of man "which emphasizes innate altruistic and cooperative propensities while playing down self-interest, aggressiveness, and competitiveness" – a vision borrowed from Rousseau, "the representative par excellence of this tradition" (ibid.). This anti-market mentality is contrasted by the principles and concepts of economic theory which, given certain "necessary but not critical modifications" (ibid.: 337), can be used in the analysis of non-market economic systems.

The formalists/substantivists debate peaked at the beginning of the 1970s with the publication of two books: Harold K. Schneider's *Economic Man* (1974) and Marshall Sahlins's *Stone Age Economics* (1972). Schneider, a student of Herskovits at Northwestern University, was an advocate of the formalist approach and his book was a manifesto for it. Sahlins's book was considered the most important contribution at that time in the field of substantivist economic anthropology.

5.2.2 Stone Age (anthropological) economics

Economy as a cultural category

In 1972 the American anthropologist Marshall Sahlins (b. 1930) – a pupil of Leslie White at the University of Michigan and then of Karl Polanyi and Julian Steward at Columbia University where he earned his PhD – published *Stone Age Economics*, a book which since then has significantly affected the debate in economic anthropology, but also has influence beyond the boundaries of the discipline. The book resulted from Sahlins's work since the mid-1960s – in fact, it collected some of his previous essays – and it was in the tradition of substantivism enhanced by the intellectual structuralist influence of the French anthropologist Claude Lévi-Strauss, with whom Sahlins worked at the *Laboratoire d'Anthropologie Sociale du Collège de France* in the years 1967–69. Sahlins writes that "the book inscribes itself in the current anthropological controversy between formalist and substantivist practices of economic theory", a debate defined "endemic to the science of economics for over a century" (Sahlins 1972: xi). What is new, he writes in the Introduction,[1] is the shift in the emphasis of the discussion:

> If the problem in the beginning was the 'naive anthropology' of Economics, today it is the 'naive economics' of Anthropology . . . 'Formalism versus substantivism' amounts to the following theoretical option: between the ready made models of orthodox Economics, especially the 'microeconomics', taken as universally valid and applicable *grosso modo* to the primitive societies; and the necessity – supposing this formalist position unfounded – of developing a new analysis more appropriate to the historical societies in question and to the intellectual history of Anthropology. Broadly speaking, it is a choice between the perspective of business, for the formalist method must consider the primitive economies as underdeveloped versions of our own, and a *culturalist study* that as a matter of principle does honor to different societies for what they are.
>
> (Ibid.: xi–xii; original emphasis)

The structure of the book is substantivist. It starts with the subject of production, and then considers distribution and exchange. Economy is considered "a category of culture" (ibid.: xii) – and for Sahlins, culture is the distinctive object of anthropology: it does not deal with the need-serving activities of individuals, but the material life process of society.[2] The book does not offer a simple methodological discussion, as many previous contributions of the debate has done; rather it addresses a fundamental issue: the positive construction of an 'anthropological economics' beyond the sterile formulations of the debate between formalists and substantivists.

As emphasized, anthropological economics considers economy as a category of culture. Culture is, for Sahlins, "a distinctive and symbolic human creation". In this sense, Sahlins's conception is alternative to the economic one, especially in the form assumed in bioeconomics and human behaviour ecology. It is worth recalling that published a few years after the publication of *Stone Age Economics*, in 1975, was Edward O. Wilson's *Sociobiology*, a book which, as previously said, gave rise to an heated controversy. Sahlins intervened with a slim and insightful book entitled *The Use and Abuse of Biology. An anthropological critique of sociobiology* (1976b). It took up arguments adduced in his *Cultural and Practical Reason* (1976a), where he developed a case against historical materialist analyses of cultural behaviour. Sahlins's main argument was that sociobiology treats human culture as a simple side-effect of human biological organization, and hence reduces the social sciences to biology.[3] In his own words:

> Sociobiology challenges the integrity of culture as a thing-in-itself, as a distinctive and symbolic human creation. In place of a social constitution of meanings, [sociobiology] offers a biological determination of human interactions with a source primarily in the general evolutionary propensity of individual genotypes to maximize their reproductive success . . . Biology, while it is an absolutely necessary condition for culture, is equally and absolutely insufficient: it is completely unable to specify the cultural properties of human behavior or their variations from one human group to another.
>
> (Sahlins 1976b: x–xi)

A constant subject of criticism in recent works by Sahlins (see Sahlins 2008a and 2013), sociobiology is correctly connected by Sahlins with the economic theories of rational choice: these contribute to making a sort of "all-purpose human science of the 'selfish gene'" purporting to explain "all manner of cultural forms by a universal human nature of competitive self-interest" (Sahlins 2008b: 319–28, 324). Sahlins does not fail to note, à la Marx, that "in this so-called human nature", "we can recognize the classic bourgeois subject" (ibid.).[4]

The domestic mode of production

The starting point of the book is a criticism of the concept of 'subsistence economy'. Although already criticized by anthropologists like Firth, the concept of subsistence economy in the hunter and gatherer societies had been traditionally and mainly considered as synonymous with: "limited leisure save in exceptional circumstances", "incessant quest for food", "meagre and relatively unreliable" natural resources, "absence of an economic surplus", "maximum energy from a maximum number of people". This was a conception, Sahlins notes, of pre-anthropological and extra-anthropological origin which went back to the time when Adam Smith was writing. However, Sahlins continues, ethnological field research do not prove this state of absence: the studies cited by Sahlins – many of them had been presented at the famous *Man the Hunter* 1966 symposium organized by the anthropologists Richard Lee and Irven DeVore at the University of Chicago, whose proceedings were published in 1968 – offer a different picture of the primitive economies. Sahlins writes:

> When Herskovits was writing his *Economic Anthropology* (1958) it was common anthropological practice to take the Bushmen or the native Australians as 'a classic illustration of a people whose economic resources are of the scantiest,' so precariously situated that only the most intense application makes survival possible.
>
> (Sahlins 1972: 14)

However this statement, he maintains, is unfounded. Today, he writes, "the 'classic' understanding can be fairly reversed – on evidence largely from these two groups" (ibid.). Two studies on the Australian natives, one by Frederick McCarthy and Margaret McArthur (1960), based on quantitative materials collected by the 1948 American-Australian Scientific Expedition to Arnhem Land in Australia, and the other by Richard Lee on the Dobe section of the !Kung Bushmen of Kalahari in Africa, showed the following different picture.

The main findings of the studies by McCarthy and McArthurs studies were:

- a The average length of time per person per day put into the appropriation and preparation of food was four or five hours.
- b The subsistence quest was highly intermittent.
- c The dietary intake of the Arnhem Land hunters was adequate – according to the standards of the National Research Council of America. Mean daily consumption per capita at Hemple Bay was more than 2000 calories.

Lee's reports showed that the Bushmen's conditions were approximately the same. In fact:

- a The average day's work for food collecting (excluding cooking) was 2 hours 9 minutes.
- b The rhythm of work was "a day or two on, a day or two off".
- c The daily per-capita subsistence yield for the Dobe Bushmen was 2,140 calories. However, taking into account body weight, normal activities, and the age-sex composition of the Dobe population, Lee estimated that people required only 1,975 calories per capita.

Similarly, James Woodburn's research on the African people of Hazda in North Tanzania estimated that "over the year as a whole probably an average of less than two hours a day is spent obtaining food" (Woodburn 1968: 54).

These estimates, Sahlins observes, confirm the information gathered by many travellers, explorers and missionaries of the past. He quotes from some of them. The English naturalist Clement Hodgkinson who explored New South Wales, Australia, in the early 1840s, wrote in an account of his explorations: "Indeed, throughout all the country along the eastern coast, the blacks have never suffered so much from scarcity of food as many commiserating writers have supposed" (Hodgkinson 1845: 227). The biologist and anthropologist Baldwin Spencer and the anthropologist Frank Gillen wrote in their *The Native Tribes of Central Australia* (1899) – the result of their scientific expeditions – about the desert people of Arunta that their "life is by no means a miserable or a very hard one" (Spencer and Gillen 1899: 7). The explorer and colonial administrator John Edward Eyre, who explored the interior of South Australia in the years 1840–41, wrote thus in his *Journals*:

> Throughout the greater portion of New Holland, where there do not happen to be European settlers, and invariably when fresh water can be permanently procured upon the surface, the native experiences no difficulty whatever in procuring food in abundance all the year round. It is true that the character of his diet varies with the changing seasons, and the formation of the country he inhabits; but it rarely happens that any season of the year, or any description of country does not yield him both animal and vegetable food . . . Of these [chief articles of food], many are not only procurable in abundance, but in such vast quantities at the proper seasons, as to afford for a considerable length of time an ample means of subsistence to many hundreds of natives congregated at one place . . . On many parts of the coast, and in the larger inland rivers, fish are obtained of a very fine description, and in great abundance.
>
> (Eyre 1845: 250–51)

In his *Journals*, the explorer and Governor of South Australia Sir John Gray wrote:

> In all ordinary seasons, that is, when the people are not confined to their huts by bad weather, they can obtain, in two or three hours a sufficient supply of food for the day, but their usual custom is to roam indolently from spot to spot, lazily collecting it as they wander along.
>
> (Grey 1841, vol. 2: 263)

The geologist Robert B. Smyth, who published in 1878 a book on the life of aborigines of the south-east of Australia, considering the hunter's movement from camp to camp, wrote that the aboriginals of Victoria were as a rule "lazy travellers": "They have no motive to induce them to hasten their movements. It is generally late in the morning before they start on their journey, and there are many interruptions by the way" (Smyth 1878 vol. 1: 125). Written in similar terms, Sahlins notes, were the Jesuits' *Relations* of the seventeenth century.

Starting from these (and other) field studies and accounts and taking two old theoretical categories – that of *oikos* or 'independent domestic economy' as used in the late nineteenth century among others by the German economic historian Karl Bucher (1893), and the Marxian one of mode of production – Sahlins tries to identify the "widespread and profound structure" of the primitive economies in the "domestic mode of production (DMP)" (Sahlins 1972: 74): "The household is to the tribal economy as the manor to the medieval economy or the corporation to modern capitalism: each is the dominant production-institution of its time" (ibid.: 76).

Sahlins founds his analysis of the mode of production on the following observation: "production is low relative to existing possibilities" (ibid.: 41). This state of under-production appears in three ways: under-use of resources, under-use of labour power, and household failure.

UNDER-USE OF RESOURCES

Drawing on the estimations of the economic capacity of traditional societies made in the already-quoted field researches by Richard Lee on the !Kung Bushman and James Woodburn on the Hazda – as well as other studies on societies practising slash-and-burn cultivation (an ancient agricultural technique of Neolithic origin that involves the cutting and burning of plants in forests to create fields) – Sahlins emphasizes that they all agree on the under-use of resources. In fact, in traditional agricultural systems, the index of population capacity for slash-and-burn agriculture shows that "the existing population is generally inferior to the calculable maximum, often remarkably so" (ibid.: 43). As for the hunter and gatherer societies, the calculation of the index of relative abundance (that is, whether or not a population exhausts all the food available from an area), shows that, to quote Lee's conclusions on the !Kung Bushman, "the habitat of the Dobe-area Bushmen is abundant in naturally occurring foods" (Lee 1968: 33).

UNDER-USE OF LABOUR-POWER

Many studies document that also the labour forces of primitive communities are under-used. Sahlins summarizes this evidence as follows:

> the work process is sensitive to interference of various kinds, vulnerable to suspension in favor of other activities as serious as ritual, as frivolous as repose. The customary working day is often short; if it is protracted, frequently it is interrupted; if it is both long and unremitting, usually this is only seasonal. Within the community, moreover, some people work much more than others.
> (Ibid.: 56)

In other words, considerable labour-power remains under-employed; hence labour is not a scarce resource in most primitive societies.

HOUSEHOLD FAILURE

This is the third dimension of primitive underproduction, "perhaps the most dramatic" one (ibid.: 69), Sahlins writes. The evidence is that a fair percentage of domestic groups persistently fail to produce their own livelihood due to an unbalanced ratio of effective workers to dependent non-producers.

In order to explain theoretically this profound tendency of under-production in primitive economies, Sahlins refers to the category of domestic mode of production (DMP). The principal aspects of the DMP are identified as:

- A division of labour by sex as the dominant form of specialization:

  > the normal activities of any adult man, taken in conjunction with the normal activities of an adult woman, practically exhaust the customary work of society. Therefore marriage, among other things, establishes a generalized economic group constituted to produce the local conception of livelihood.
  >
  > (Ibid.: 79)

- The correlation between the domestic mode, atomized and small scale, and a technology of similar dimensions: "the basic apparatus can usually be handled by household groups; much of it can be wielded autonomously by individuals . . . productive processes are unitary rather than decomposed by an elaborate division of labour" (ibid.).
- But this technological simplicity, Sahlins notes, is such only for the primitives who understand that technology, because "the world's most primitive peoples – judged as such on the plane of overall cultural complexity – create unparalleled technical masterpieces" (ibid.: 80):

  > Dismantled and shipped to New York or London, Bushman traps lie now gathering dust in the basements of a hundred museums, powerless even to instruct because no one can figure out how to put them back together again. On a very broad view of cultural evolution, technical developments have accumulated not so much in ingenuity as along a different axis of the man-tool relationship. It is a question of the distribution of energy, skill, and intelligence between the two. In the primitive relation of man to tool, the balance of these is in favor of man; with the inception of a "machine age" the balance swings definitively in favor of the tool.
  >
  > (Ibid.)

- Production for livelihood, that is 'production for use': Sahlins takes from the classics and Marx the distinction between 'production for use' and 'production for exchange' already used in anthropology by Thurnwald (1932).

Sahlins's conclusion is that "economics is only a part-time activity of the primitive societies, or else it is an activity of only part of the society" (ibid.: 86): its economic goals are limited, "qualitatively defined in the terms of a way of living rather than quantitatively as an abstract wealth" (ibid.). Accordingly, work is unintensive. Otherwise said, Sahlins adds:

> the DMP harbors an anti-surplus principle. Geared to the production of livelihood, it is endowed with the tendency to come to a halt at that point. Hence if 'surplus' is defined as output above the producers' requirements, the household system is not organized for it. Nothing within the structure of production for use pushes it to transcend itself.
>
> (Ibid.)

Owing to the intrinsic tendency of under-production, the domestic group may be – paradoxically, Sahlins notes – unable to produce its livelihood. In order exactly to appreciate this non-intensive use of productive forces, Sahlins introduces Chayanov's rule – the reference is to the Soviet agrarian economist Alexander Chayanov (1888–1937) and his work *The Theory of Peasant Economy* (1966 [1925]) – which reads as follows: "in the community of domestic producing groups, the greater the relative working capacity of the household the less its members work" (ibid.: 87), or, put in another way, productive intensity is inversely related to productive capacity. This means that the households of greater working capacity do not automatically extend themselves on behalf of the poorer, so that "the plight of the least effective domestic groups, especially the substantial percentage that do not meet their own requirements, seems all the more serious" (ibid.: 91). Then comes the dramatic alternative: "The economic defects of the domestic system are overcome, or else the society is overcome" (ibid.: 101). However, Sahlins notes, the total final material product of the society is "above the domestic propensity" (ibid.: 102). In fact, certain domestic groups well endowed with workers function beyond their own necessity for the community. Sahlins notes that "the grand strategy of economic intensification enlists social structures beyond the family and cultural superstructures beyond the productive practice" (ibid.). Kinship and politics explain this result: "kin and political relations between households, and the interest in others' welfare these relations entail, must impel production above the norm in certain houses in a position to do so" (ibid.: 103). Kinship relations counter the centrifugal movement of the DMP. Kinship solidarities develop a wide cooperation, generating a surplus tendency.

However, Sahlins maintains, it is the political system that plays the crucial role. As the structure is politicized, passing from the formal solidarity of the kinship structure to its political aspect, "especially as it is centralized in ruling chiefs, the household economy is mobilized in a larger social cause" (ibid.: 130). Chieftainship is a political differentiation of a kinship order, Sahlins writes, and leadership is simply "a higher form of kinship, hence a higher form of reciprocity and liberality" (ibid.: 132) – as the ethnographic descriptions of all the primitive societies maintain.

Political life is "a stimulus to production" (ibid.: 135) through the role of the chief. It is certainly "a matter of prestige", Sahlins says, "but more profoundly, his generosity is a kind of constraint" (ibid.: 133). The Melanesian big-man is the exemplary case. He has to work harder that anyone else: as the native say "his hands are never free from earth, and his forehead continually drips with sweat."[5]

Reciprocal exchange in primitive societies

In the *Argonauts*, Malinowski developed a classification of Trobriand exchanges, from the pure gift (the extreme case) – that is, an offering for which nothing is given in return – to genuine barter, through many customary forms of gift and other forms of exchange where more or less strict equivalence is observed. Sahlins takes Malinowski's perspective beyond the Trobrianders and applied it broadly to reciprocal exchange in primitive societies. Sahlins lays out "a continuum of reciprocities, based on the 'vice-versa' nature of exchanges, along which empirical instances encountered in the particular ethnographic case can be placed" (ibid.: 193). According to this schema, reciprocity can be ordered as follows:

- *Generalized reciprocity*: this refers to transactions that are "putatively altruistic" (ibid.) – Malinowski's pure gift, sharing, hospitality, free gift, generosity, are the formulas used in ethnographic accounts. It can also be termed "weak reciprocity" (a term introduced by the American anthropologist John A. Price (Price 1962) "by reason of the vagueness of the obligation to reciprocate" (Sahlins 1972: 194).
- *Balanced reciprocity*: this refers to an exchange where "in precise balance, the reciprocation is the customary equivalent of the thing received and is without delay" (ibid.).
- *Negative reciprocity*: this refers to "the several forms of appropriation, transactions opened and conducted toward net utilitarian advantage" (ibid.: 195). It corresponds to haggling, gambling and barter.

Empirical exchanges, Sahlins maintains, fall somewhere on the line linking these different points: social or economic circumstances, like kinship distance and kinship rank explain the position. On this basis, Sahlins outlines a 'tribal plan', or "a series of concentric spheres, beginning in the close-knit inner circles of homestead and hamlet, extending thence to wider and more diffuse zones of regional and tribal solidarity, to fade into the outer darkness of an intertribal arena" (ibid.: 279).

This is at once "a social and moral design of the tribal universe", Sahlins maintains, "specifying norms of conduct for each sphere" (ibid.). Hence reciprocity is generalized in the innermost sectors. But on leaving these internal spheres,

> one discovers a sector of social relations so tenuous they can only be sustained by an exchange at once more immediate and balanced. In the interest of a long-term trade, and under the social protection of such devices as "trade partnership," this zone may even extend to intertribal relations.
>
> (Ibid.: 280)

Beyond the internal economy of reciprocity, there is a sphere, of greater or less expanse, marked by some correlation between the customary and de facto rates of equivalence: "Here, then, is the area of greatest promise to research on exchange rates" (ibid.). As well-documented in ethnographic research, the indeterminacy of the rates is a characteristic feature of primitive exchange: "In different transactions, similar goods move against each other in different proportions – especially so in the ensemble of ordinary transactions, the everyday gift giving and mutual aid, and in the internal economy of kinship groups and communities" (ibid.: 278).

It is also well known that in the different spheres of exchange, goods have different ranks in a ethical hierarchy of virtues. Only in the more external spheres of exchange can constant relations of equivalence be found: "not only is balanced dealing there enjoined, but the exchange circuits of the internal economy tend to disintegrate and combine, as the immorality of 'conversion' is rendered irrelevant by social distance" (ibid.: 280). Sahlins examines three real exchange networks in the Pacific area: the Vitiaz Straits and Huon Gulf systems of New Guinea, and the intertribal trade chain of northern Queensland, Australia. In all these cases, demand and supply influence the rates of exchange, but in a particular system of relations where:

> The traffic is canalized in parallel and insulated transactions between particular pairs. Where trade is handled through partnerships, exactly who exchanges with whom is prescribed in advance: social relations, not prices, connect up "buyers" and "sellers." Lacking a trade contact, a man may not be able to get what he wants at any price. There is no evidence anywhere, so far as I know, of competitive bidding among members of a trading party for the custom of each other's partners; there is only the occasional observation that it is expressly forbidden.
>
> (Ibid.: 298)

Sahlins thinks that there are no 'markets' properly so-called in primitive societies, and that it is not correct to speak in this context of a 'market principle', even peripheral, as Bohannan and Dalton (1965) did as regards the African 'markets'. Sahlins prefers say that "the sensitivity we have observed in Melanesian exchange values remains an intriguing mystery" (Sahlins 1972: 301).[6]

5.2.3 On the paradox of 'primitive affluence': Zen strategy and substantive rationality

Sahlins's substantivist perspective offers a picture of the functioning of the economy in the primitive societies very different from that of economics. He describes a society where the average amount of time devoted to work is low, the pace of work is slow, and the diet more than satisfying in terms of calorific contribution and protein content. Sahlins calls it an "affluent society". Sahlins's analysis may be summarized as follows. The primitive domestic mode of production is characterized by a tendency to under-production and under-exploitation of resources. The available technology, evaluated on the basis of its capacity to satisfy in a certain environment the needs of society in the long run, is not definable as inferior or inadequate. According to the archaeological and ethnological information used by Sahlins, primitive technology is adequate and effective, and therefore it is not the cause of the absence of surplus; on the contrary, it is the result of a voluntary limitation, a choice of the savages. From the perspective of economic development, it is an opportunity not exploited.

How to explain this fact, which appears as a paradox from the economist's point of view? Sahlins's explanation is that the need motivation is less strong in a primitive society than in any other society:

> There is . . . a Zen road to affluence, departing from premises somewhat different from our own: that human material wants are finite and few, and technical means unchanging but on the whole adequate. Adopting the Zen strategy, a people can enjoy an unparalleled material plenty with a low standard of living. That, I think, describes the hunters. And it helps explain some of their more curious economic behaviour: their 'prodigality' for example – the inclination to consume at once all stocks on hand, as if they had it made. Free from market obsessions of scarcity, hunters' economic propensities may be more consistently predicated on abundance than our own. Destutt de Tracy, 'fish-blooded bourgeois doctrinaire' though he might have been, at least compelled Marx's agreement on the observation that 'in poor nations the people are comfortable' whereas in rich nations 'they are generally poor'. This is not to deny that a preagricultural economy operates under serious constraints, but only to insist, on the evidence from modern hunters and gatherers, that a successful accommodation is usually made.
>
> (Ibid.: 2)

It follows from Sahlins's analysis that the economy of primitive societies is not characterized by the neoclassical rationality, that is, by maximum output with minimum efficient effort. On the contrary, it is characterized by making the effort able to obtain, with a low rhythm of work, what is necessary for a good 'satisfying' life.[7] This is 'primitive' rationality, what we could call *substantive rationality* (Sahlins 1969, Marchionatti 2012): a coherent behaviour, culturally determined, appropriate to the achievement of the social end of a material reproduction of a society ecologically sustainable in the long run, without the pressure of the scarcity of resources, which is largely a social construct, not a natural property of human existence, and without the need to assume a maximizing behaviour.

5.3 The debate on *Stone Age Economics* in the 1980s and 1990s

5.3.1 The controversy about the 'original affluent society' thesis

Since the early 1980s, several field works have called into question the validity of the data used by Sahlins to support his 'original affluence' argument. Kristen Hawkes and James O'Connell (1981), analysing the subsistence production of the Alyawara, a central Australian hunting group, maintained that "the cost of subsistence is sometimes quite high, far higher than the current conventional wisdom regarding hunters would suggest" (Hawkes and O'Connell 1981: 622). John Altman (1984) examined data collected among Australian North-Central Arnhem Landers regarding subsistence production and criticized the reliability of McCarthy's and McArthur's time allocation studies conducted in 1948 in Arnhem Land and reported by Sahlins. Firstly, he maintained that they had been conducted over a short period and were therefore unrepresentative of the seasonal cycle; then, and more in general, that the data were collected under artificial circumstances. The new studies seemed to show that the old studies over-estimated the amount of leisure time available to Aborigines in the past. Bettinger (1991) noted that the data supporting the 'affluent society' thesis were not overwhelming. David Kaplan (2000) examined data that cast doubts on the notion of hunter-gatherers' affluence. He confirmed the opinion expressed by Altman on the studies by McCarthy and McArthur:

> The artificial conditions under which the survey was done, the brief length of the study, and modern features (e.g. metal tools) which may have influenced the outcome of the survey, . . . should make us wary about relying too heavily or exclusively on the Arnhem Land data.
>
> (Kaplan 2000: 307)

As regards the !Kung San of Southern Africa, Hawkes and O'Connell (1981) criticized Lee's procedure of calculation of the work effort on the grounds that it had not taken account of the time spent processing food. However, new calculations by Lee (1984) indicated that the typical work effort of a Bushman group was just more than 40 hours each week, confirming his thesis that the !Kung had the combination of an adequate diet and a short working week. In fact, while these studies introduce doubts on the reliability of ethnographic data and raise a note of caution concerning the empirical work of anthropologists, there is still broad consensus that Sahlins's 'affluent society' idea is valid. This is the view of specialists in hunter-gatherer societies like Alan Barnard and James Woodburn (1988), Nurit Bird-David (1992) and Elisabeth Cashdan (1989). In an essay on the affluent society argument, Bird-David (1992) has written that "Sahlins's argument, duly updated and reconceptualized, does indeed hold" (Cashdan 1989: 27). Barnard and Woodburn (1988) observe that "the crux of the theory has . . . stood up well to twenty years of additional research" (Barnard and Woodburn 1988: 11). In a review of economic research on hunter-gatherers, Cashdan wrote: "Although later research has shown [the affluent society idea] to be an overstatement, it remains true that among many hunter-gatherers subsistence work is intermittent, leisure time is abundant and nutritional status excellent" (Cashdan 1989: 22–3).

More recently, in his 1996 PhD dissertation, the American anthropologist Ross Sackett tested the 'primitive affluence' hypothesis. He examined cross-cultural variation in adult time allocation and energy expenditure in a global ethnographic sample of small- and large-scale societies. The time allocation data (102 cases from 76 societies) indicated that (1) average daily adult time in production increases from 4 hours in small-scale societies (foragers and horticulturalists) to 5½ hours in large-scale societies (agriculturalists and industrialists); (2) housework time shows little trend with scale, averaging 3 hours per adult day; (3) total work time (production plus housework) increases from 6–7 hours in small-scale societies to about 9 hours in large-scale societies. These findings are generally consistent with the primitive affluence hypothesis.

5.3.2 A 'behavioural ecology' interpretation of the 'original affluence': Winterhalder's re-visitation (and misunderstandings)

Adopting an evolutionary ecology approach to the analysis of hunter-gatherer subsistence, Bruce Winterhalder (1992) offered an explanation of limited work effort which is alternative to Sahlins's 'Zen strategy' and, in the author's opinion, appears compatible both with the hypothesis of individual economic rationality and with ethnographic data. Reversing Herskovits's (1952: 69) proposition that "only intense application makes survival possible", Winterhalder claimed that in primitive economies, "poverty and loneliness are the sure outcomes of long hours in the food quest" (Winterhalder 1992: 323). To prove the hypothesis, he developed a model where resource selection and individual behaviour are related to the availability, characteristics and distribution of those resources.

Winterhalder formulated a simulation model which incorporates three components – a logistic resource population model, a diet choice model, a human population model – linked by four functional relationships: human population growth as function of foraging efficiency, diet selection as function of resources densities, demand for resources as function of the size of population, and resource population density as a function of which resources are harvested, in what amounts, and their capacity to recover. Parameters were chosen to be representative of actual hunter-gatherers. The model showed that "ecological relationships alone may lead to limited work effort and a state of original affluence" (ibid.: 328). But, Winterhalder wrote, it could not (in its then state of development) allow researchers to predict that hunter-gatherer societies actually will evolve to this condition.

Let us consider rational individual behaviour. If individuals respond to declining rates of harvest by foraging somewhat longer each day, in order to gather sufficient food, they will deplete resources to yet lower levels: that is, "rational short-term decisions by individuals about effort have unhappy long-term consequences for yield" (ibid: 329). As the daily duration of foraging effort increases, production will show decreasing marginal returns and an intermediate peak of yield. Given the population ecology of their resources, foragers who exceed a moderate commitment of time will soon encounter the impediment of low net and absolute returns. In conclusion, individual-level decisions lead to poverty. However, Winterhalder observes, there is ethnological evidence that the system stabilizes at low levels of work effort and a relatively high level of population density. The model shows that limited work can occur, but, "without some additional consideration or factor, the evolutionary dynamic of the model implies that it would not occur" (ibid.). In other words, the model does not allow researchers to infer that the society will actually evolve to the condition of limited work effort and a state of original affluence – that is, the state at which primitive systems stabilize in reality. "Quite the opposite" (ibid.: 328): consistent application of an individual-level, selectionist perspective would lead one to predict harsh poverty. The solution to the puzzle lies in a more general framework which comprises sociocultural or institutional factors.

Winterhalder therefore considers the distribution and consumption dynamics able to explain the "time reward" to work (foraging) activity. The distribution dynamics determine how and to what degree labourers retain or benefit from the immediate product of their work. Consumption dynamics determine how material products are consumed. As regards the former dynamics, food sharing, interpreted as rational response to "the risk on resource selection" (ibid.: 331), appears to be "a necessary and highly effective concomitant of dependence on unpredictable resources" (ibid.): it disperses the products of an individual's work among the band, thereby dissipating his incentive to engage in exceptional effort. As regards consumption dynamics, "the mobility-portability argument . . . entails a sharp consumption constraint for material goods and also for reproduction" (ibid.: 332). Hence these factors can help explain why hunter-gatherers might engage in limited effort foraging: "after constraints are met . . . the opportunity costs of alternative activities [non-subsistence activities] should be appraised relative to the net benefits of foraging" (ibid.).

In the last part of his paper, Winterhalder revisits the original affluent society argument as discussed by Sahlins. Sahlins's reasoning is reconstructed as follows:

> There is an empirical fact: workers in a market economy put in long hours. And there is an associated neoclassical interpretation: they do so because they have unlimited wants, very limited means and as a consequence, live in condition of scarcity. By contrast, foragers labour for only a few hours, their limited effort the antithesis of that characteristic of workers. By extension, the postulates of their Zen economics must negate those of Smith and Ricardo. Thus, the forager has limited wants and sufficient means, and thereby lives in a situation of relative plenty.
>
> (Ibid.: 333–4)

Hence, Zen economics should be interpreted as "the inversion of the neoclassical sort: the hunter is the 'uneconomic man'" (ibid.: 334). Sahlins assumes means available to foragers to be low, and their wants even more limited. The fundamental fact is, Winterhalder comments, that the necessity to do so is of an ecological character: they are faced with diminishing returns. "The ecological relationship that Sahlins places at the core of the Zen economy – the imminence of diminishing returns at a locality", Winterhalder maintains, "nearly anticipates a key model of optimal foraging theory, the marginal value theorem" (ibid.: 335), according to which "the optimal forager moves when the marginal return in the present locale drops to the average return for the habitat as a whole." As a consequence, there would be "perfect conformation between the evolutionary ecological model and Sahlins's argument". On the other hand, Winterhalder can argue that "Sahlins professed allegiances are with substantivism, but his argument is so closely aligned to micro-economic principles that one might almost suspect it of being a cleverly disguised ruse"; in fact, "the Zen economy is the neoclassical formulation preceded by a minus sign" (ibid.). Winterhalder concludes that Sahlins's structuralist concept of the Zen economy is de facto useless: the 'evolutionary ecology' approach, based on formalist assumptions, suffice, and needs not be substituted or complemented, to explain limited production effort and other fundamental characteristics of primitive economies.

Winterhalder's 'evolutionary ecology' interpretation of primitive economic behaviour and organization contains, however, some misunderstandings, which need to be clarified (see Marchionatti 2012), the most important regarding the relationship between the evolutionary ecological model and neoclassical economics. Winterhalder argues that his approach is a microeconomic one which applies the neoclassical assumptions of scarcity, rational choice and optimization to an ecological (rather than market) setting. In fact, Winterhalder interprets hunter-gatherers' behaviour as the result of individual rational choices in a context of scarcity of resources compared to the means: this view is coherent with a neoclassical economic approach. Consequently, Winterhalder can claim that 'behavioural ecology' analysis accommodates the intuition that foraging economies are profoundly different from other societies, while simultaneously insisting that the same analytical tools employed to analyse these latter societies can be applied to understand forager behaviour.

Behavioural ecology appears to be reductionist when emphasizing the role of ecological-economic factors (representing the 'structure' of society, to use a Marxian concept) in necessarily determining the political and cultural development of societies. This makes the analogy with the economic approach appear a strong one, but further considerations on the use of the concept of scarcity and optimization in the model can easily weaken it. Winterhalder recognizes that scarcity of resources is not perceived by primitives, so that one has to adopt it as an axiom:

> We retain scarcity as an axiom because it helps to explain a society in which scarcity as a perception of inadequate provisions or as a material fact is less common than we may expect. We must acknowledge that materialist analysis need not entail the culture of accumulative materialism so evident in Western industrial societies.
>
> (Winterhalder 1992: 336)

But this inevitably reinforces the substantivist critique and the claim that the concept of scarcity is simply not applicable to primitive societies, for the institutional and cultural conditions that lie at the origins of the concept itself are lacking.

As regards optimization, the ecological approach confirms that primitive societies are ecologically efficient in managing natural resources. One could interpret this evidence, as Winterhalder does, as the application of maximizing behaviour, but the hypothesis seems largely unnecessary. Consistently with ethnological evidence, we can hypothesize that selective mechanisms operating on cultural inheritance and gained experience, within a peculiar cultural and institutional context, determine the adoption of behavioural routines that prove to be effective and adequate to the social aim of material reproduction. It follows that the use of concepts borrowed from neoclassical economics is misleading or wrong. The ecological approach cannot establish that neoclassical economic science furnishes the required theoretical tools and general intellectual framework able to explain hunter-gatherers' behaviours. On the contrary, it simply demonstrates that such behaviour in the field of subsistence and management of natural resources is effective, and, as a consequence, it can be described by using analytical tools of neoclassical microeconomics. Furthermore, the assumption that primitives are neoclassical optimizers is not necessary. In the culturalist context suggested by Sahlins, this behaviour can be regarded, as said, as the result of a lifestyle that is culturally adapted to nature, expressing the 'substantive rationality' of the community. There is no need to invoke an optimal use of resources in the neoclassical economics sense – adaptation, as Sahlins (1969: 30) had already established, "is normally a principle of non-optimal resource use". Work effort in primitive societies is devoted to obtaining a socially 'satisfying' situation.

Instead of following a logic of adaptation to ecological necessities, as the behavioural ecological approach is compelled to argue, this behaviour results in sum from a cultural choice. As Richard Lee, following Clastres's political anthropology (see section 6.2), writes, "what sets hunter-gatherers apart is their ability to reproduce themselves *while severely limiting* the accumulation and concentration of wealth and power" (Lee 1992: 43; original emphasis).

They have, Lee writes, a dynamic of a sort different from that of Western societies, what the British anthropologist Tim Ingold has called a "different type of sociality" (Ingold 1990: 130). Commenting on the subsistence strategy of the !Kung Bushmen of Kalahari, and referring to Lee's work on them, the ethologist Irenaus Eibl-Eibesfeldt writes that "there are no primitive cultures but only cultures that have preserved archaic traits that continue to be adaptive in a particular ecological niche" (Eibl-Eibesfeld 1991: 56). The biological concept of 'ecological niche' refers to the fact that "a particular environment offers options for different life-styles" and "peoples adapt culturally to different subsistence strategies": "The adaptations are reflected in their material cultures, skills, customs, and ideology, which are interlocked in a functional system" (ibid.: 55). Eibl-Eibesfeldt concludes that the material culture of the Bushmen (and, we may say, of the primitive societies in general) and their knowledge of the environment "reflect a highly sophisticated set of adaptations" that allow resources to be efficiently exploited. Consequently, "in general they fare well and enjoy a life that could be characterized as 'leisure-intensive'" (ibid.). In Sahlins's terms, they live in an affluent society.

Notes

1 The original introduction to the volume, written three years earlier, when the book was nearing completion, was then published as a separate essay with the title "Economic Anthropology and Anthropological Economics" (Sahlins 1969).
2 Thus, in a substantive sense, "the individual is not thought independently of the society but as a member, inscribed in the society and 'enculturated' in its practices" (Sahlins 1969: 19).
3 "Sociobiology challenges the integrity of culture as a thing-in-itself, as a distinctive and symbolic human creation. In place of a social constitution of meanings, [sociobiology] offers a biological determination of human interactions with a source primarily in the general evolutionary propensity of individual genotypes to maximize their reproductive success . . . Biology, while it is an absolutely necessary condition for culture, is equally and absolutely insufficient: it is completely unable to specify the cultural properties of human behaviour or their variations from one human group to another" (Sahlins 1976b: x–xi).
4 In a footnote of *What Kinship Is – and Is Not* (Sahlins 2013a), Sahlins says that sociobiologists miss the point in comparing humans to "subhuman primates" in terms of reciprocity or altruism: "The point is that humans subsume self and other in a single collective entity, a 'we-ness,' which apes cannot do. In the terms of this book, they are not our 'closest relatives' – one more evidence that kinship is not genealogy" (Sahlins 2013: 38).
5 The role of chiefs and more generally of power in the primitive societies has been investigated in masterly manner by the French anthropologist Pierre Clastres in two books: *La société contre l'état* (1974) and *Recherches d'anthropologie politique* (1980). On Clastres and the literature on his work, see Marchionatti 2013.
6 On this matter, see one of the chapters of *Trade and Markets*, on the African "Explosive markets: The Berber Highlands", by Francisco Benet (1957). In particular, especially interesting is Benet's quotation from an old 1874 article written by J. Nil Robin and published in the *Revue Africaine*, where the author attests to the great importance of the market in Berber life and polity: "The markets are the forum of the tribe. Ideas and business affairs are dealt with here once a week between individuals who live at a considerable distance. It is here that collective sentiments form and manifest themselves. Villages and families fuse their emotions into that often entirely different product which grows from mass contacts. The market creates the external individuality of the group often so dissimilar from the feelings of the individuals composing it. The egotism of the tribe or the douar [village] takes the place of egotism of the individuals" (Polanyi et al. 1957: 193).
7 The idea of a Zen strategy appears to share the same spirit of Ernst F. Schumacher's 'Buddhist economics'. The German economist and philosopher, protegé of Keynes during the Second World War, coined the term in 1955, when working in Burma as economic consultant. The essay "Buddhist Economics" was first published in 1966 and then in Schumacher's volume *Small is Beautiful* (1973).

6 The intelligibility of primitive economic organization

Sahlins, Lévi-Strauss and Clastres on Mauss's political philosophy

6.1 Claude Lévi-Strauss and Marshall Sahlins on the primitive social contract

Chapter 4 of Sahlins' *Stone Age Economics*, entitled "The Spirit of the Gift", conducts an original discussion of Mauss's *Essai*, and in particular of what the French anthropologist considers to be its key concept – the Maori *hau* – together with the theme of the social contract reiterated throughout the *Essai*. In this way, Sahlins maintains, it is possible to appreciate "in another light certain fundamental qualities of primitive economy and polity" (Sahlins 1972: 149).

Mauss had written that, on one hand "to refuse to give, to fail to invite, just as to refuse to accept, is tantamount to declaring war" (Mauss 1990 [1923–24]: 17), on the other hand, the obligation to reciprocate is imperative because gifts convey a power contained in them, the *hau*. It is "the power . . . in the object given that causes its recipient to pay it back" (ibid.: 4). Sahlins discusses this controversial issue and restores the disputed text to its nature "as an explanatory gloss to the description of a sacrificial rite" (Sahlins 1972: 157). According to Sahlins, Tamati Ranapiri's text states a fundamental fact: that "withholding goods is immoral" (ibid: 162). This the interpretation proposed by Sahlins:

> We have to deal with a society in which freedom to gain at others' expense is not envisioned by the relations and forms of exchange. Therein lies the moral of the old Maori's economic fable. The issue he posed went beyond reciprocity: not merely that gifts must be suitably returned, but that returns rightfully should be given back.
>
> (Ibid.)

Sahlins discusses the political philosophy of the *Essai*, by reprising what Lévi-Strauss had said: that in Mauss there is a possible answer to the question of why primitive society is founded on reciprocity – that is, the idea of the exchange as a political contract. According to Sahlins, when Mauss discussed the political issues of philosophers such as Rousseau, Locke, Spinoza and Hobbes, he gave "a new version of the dialogue between chaos and covenant" (ibid.: 169):

> Like famous philosophical predecessors, Mauss debates from an original condition of disorder, in some sense given and pristine, but then overcome dialectically. As against war, exchange. The transfer of things that are in some degree persons and of persons in some degree treated as things, such is the consent at the base of organized society. The gift is alliance, solidarity, communion – in brief, peace, the great virtue that earlier philosophers, Hobbes notably, had discovered in the State . . . The primitive analogue of social contract is not the State, but the gift. The gift is the primitive way of achieving the peace that in civil society is secured by the State.
>
> (Ibid.)

For the philosophers, the social contract was an agreement of incorporation: to form a community out of previously separate and antagonistic parts, the state, that would exercise the power subtracted from each to the benefit of all. On the contrary, Sahlins explains, the society organized through the gift system does not dissolve its separate parties within a higher unity: "Except for the honor accorded to generosity, the gift is no sacrifice of equality and never of liberty" (ibid.: 170). The exchange of gifts, he continues, removes the original condition of disorder and realizes the condition of peace: from Hobbes's state of war of all against all (that is, the state of nature) to peace through the exchange of everything between everybody. Constantly menaced by deterioration into war, primitive groups are nevertheless reconciled by festival and exchange. By the end of the essay, Sahlins writes, "Mauss had left far behind the mystic forest of Polynesia":

> The obscure forces of *hau* were forgotten for a different explanation of reciprocity, consequent on the more general theory, and the opposite of all mystery and particularity: Reason. The gift is Reason. It is the triumph of human rationality over the folly of war.
>
> (Ibid.: 175)

According to Sahlins, in the *Essai* Mauss "transposes the classic alternatives of war and trade from the periphery to the very center of social life, and from the occasional episode to the continuous presence" (ibid.: 182). It follows that the primitive society may be defined, in this perspective, a "society against war". All exchanges, Sahlins says, must bear in their material design some political burden of reconciliation, or to quote what a Bushman said to the American anthropologist Lorna Marshall: "The worse thing is not giving presents. If people do not like each other but one gives a gift and the other must accept, this brings a peace between them. We give what we have. That is the way we live together" (Sahlins 1972: 182).

From this derive the basic principles of what Sahlins calls an "economics properly anthropological", in particular, the principle that "every exchange, as it embodies some coefficient of sociability, cannot be understood in its material terms apart from its social terms" (ibid., 183).

6.2 Pierre Clastres on the relationship between war and gift exchange in societies "against the state"

The idea that the primitive society is a society against war had been supported, as already mentioned, by Lévi-Strauss. "There is a link," he wrote, "a continuity, between hostile relations and the provision of reciprocal prestations. Exchanges are peacefully resolved wars and wars are the result of unsuccessful transactions" (Lévi-Strauss 1959: 67). From this perspective, war is a failure, the failure of the primitive social being, because primitive society is essentially a society for exchange and war is the break-up of exchange. The French anthropologist Pierre Clastres (1934–77), pupil of Lévi-Strauss, dealt with this question in an essay on "the archeology of violence" and criticized Lévi-Strauss's thesis, offering an interesting contribution to the debate on the relationship between war and exchange. He wrote: "Primitive society is a space of exchange, and it is also a place of violence: war, on the same level as exchange, belongs to the primitive social being" (Clastres 1994 [1980]: 152).

The "exchangist conception of society" is symmetrical and inverse to that of Hobbes, Clastres maintains; for Hobbes, primitive society was a war of all against all while for Lévi-Strauss, primitive society is the exchange of each with each. According to Clastres, "Hobbes left out exchange, Lévi-Strauss leaves out war" (ibid.). Clastres offers a different interpretation of the relationship between war and exchange in primitive societies. Primitive society is self-sufficient on the economic level and independent on the political level. Therefore

> one would assume . . . a general absence of violence: it could only arise in rare cases of territorial violation, it would only be defensive, and thus never produce itself, each group relying on its own territory which it has no reason to leave.
>
> (Ibid.: 154)

However, ethnological studies show that war is widespread and very often offensive in the savage world. Hence the relationship between war and society "has yet to be illuminated" (ibid). Two sociological properties of primitive society make its social being and war intelligible: "the primitive community is at once a totality and a unity" (ibid.: 155), Clastres maintains: "A unity in that its homogeneous being continues to refuse social division, to exclude inequality, to forbid alienation . . . A totality in that it is a complete, autonomous, whole ensemble, ceaselessly attentive to preserving its autonomy" (ibid.).

Clastres defines it, in his best-known book, *a* "society against the state" (Clastres 1974). He writes:

> Faced with neighboring communities or bands, a particular community or band posits itself and think of itself as absolute difference, as irreducible freedom, as a body possessing the will to maintain its being as a single totality. Here then I show how primitive society concretely appears: a multiplicity

> of separate communities, each watching over the integrity of its territory, a series of neo-monads each of which, in the face of others, asserts its difference. Each community, in that it is undivided, can think of itself as a We.
>
> (Clastres 1994 [1980]: 156)

It follows that "the possibility of war is inscribed in the being of primitive society" (ibid.: 157). However, the Hobbesian war of all against all is prevented, Clastres writes, because it would lead to the institution of a political hierarchy, the establishment of nomination and power of the victor over the vanquished, the political division of society into Masters and Subjects: "precisely the political relationship that primitive society works constantly to prevent" (ibid.: 158), because in the case of war of all against all, the community would lose its homogeneous unity through the irruption of social division. Then, "the impossibility of war of all against all for a given community immediately classifies the people surrounding it: Others are immediately classified into friends and enemies" (ibid.: 159). With the former, one will attempt to form alliances; with the latter, one accepts the risk of war. "Why does a primitive society need allies?", Clastres asks. He answers: because it has to be assured of its strength: "It never launches into a war adventure without first protecting itself by means of diplomatic acts –parties, invitations – after which supposedly lasting alliances are formed, but which must constantly be renewed, for betrayal is always possible" (ibid.).

As travellers and ethnographers show, Clastres notes, alliances change, but the division of others into allies and enemies remain: alliance is a means to attain at the lowest risk and at the least cost a goal that is the war enterprise: "the strategy is . . . to persevere in their autonomous being, to conserve themselves as what they are, undivided We's" (ibid.: 160). So the relationship between exchange and war becomes clear, Clastres writes:

> Through the will for political independence and exclusive control of its territory manifested by each community, the possibility of war is immediately inscribed in the functioning of these societies: primitive society is a locus of a permanent state of war . . . seeking an alliance depends on actual war: there is a sociological priority of war over alliance. Here, the true relationship between exchange and war emerges. Indeed, where relations of exchange are established, which sociopolitical units assume a principle of reciprocity? These are precisely the groups implicated in the networks of alliance: exchange partners are allies, the sphere of exchange is that of alliance.
>
> (Ibid.)

In exchanges with allies, Clastres emphasizes, there is exchange because there is alliance. It is essentially exchange of gifts and especially exchange of women, in order to reinforce the political alliance, which confirms the political significance of the gift:

> the establishment of matrimonial relations between different groups is a way of concluding and reinforcing political alliance in order to confront enemies

> under the best conditions. From allies who are also relatives, one may hope for more constancy in war-like solidarity.
>
> (Ibid.)

6.3 Primitive economic organization in the light of Mauss's political philosophy

The idea of a primitive social contract, as elaborated, in the Maussian tradition, by Lévi-Strauss, Sahlins and Clastres, makes the place of economy in primitive societies understandable. The social contract establishes the society's political independence and its internal equality as common goods *par excellence* to be preserved.

The aim of safeguarding independence and equality entails two order of conditions, one internal and the other external to the community: a condition of autarchy (or an "internal subsistence economy", to use Firth's term), internally, accompanied by reciprocity and inhibition of accumulation – gift exchange with allies, externally, and peripherality of markets.

Autarchy means economic independence from other groups. Inhibition of accumulation and internal reciprocity protect unity and equality in the community. External reciprocity (through gift exchange) involves a system of alliances and territorial independence. Moreover, inhibition of accumulation and internal reciprocity impede the formation of stable surplus. This result, together with limited wants (the Zen strategy is at work), is not the necessary outcome of technological and knowledge backwardness, as conjectured in the economicist interpretation. Two reasons explain why surplus accumulation is not pursued. On the one hand, when needs are intentionally limited, and the aim of material self-sufficiency is easily obtained, social incentives to accumulate fall down. On the other hand, surplus accumulation tends to generate material differences in the community, as well as incentives for market exchanges outside communitarian borders, with consequent risk of decreasing, or loss of independence – thus, the only possibility left is to destroy surpluses.

In this context, the place of economy in primitive societies is subordinate to the political strategy adopted: this is the fundamental reason why Polanyi, along Maussian lines, can use the notion of embeddedness when dealing with the economy in archaic societies. It follows that the social institutions that are extraneous to such political strategy are excluded, or channelled into paths that can render them innocuous or even functional to the political strategy: private property is often absent, while ownership of goods is limited by norms concerning the obligation to give and to destroy goods after the owner's death.

This social logic can explain the social control of power through the obligation (for the chief) to display generosity – a form of inextinguishable debt towards the community – and casts light on both the peripherality of market relations, outside the community, and, at the same time, the complex nature of primitive markets.

Part III

The problem of the 'other'

Economics and unselfish behaviour

Part III proposes a historical perspective on the developments in economic theory made necessary by the attempt to address the problem of the 'other' – read, unselfish behaviour.

Chapter 7 focuses on the 'economics of unselfishness' as developed since pioneering studies on philanthropy in the 1960s. The resulting economics of altruism represents the most intriguing contribution offered by the economic discipline to the post-war social sciences debate about the foundations of modern human aggregates. Still, the chapter shows that the 'mainstream' and even 'imperialist' character of the early economics of altruism impeded the reformulation of the *homo oeconomicus* paradigm and the removal of the bias necessarily produced by economics' emphasis on self-interest, rationality and maximization. Adequate importance is given to the reception of Richard Titmuss's *The Gift Relationship*, showing the difficulties economics encounters in dialoguing with other social disciplines, and to the non-qualified use economic science has subsequently made of the concept of gift.

The chapter closes by introducing the recent "economics of reciprocity", building upon laboratory and field experiments whose results clearly violate the main assumptions of the *homo oeconomicus* paradigm. Chapter 8 further investigates the importance of this research programme, and discusses in particular Herbert Gintis's suggestion of a new theoretical framework for behavioural sciences, intended to make the variety of approaches proposed in social sciences compatible with one another. The chapter highlights the influence of sociobiology (and its 'competing' imperialism) on the proposal.

7 Economics on altruism, giving and reciprocity

Given much increased insistency (and seemingly more powerful tools available, those of behavioural economics, to reach the goal) on the necessity of more realism in the analysis of individual behaviour, the ambition to revise the egoistic assumptions of the *homo oeconomicus* paradigm is today a more realistic perspective than it was in the decades of the economics of unselfishness. This latter term (as is much of the reconstruction that follows) is borrowed from Philippe Fontaine's (2007, 2012) accurate account of this specific subfield of economics, whereby the evolution of the economics of unselfishness from philanthropy to altruism to a more recent, however defined movement "beyond altruism", ends up with minimizing the ethical dimension of unselfish behaviour in economics. The apparent paradox owes to the initial motivations justifying the incursion of economics into the realm of altruism: that is, the perception of the impossibility of relying on selfishness exclusively to ensure social cohesion in Western societies. Less paradoxically, it appears that economics continues to be "conspicuously absent from a topic [the gift] that seems to lie well within its purview" (Osteen 2002: 31). More in general, "neglect of anthropology is nearly ubiquitous in economics, often accompanied by convictions that it has little or nothing to offer the modern social scientists" (Mirowski 1994: 313). But it must also be noted that the economics of altruism quite easily pushed the gift outside its own borders, confining it into the research and, more generally, the imaginary of the few somewhat "heretical" economists trying to investigate the motivations lying behind gift relationships. The result is that virtually any social study of the gift, to borrow from Osteen, is "silent about economics because economics has been almost totally silent about the gift" (Osteen 2002: 32). "How can scholars in the humanities and researchers in the social sciences engage in dialogue", Osteen (ibid.) wonders, "if one side remains mute"?

7.1 From philanthropy to altruism

The public launch of the economics of altruism was a New York City conference in March 1972, convened by the American economist Edmund Phelps (winner of the 2006 Nobel Prize in economics). In explicitly addressing 'The Theory of Altruism', the conference made a significant innovation with respect to the one on philanthropy held in Southampton, Long Island, New York in 1961 and sponsored by the National Bureau of Economic Research, which was conducting at the time a study on philanthropic behaviour, financed by a Russell Sage Foundation grant. Associated with this research were pioneering attempts to analyse unselfishly oriented behaviour by Gary Becker (1961), Kenneth Boulding (1962) and William Vickrey (1962). Their three essays were already representative of the two alternative modalities since then employed to face the problem of altruism in economics, alternatives whereby the economic discipline somehow internalized the more general dichotomy in social sciences between normatively oriented behaviour and self-interested action. In economics, it is now commonplace to adopt the 1998 Nobel Prize winner Amartya Sen's (1977) terminology as concerning individual preferences in relation to altruism. On denouncing the absurdity of the "rational fools" representation of individuals as endowed with a rationality that requires universal selfishness (see Sen 1977), he named "sympathy" the somewhat "egoistic" concern for others, and "commitment" the ensemble of good reasons individuals can have to pursue objectives that cannot be assimilated with utility maximization. Becker's 1961 study was motivated by the desire to redefine the individual utility function by including arguments related to others and thereby come to expand the boundaries of economics to non-economic topics. Treating philanthropy as the result of human beings' "capacity for empathy", Boulding's work (1962: 61) already presented the Polanyian flavour of his more mature writings. It was exactly after the conference on philanthropy that Kenneth Boulding (1910–93), one of the most important unorthodox American economists, could finalize his first suggestion of a general theory of social interaction. There, the "economic", that is "exchange", coexists with "love", or (the term appeared in Boulding's 1963 restatement of the theory) "integrative relationships" (the social dimension), and "threat" (the political dimension, and the state) in their quality of "social organizers" of three specific but "large, overlapping, and interpenetrating systems" which, together, form the social system. Considering grants as the material representation and measure of the integrative system, Boulding (1968) came to associate unselfish behaviour with a "heroic ethic", based on an individual's identity and sense of belonging to a community, the opposite of the "economic ethic" which guides cost-benefit calculus. In *The Economy of Love and Fear* (1973), Boulding will complete his journey outside the wall of economics imperialism. He explicitly called upon other social disciplines to reconstruct economics – "integration of the social sciences rather than their unification around the self-interest motivation" (Fontaine 2007: 29). While Becker's work on philanthropy was just a (rather marginal) step towards the much more general program of extending maximization outside the "economic" sphere, Boulding, a "moral" scientist,[1] showed on the contrary a real interest in the possibility of a grant (or gift) economy (Fontaine 2007, Mirowski 1994).

Hirshleifer (1987 [1967]) immediately rejected this possibility, arguing that other-interested behaviour as field of research is in truth of little if any relevance. Hirshleifer's stance owed much to the reading of Mancur Olson's *The Logic of*

Collective Action (1965), investigating group and organizational behaviour by applying economic analysis and categories. The volume was instrumental in setting economists on a path that would compel them to acknowledge the importance of collective action, goods and externalities for social cohesion. In this perspective, individuals can adopt altruistic behaviour when induced to do so by the risk of social disintegration: this does not justify special treatment (read: considering different behavioural assumptions) by the economic discipline. De facto, this (economics-imperialism) logic prevented Boulding's interests in grants from developing into a collective interdisciplinary research programme on (also) the motivations of altruistic behaviour: as Fontaine (2007) argues, it was public-choice economist and 1986 Nobel Prize winner James Buchanan who dismissed the possibility to orient economic research in this direction. Having read Boulding's 1963 article on "threat systems" to prepare his 1963 presidential address to the Southern Economic Association, Buchanan later commented in 1969 on the 1964 second edition of Alchian and Allen's *University Economics* textbook. He argued that while the individual utility function can include arguments of a non-economic essence (provided, following the two famous American economists, they can be treated as "goods"), a reduction to economics' selfish dimension was absolutely required to explain non-economic behaviour. But this meant, according to Buchanan, that economists could not say anything relevant on the various specific and heterogeneous motivations that can justify such attitudes (Fontaine 2007): "non-economic models of behavior" (Buchanan 1972: 18) are rather needed for analysing non-market behaviour.

As Fine and Milonakis (2009) note, Buchanan's reservations about the 'primacy' of economics – in a similar vein, McKenzie and Tullock (1978) will stress the "limits of economic analysis", and the need of social sciences to investigate the origins of preferences and values – are indicative of a more nuanced position with respect to Becker's fully imperialist stance. This latter's contributions on altruism and gift-giving make no exception. In "A Theory of Social Interactions" of 1974 (the article where Becker exposes the famous "rotten kid" theorem), Becker rejected the normatively oriented approach to gift-giving and described it in terms of individual rationality – coherently with his general strategy of making the "non-economic" unnecessary, which requires treating any behaviour 'as if' it were the consequence of economic and rational choices. Altruism itself on the part of the benevolent member of the family or, by extension, of the whole society was in truth 'as if' altruism. The important point is that purely selfish behaviour is a self-defeating strategy, in presence of charitable ("sympathetic", Sen would say, since their income is affected by concern for others) persons, who will offset egoists' wrongdoings by increasing in volume their transfers to other members. After Becker's imperial model of 'social interactions', Buchanan's doubts will become Sen's (1977) condemnation of the poorness of maximization as sole explanation for the complexity of social interrelationships.

Phelps's 1972 conference on the theory of altruism, though open to other disciplines (it saw the participation of philosophers John Rawls and Tom Nagel, as well as sociologist Erving Goffman and political scientist Edward Banfield), was essentially conceived (the first among other reasons), as an exercise in economics expansionism. Together with Becker's "A Theory of Social Interactions", the volume gathering (quite heterogeneous) articles presented at the conference, *Altruism, Morality, and Economic Theory* (Phelps 1975), is a milestone in the story of the economics of altruism, being at the origins of an extensive successive literature which brought altruism economics into the mainstream of the discipline. "Sympathy" was clearly destined to triumph on "commitment": the incorporation of unselfish behaviour into the discipline occurred at the expenses of its ethical dimension (Fontaine 2007). The most evident illustration of this tendency is the reception of Richard Titmuss's *The Gift Relationship. From Human Blood to Social Policy*, of 1970.

7.2 Richard Titmuss's *The Gift Relationship* and economists' embarrassment

Professor of social administration (the former expression of the discipline of social policy, which he founded) at the London School of Economics, Richard Titmuss (1907–73) was a leading figure in social sciences in view of the decisive contributions he offered in shaping the post-war Britain's welfare state and of his work on social policy. But Titmuss's work is also famous for having "disconcerted economists" (Fontaine 2002: 433), with a book centred on the defence of blood donating as against its commercialization. The volume was celebrated as one of the seven most important books to appear in 1971 by the *New York Times Book Review*. It collected a huge amount of statistical data from several fragmented sources concerning the demand and supply of blood in the United States and Britain, but the debate it generated mostly focused on the social and moral values advanced by Titmuss in praise of the British voluntary system of blood collection as against its commodification in the United States. The comparison between the two systems clearly favoured the British one: to borrow from Jeremy Shearmur (2001), Titmuss reached the conclusion that when blood is donated by volunteers, it is not affected by problems of adverse selection – blood sellers are in fact more likely, according to Titmuss, to be disadvantaged people and the bearers of diseases – and rather is nurtured by the strength, to say it in more modern terms, of intrinsic motivation (blood donors include also individuals who would not sell their blood in a system where it is commercialized; see Sandel 2012). Moreover, by commercializing blood, a market system raises a problem of donor truthfulness (which is highly relevant in view of the possibility of transfusion-transmitted infections): paid donors will scarcely reveal their medical history, Titmuss argued, or information about their lifestyle, fearing that this may disqualify them as donors.

Curiously enough, if one holds in mind the book's title, Titmuss had started working on the subject without awareness of the anthropological literature on the gift. Paradoxically, again, direct references included in the gestation of the book to this corpus of study, and in particular to Mauss's work, which Titmuss discovered in 1967, were among the most immediate causes of the tremendous impact the volume had on social sciences. The theoretical link between the two scholars is hardly surprising. After all, Mauss himself had devoted some pages of the conclusions of *The Gift* to the embryonic (if compared to modern times) welfare state society, wherein he could detect signs of the continuing topicality and relevance of the gift. Mauss noted that the French legislation on social insurance was inspired by a principle according to which the worker "has given his life and his labour, on the one hand to the collectivity, and on the other hand, to his employers". Representing that "collectivity", the state consequently "owes him . . . a certain security in life, against unemployment, sickness, old age and death" (Mauss 1990 [1923–24]: 67). But then, this means that:

> the state and its subordinate grouping desire to look after the individual. Society is seeking to rediscover a cellular structure for itself. It is indeed wanting to look after the individual. Yet the mental state in which it does so is one in which are curiously intermingled a perception of the rights of the individual and other, purer sentiments: charity, social service, and solidarity. The themes of the gift, of the freedom and the obligation inherent in the gift, of generosity and self-interest that are linked in giving, are reappearing in French society, as a dominant motif too long forgotten.
>
> (ibid.: 68)

As Fontaine remarks, Titmuss was an eclectic scholar, showing no fear of trespassing disciplinary boundaries. The resulting "bricolage" (Fontaine 2002: 418) of *The Gift Relationship* is what confers originality to the book, but it was also a reason for disappointment for specialized scholars like anthropologist Mary Douglas. Douglas saw the bricolage as the impossible union of two books in one (one was the study of alternative modalities of organizing the collection and delivery of blood to hospitals, the other on the author's "own social philosophy") – "not usually a good formula for a book", all the more so since the second book is not more than "a confused collection of slogans" (Douglas 1971: 499). Probably an unfair criticism, surely one – *ex post* at least – that missed the point, Douglas's reaction is however understandable. Titmuss (1970: 71) explicitly declared that: "to give or not to give, to lend, repay or even to buy and sell blood leads us, if we are to understand these transactions in the context of a particular society, into the fundamentals of social and economic life."

Yet the story of how Titmuss came to write *The Gift Relationship* is highly instructive in this regard. For the book is also the final step in his criticism of the approach of the Institute of Economic Affairs (IEA), a London-based think tank inspired by Friedrich von Hayek and destined to acquire decisive importance in the years of Prime Minister Margaret Thatcher's rule, to medical care and in general to non-economic topics. A radically pro-market imperialist attitude undersized, in Titmuss's (1963) view, the "social", as well as any ethical implication for public policies in stimulating ethical behaviour, without considering the negative consequences for social cohesion of the extension of markets to social services (see Fontaine 2002). Remarkably, Titmuss believed to have found in Kenneth

Arrow's 1963 article 'Uncertainty and the Welfare Economics of Medical Care' (published in the *American Economic Review*) a powerful theoretical ally in his struggle against the "economic approach" to social services. In the article, the future Nobel Prize winner discussed the structural factors, broadly related to the intrinsic uncertainty characterizing the general framework shaping the relationships between sellers of medical care, doctors and patients, that might prevent people from considering medical care as a commodity – contrary to the IEA's approach of considering "social services in kind" as having "no characteristics which differentiate them from goods in the private market" (Titmuss 1966: 145). Arrow was thus unwittingly instrumental in bringing Titmuss on a Polanyian path that – culminating in *The Gift Relationship* – will lead this latter to explore the issue of "fictitious" commodities (see Steiner 2003).

After reading Boulding's 'The Boundaries of Social Policies' (1967), and now being also familiar with Mauss's *The Gift*, Titmuss came to consider the gift – one of the examples made was the gift of blood – as "the distinguishing mark of the social" (1967: 22). *The Gift Relationship*, he was to write in the introduction to the book, originated "from a series of value questions formulated within the context of attempts to distinguish the 'social' from the 'economic' in public policies and in those institutions and services with declared welfare goals" (1970: 15). By 1967, therefore, Titmuss had realized that blood giving was a most useful illustration of the "social" (Fontaine 2002), and a stimulus to write *The Gift Relationship* came from criticisms directed towards a study for the IEA on the supply of blood produced by Michael Cooper and Anthony Culyer (1968) of the University of Exeter, where the economicist view was defended, in that, by paying donors, a system could avoid shortages and waste. Titmuss was highly critical of the assumptions implicit in this perspective, and on reading Cooper and Culyer's study, he focused on the authors' belief that unselfish behaviour could develop only amongst families or closed communities. Hence the importance, in Titmuss's vision, of the "stranger", and the idea that social policy should have the aim of stimulating unselfishness in the large social groups normally considered as made up of individuals who are essentially strangers to one another.

Chapter 5 of *The Gift Relationship* presents a typology of donors entering into a gift relationship with strangers – a diametrically different situation, Titmuss himself notes, from other types of gifts in modern societies, these latter being all characterized by the absence of anonymity. In introducing the chapter, he observes that:

> The forms and functions of giving embody moral, social, psychological, religious, legal and aesthetic ideas. They may reflect, sustain, strengthen or loosen the cultural bonds of the group, large or small . . . Customs and practices of non-economic giving – unilateral and multilateral social transfers – thus may tell us much, as Marcel Mauss so sensitively demonstrated in his book *The Gift*, about the texture of personal and group relationships in different cultures, past and present.
>
> (Titmuss 1970: 71–2)

Titmuss then summarizes the anthropological literature on gift-giving, stressing the "pervasiveness of the social obligation . . . to give and to repay" (ibid.: 72) and of sanctions; in other words, he insists on the "elements of moral enforcement" (ibid.) attached to gift practices in non-industrialized societies, but calls on Mauss himself (the Mauss of the last pages of the *Essai sur le don*) in support of his own attempt to apply the anthropological reasoning on the gift to blood donation in Western contemporary societies. Blood gifts configure impersonal situations, wherein recipients and donors do not know each other, so that givers cannot reasonably expect corresponding gifts in return. But givers neither require nor wish such a countergift, and there is no sanction for not giving (recipients themselves are not required to give in their turn). The trustfulness of the giver determines the quality of the gift, and intermediaries play a fundamental role.

In treating the relationship produced by blood donation as gift relationship, Titmuss raised the disapproval of anthropologists who most easily identified themselves with the political philosophy of the *Essai sur le don*. Curiously enough, while reviewing Titmuss's book, Arrow himself (1972: 360) criticized Titmuss's interest in "impersonal altruism", or a "diffuse expression of confidence by individuals in the workings of a society as a whole", which is "as far removed from the feelings of personal interaction as any marketplace". But Titmuss at once created, *ex nihilo*, the concept of the unilateral gift to strangers, that – after exposing, in general, Titmuss to sociologists' criticisms (Alvin Gouldner (1971) believed that Titmuss had too easily passed over social norms implied in the relationships under investigation) – would have compelled social scientists (see Godbout 2000) to investigate the constitutive "difference" of gifts in modern societies.

According to Mary Douglas (1971: 500), Titmuss's references to Mauss were just a matter of cosmetics, serving to "decorate the reiterated theme that altruism is a very good thing". Engaged in what Titmuss defined as gift relationships – and wrongly so: there is no gift, as there are no relations between givers and receivers – were a "whole complex of paid professionals and advertising agencies" (ibid.). Canadian sociologist Jacques T. Godbout came to affirm that Titmuss treats receivers as economists would do – abstractly, and in economic terms. Still, Godbout also holds that the gift of blood – a "tiny initial difference" with respect to systems of blood commercialization, for this gift is a gift that has no receivers, de facto – allows the "spirit" of the gift to circulate – a radical difference with respect to market approaches to blood supply. By – unduly – playing with Mauss's scheme to adapt it to the gift of blood, Titmuss exploits what in Mauss does not pertain to a morals of equivalence and reciprocity; in other words, what in Mauss does not pertain to the habitual model of the anthropological gift (Godbout 1998).

This remark can be useful in shifting the focus on economists' reactions to the book, mainly centred upon the "Titmuss dilemma", as moral philosopher (and professor of bioethics) Peter Singer (1973) called it on commenting Arrow's review of *The Gift Relationship* (which he prepared for the 1972 conference on

'Altruism and Economic Theory' at the Russell Sage Foundation). Paradoxically unaware of the influence he exerted on Titmuss himself, Arrow recognized that the book provided a

> searchlight to illuminate a much broader landscape [than the workings of peculiar blood supply systems]: the limits of economic analysis, the rival use of exchange and gift as modes of allocation, the collective or communitarian possibilities in society as against the tendencies toward individualism.
>
> (Arrow 1972: 343)

What Arrow found particularly disturbing were not Titmuss's "four testable non-ethical criteria" upon which to (negatively) evaluate the commercialized blood market (economic inefficiency, with chronic shortages, and the resulting illusory character of the equilibrium between demand and supply; administrative efficiency; costs for patients; probability to distribute contaminated blood). Rather, Arrow concentrated his criticism on Titmuss's arguments about the "erosion of motivation" (Archard 2002) produced by the passing from voluntary to commercial means of collecting blood. According to Titmuss

> private market systems . . . deprive men of their freedom to choose to give or not to give . . . policy and processes should enable men to be free to choose to give to unnamed strangers. They should not be coerced or constrained by the market. In the interests of the freedom of all men, they should not, however, be free to sell their blood or decide on a specific destination of the gift. The choice between these claims – between different kinds of freedom – has to be a social decision; in other words, it is a moral and political decision for the society as a whole.
>
> (Titmuss 1970: 242)

The creation of a market, consequently, does not enhance individual freedom, as the received view in economics would maintain. In Titmuss's view, on the contrary, the problem of individual freedom cannot be dealt with if not within the broader socio-political context (Archard 2002). Arrow simply found unacceptable Titmuss's dilemma: for it is exactly the creation of a market that adds to the voluntary system by "expand[ing] the individual's range of alternatives" (Arrow 1972: 350). As Singer (1973: 313) observes, Titmuss may have presented the argument in a misleading form (see also, for a much more critical comment, Glazer 1971). The choice, he held, is not between the "incompatible freedoms, or between a 'right to give' and a 'right to sell'". Still, "there remains there remains a real dilemma. For what Titmuss is really asserting is that a voluntary system fosters attitudes of altruism and a desire to relate to, and help, strangers in one's community" (Singer 1973: 313–14), whereas the introduction of a market has exactly the opposite effect. As against Arrow, Singer finds in Titmuss's study evidence that commercialization drives out voluntary donors. In systems where blood is freely given, the number of donors has risen, Singer argues after Titmuss, whereas where the opportunity exists to sell it, the number of volunteers has fallen, "and can only with difficulty, if at all, be made good by increases in the amount of blood bought" (ibid.: 315).

To say it with philosopher David Archard (2002), Titmuss's thesis rests upon (not that the distinction is not explicit in the text) two "domino" arguments. These are a "contamination of meaning" argument – where monetary terms are used, the meaning of the gift is corrupted – and an "erosion of motivation" argument – a sort of Gresham's law applied to blood supply: market and non-market exchanges cannot coexist (see also Frey's 1997 exploration of "intrinsic" motivations). Titmuss's attention went in large part to the erosion of motivations: "the emphasis [in the book] is less upon the extent, or quality, of individual freedom than the quality of social relationships" (Archard 2002: 91). In Titmuss's reasoning as restated by Singer, not only institutions matter, but they can act in 'transformative' ways: they can, in other words, affect the quality of individual behaviour, and transform unselfishness into utility maximization or vice versa (see Archard 2002, Steiner 2003): "Commerce replaces fellow-feelings" (Singer 1973: 316). Not without reasons, in the effort to hold such arguments together, Archard insists on the "imperialism" of blood markets; as he puts it:

> I simply see no need to give since others are prepared to sell their blood to those who are willing to buy. It is not that I cannot see my gift of blood as a gift; it is that I see no social 'space' for my gift.
>
> (Archard 2002: 94)

Titmuss's dictum is famous: "the commercialization of blood and donor relationships represses the expression of altruism, erodes the sense of community" (1970: 245). Arrow's reply shows, however, that economists have their own preferences, as Singer observed. In criticizing Titmuss for recurring to ethical reasons, Arrow explicitly admitted that he did "not want to rely too heavily on substituting ethics for self-interest":

> I think it is best on the whole that the requirement of ethical behavior be confined to those circumstances where the price system breaks down as suggested above. Wholesale usage of ethical standards is apt to have undesirable consequences. We do not wish to use up recklessly the scarce resources of altruistic motivation, and in any case ethically motivated behavior may even have a negative value to others if the agent acts without sufficient knowledge of the situation.
>
> (Arrow 1972: 354–5)

Yet the idea that altruism can be considered as a "scarce resource" is left unwarranted. Singer can thus easily oppose this argument by observing that one surely finds it "hardest to act with consideration for others when the norm in the circle of people I move in is to act egoistically. When altruism is expected of me, however, I find it much easier to be genuinely altruistic" (Singer 1973: 319).

Singer concludes his review stressing that Titmuss's book contained an important message for economists. The idea had already been advanced by the American economist Robert Solow, who identified the polemical target of *The Gift Relationship* in the "misuse" (Solow 1971: 1696) of economic reasoning, although not economic reasoning itself: problems are caused by economists' narrow-mindedness, with resulting "invalid overextensions of economic reasoning" (ibid.: 1709). As Fontaine puts it, "*The Gift Relationship* had much to antagonize a large segment of the economics profession, and it did. Yet at the time the book came out, economics was going through a transitional period" (Fontaine 2002: 425).

The Institute of Economic Affairs' response to Titmuss, the volume *The Economics of Charity* (with the lengthy subtitle *Essays on the comparative economics and the ethics of giving and selling, with applications to blood*) (Seldon 1973) appeared after a long gestation in 1973, with Armen Alchian, R.G.D. Allen, Gordon Tullock, Anthony J. Culyer among contributors. Remarkably, as Fontaine suggests, it was the breadth of the debate around Titmuss's book, and the names involved in the discussions, all leading figures in specific social disciplines, to convince IEA President Arthur Seldon that

> refuting Titmuss required not only rebutting his claim concerning the undesirable consequences of blood commercialization but also showing that economists had their own theory of giving, which would allow them to claim some expertise in areas that were usually considered the province of other social sciences.
>
> (Fontaine 2002: 428)

Made up, de facto, of two volumes, originally conceived as outcomes of separate research programmes, one on blood and Titmuss's book, the other on the economics of philanthropy, *The Economics of Charity* served this purpose, but Arrow's and Solow's reviews had already occupied the scene. It is after the two Nobel Prizes winners (Arrow was awarded the prize in 1972, while Solow would follow in 1987) had not negatively commented on Titmuss's books that, "largely unprepared" for its main message (about the importance of moral norms), economists came to realize, at least, that it would have now been difficult to "dismiss Titmuss's emphasis on the role of gift-giving in the working of society as mere softheartedness" (Fontaine 2002: 433).

But this does not mean that Titmuss won the battle. Among other factors (dealt with in the following pages), the ambiguity intrinsic in Arrow's comments on *The Gift Relationship* may partly explain why economics lost the opportunity to develop a non-imperialistic attitude to the fundamental issue at stake – which was also the main legacy of Titmuss's book. That is, in Singer's words, the reflection economists should necessarily make when facing the problem of

> the social utilities involved in the possibilities for altruistic behaviour which are lost when economic relations are substituted for voluntary donations.

> Here we must ask ourselves not 'How can we obtain the most blood at the least cost?' but '*What sort of society do we want*?"
>
> (Singer 1973: 320; emphasis added)

In this regard, Mirowski (2001) has advanced an intriguing interpretation of the (perhaps even unintended) essence of Arrow's defence of economics against the potential primacy (de facto explicit in Titmuss's work) of ethics: this would be but a typical illustration of the "futility thesis" in neoclassical economics:

> In all its various manifestations, the common denominator is some assertion that the world is so structured and interlinked that anything one might wish to accomplish will be offset – usually in some unexpected or unanticipated manner – returning you to the original situation.
>
> (Mirowski 2001: 435)

Economics' sudden, unprepared detour towards the socio-anthropological dimension of gift-giving (in a broader context of increased attention to unselfishness) ends up with denying any consistency to the concept. Mirowski sees Arrow's profound objection to Titmuss in the rejection of the idea that gifts can be of indispensable help to the economy:

> The aspect of Titmuss's work that will probably have the most striking effect both immediately and in the long run is his argument that a world of giving may actually increase efficiency in the operation of the economic system. This is on the face of it a direct challenge to the tenets of the mainstream of economic thought . . . since the time of Adam Smith.
>
> (Arrow 1972: 351)

Mirowski's view is that Arrow simply cannot tolerate the idea that "gift-giving, *if it exists*, could outperform the market in any way, shape or form" (Mirowski 2001: 437; original emphasis). Arrow seems to oscillate between assertion that gifts are impossible, on one side, and recognition that although possible, they are also not so widespread as Titmuss would induce readers to believe, or that economic motivations can in truth explain the recurrence of such practices – which are in truth camouflages.

7.3 Mainstream economics and the gift

The "most basic law" of the economic discipline being, according to British economist and first biographer of Keynes, Roy Harrod, "that one cannot get something for nothing" (1948: 36), it is not surprising that the gift had to wait for a "favourable" intellectual climate to be allowed to enter economics. The advent and relative success of the economics of altruism, and the 'Titmuss affair' were instrumental in bringing the relevance of the gift as object of study to the attention of economists. Concern for others was destined to become "the new frontier of economics", to borrow from Serge-Cristophe Kolm and Jean-Mercier Ythier's (2006: 5) introduction to the *Handbook of the Economics of Giving, Altruism and Reciprocity*. And while Kolm and Ythier take pains to demonstrate that altruism was in truth economics' "oldest concern and tradition", the economics of altruism has a peculiar "story", as seen, dating back to the 1960s and 1970s, as well as definite "founders".

Economists who oriented their research work to the problem of altruism after Becker's (1974) and Phelps's (1975) seminal contributions were less concerned with the issues raised by the introduction into mainstream economics of what appears as a somehow 'external' issue. As Fontaine remarks, they quite easily accepted – together with Becker's theoretical framework – the utility-maximization hypothesis, thus "positing the essentially economic character of unselfish behavior". "The price paid by the discipline to incorporate unselfish behavior", Fontaine continues, "was a minimization of its ethical dimension" (2002: 40). The excursion of economics into the realm of other social sciences, also in response, at least in part, to the competing imperialism of sociobiology in the mid-1970s (as already hinted at above), finally resulted in a growing insistence on the relevance of selfishness in explaining unselfishness. Less and less room was thus left to unselfishness itself, in its autonomy, in economics.

In his 1973 inaugural lecture at the London School of Economics, "Behaviour and the Concept of Preference", the Indian economist and philosopher Amartya Sen posited the need to go beyond the narrowness of maximization as 'as if' hypothesis – with its almost linear correspondence between choice, preference and welfare – about human behaviour in society. "Commitment" (as opposed to "sympathy") would simply break this correspondence, and instead transform it into a complex relationship, relegating utility maximization to being only one of many considerations influencing its precise shape. Sen was not alone in criticizing the behavioural foundations of economics, and in stressing the need for the discipline to avoid neglecting ethical-oriented behaviour. Boulding's taxonomy of social organizers evidently called into question the separation between economics and contiguous disciplines. Even Dennis Mueller's (1973) pioneering attempt to demonstrate (by making use of Rawls's *A Theory of Justice* of 1971) the relevance of empathy in public finance theory – despite the limitations Mueller himself imposed on the notion in explaining provision of public goods – was an important step in the construction of an alternative framework to Becker's "closed" model wherewith to analyse unselfish behaviour. The contribution written for Phelps's *Altruism, Morality, and Economic Theory* by Buchanan (1975), who had already expressed doubts, as seen, about the 'sufficiency' of purely economic motivations in the analysis of individual's utility functions, recognized the relevance of unselfish behaviour as a social-in-nature remedy to the "Samaritan's dilemma".

Yet, even the 'competing imperialism' of sociobiology, to say it with Hirshleifer, and despite the fundamental challenge this posed to a self-contained, or inward-looking mainstream economics (as Hirshleifer himself enthusiastically admitted), brought about a defence of the economic approach to altruism. Landes and Posner's 1978 article on altruism in law and economics, or Tullock's 1978 contribution on altruism and public goods were evidence that economists were disposed to concede ground to sociobiology on the issue of the foundations of unselfishness, but much less so when it came to the analysis of the factors motivating unselfish behaviour in contemporary societies (see Fontaine 2012). Then, "with economics imperialism gradually entering the mainstream . . . the need for economists to assert their expertise over social phenomena and seemingly unselfish behavior became less pressing than before" (ibid.: 205). But Becker's intention had never been to explore the motivations underlying unselfishness; his interests were both more practical and restricted (to concrete behaviour and policy implications). While Sen's (1977) famous article on the "rational fools" was inspired by the ambition to reaffirm the importance of non-market social organizers,[2] the economics of altruism that famously developed in the 1980s starting from Becker's contributions did not put into question such foundations. Somehow paradoxically, after building on Becker's contributions (extended beyond the family borders, to embrace society as a whole), *that* economics of altruism flourished by rejecting Becker's main results in terms of the necessity of unselfishness to counteract the undesired consequences of opportunism. Rather, perhaps also due to the modified political climate, altruism was shown to generate opportunism (Lindbeck and Weibull 1988). While Bernheim and Bagwell (1988) had argued against the relevance of Becker's extended interfamily relationships to analyse the effects of public policies, James Andreoni's (1988) studies on public goods provision attempted at demonstrating not only that altruistic transfers could not establish social policies neutrality, but they even caused inefficiencies which governments could counteract by appropriate tax reduction policies.

In general, Sen's attempt to formulate the possible contribution of economics to the general problem of social cohesion was made difficult by the perceived impossibility (on the part of mainstream economists dealing with altruism) to extend unselfishness to strangers – that is, outside the family or close-knit groups – as well as by the related tensions (in general, see Sen 1988) between economics and ethics. These two were also, unsurprisingly, the obstacles that prevented economists from considering the complexity of the gift since the 'Titmuss affair'.

The 1980s in particular saw an upsurge of studies employing the sociological-anthropological concept of gift to throw light on economic phenomena that require for their understanding consideration for undesirable consequences of individual actions (as already anticipated by Phelps 1975), but not necessarily broader notions of rationality than the (narrow) standard neoclassical one (see Batifoulier, Cordonnier and Zenou 1992). In a research context shaped first by the development of the information-theoretic approach (see Fine and Milonakis 2009) and, secondly, by Axelrod's 1984 now classic study *The Evolution of Cooperation*, such works addressed the problem of coordination in a variety of market contexts (see Cordonnier 1997), indirectly but explicitly trying to investigate how cooperation can emerge from self-interested individuals. Ukrainian economist Leibenstein's (1982, 1987) and the 2001 Nobel Prize winner George Akerlof's (1982) contributions in this regard focused on efficiency wages. In exploring the reasons underlying the lack of correspondence between conventional neoclassical theory of competition and reality, Leibenstein suggested there was the need to relax the assumption of utility maximization and consequently the introduction of the concept of "X-efficiency" to allow for non-allocative inefficiencies in organizations such as firms. A variety of factors, among which "local conventions" whereby workers freely offer effort, and care about this latter's quality, could explain differences in productivity and outcome of otherwise identical firms. Employees and employers solve their "prisoner's dilemma" problem by agreeing to a tacit convention which, though not leading to Pareto-optimal results, can be conceived as the result of an equilibrium of a coordination game (requiring effort discretion), which is to be strictly preferred to non-cooperative solutions. Leibenstein thus allowed a collective dimension (inducing individuals to adapt themselves to the cooperative solution of the "effort convention") and other – sociological, psychological, like confidence, equity, and so on – factors than wage to enter the efficiency wages framework. As Batifoulier, Cordonnier and Zenou (1992) note, the substitution itself of inducement for motivation amounts to recognition of the relevance of non-market legitimizing principles for coordination.

Akerlof's 1982 work on the microfoundations and implicit components of labour contracts directly draws on Mauss's *The Gift*: employment arrangements are described as having a "gift-exchange" (Akerlof 1982: 544) nature, emphasizing the importance of endogenously determined norms of behaviour. Explicitly situating his own analysis in line with Leibenstein's (1976), Akerlof – elaborating on Homans' (1954) study of a small group of "Cash Posters" in New England, who were reported to significantly exceed, as against neoclassical assumptions, the minimum work standard – offered an explanation of excess effort supply as gift: as persons

> share gifts as showing sentiment for each other, it is natural that persons have utility for making gifts to institutions for which they have sentiment. Furthermore, if workers have an interest in the welfare of their coworkers, they gain utility if the firm relaxes pressure on the workers who are hard pressed; in return for reducing such pressure, better workers are often willing to work harder.
>
> (Akerlof 1982: 550)

The gift-counter-gift dynamics just described is thus illustrated by the implicit exchange between working harder and the firm's offer of a fair wage: since labour contracts are in truth partial gift exchanges, wages are (partially) determined by, and at the same time (partially) determine norms of (effort) behaviour.

Six years later, Camerer (1988) published an article on gifts as "economic signals" and "social symbols", which could provide the theoretical explanation for Akerlof's labour contracts as gift exchanges. In effect, Akerlof has been criticized (by Insel 1991) for failing to outline the micro-sociological (individual) device that induces cash posters to submit themselves to the collective norm concerning the effort workers should offer. Camerer's starting point is different from Akerlof's (although he sees the case of cash posters as an application of his own theory): his ambition was to challenge anthropologists and sociologists on the inefficiency of gift-giving – "givers spend money on gifts differently from the way receivers would – and it seems to be necessarily so" (Camerer 1988: 199). Explanations provided by other social sciences, he observed, "seem either too primitive or too complicated to be useful, and neither [anthropology nor sociology] describes a function for inefficiency" (ibid.). The economic approach to gift-giving seems on the contrary able to clarify both the role of gifts and their inefficiency: individuals who expect to engage in long-term, business, or personal relationships normally run the risk of falling victim of non-cooperative results, since the desired kind of relationship necessarily requires partners to invest in it. Gifts can thus act as "signals of information": by engaging in inefficient practices of gift-giving, givers signal their intention to invest in a relationship, while at the same time providing (symbolic) information on the cooperative nature of their behaviour. Inefficient gifts are required to preserve their efficiency: to perform their function, gifts need to be inefficient; that is, they must involve high costs for givers (so as to discourage attempts to simulate cooperation) and offer little value to receivers (so as to avoid opportunism on the part of receivers themselves).

If seen from the perspective of the relationships between economics and other social disciplines, such studies provide evidence of a structural difference with respect to Becker's approach. This latter, relying on "extendable" utility functions, rejects in fact the need to distinguish between ethical and personal preferences, and at the same time the need of a theory of preference formation (see Fine and Milonakis 2009). Implicit in Camerer's criticism of anthropological and sociological theory as primitive or too complicated might appear a residual of Tullock's (1972) demarcation (later revived, as seen, but in a radical form, by Lazear 2000) between economics as the – imperial – "science of choice" and other social disciplines as "sciences of preferences". Yet the gulf between such new approaches and the neoclassical paradigm of utility maximization is explicitly recognized. And, as regards the relevance of ethics, Becker's solution (and Arrow's corollary about the importance not to substitute ethics for price mechanisms) to avoid the conflict between economic (rational) and non-economic (non-rational) behaviour – that is, to deny any distinction, by treating all behaviour as economic and rational – is ruled out from the beginning. On incorporating gift-giving into economic analysis, Akerlof and Camerer have however reaffirmed the instrumental nature of rationality as suggested and employed in the economic discipline. Though present, the collective dimension of the exchange is not addressed as such, nor is the system of rules of reciprocity on which such exchanges rest; while the non-utilitarian content of the gifts is victim of ubiquitous market metaphors. As Batifoulier, Cordonnier and Zenou observe, the (early) rediscovery of gift-giving in economics occurs through models of "sophisticated barter wherein circulating 'objects' represent a rupture with the ordinary conception of economic goods" (1992: 939, our translation). But this does not justify the use of a gift-counter-gift dynamics.

More, the strategic dimension in which such 'gift' exchanges would occur in contexts shaped by information asymmetries provide support to Fine and Milonakis's argument about the "new economics imperialism" which substituted for its old, Chicago-style version. While this latter "sought to push out the boundaries of the economic (approach) to incorporate the subject matter of the other social sciences", new economics imperialism "has recognized these boundaries by pushing out its own method both to transgress and, in a sense, to respect those boundaries" (Fine and Milonakis 2009: 74). The development, in particular, of the information-theoretic approach (with pioneering analyses by Akerlof himself, 1970, and Stiglitz (see 2000), and the concomitant incorporation of institutions, culture, norms – borrowing from other disciplines – allowed economics to accept the challenge of non-market behaviour, and to provide an explanation of this apparently non-rational behaviour in terms of market and information imperfections (see also Mirowski 2000). In Fine and Milonakis's words:

> The latest phase of economics imperialism is explicit about addressing the social, albeit only in the sense of moving outside the confines of the 'as if' market rather than as a rejection of a special type of methodological individualism. On the basis of market/informational imperfections, neoclassical economics has squared the circle of explaining the social, rather than taking it as exogenously given and hence the prerogative of the non-rational and other disciplines.
>
> (Fine and Milonakis 2009: 116)

While Akerlof's (1990; and others) insistence on the novelty of the approach, which explicitly rests on borrowing concepts from other disciplines with a view to investigating economic issues, evidently represents a break with respect to Becker's old imperialism, it is nevertheless true that there is substantial neglect of "close scrutiny of any literature concerned with the meaning of [the] categories of analysis, in ethical or other content" (Fine and Milonakis 2009: 120) used in these works. At best, the above-mentioned literature configures cases of "limited borrowing" on gift-giving from other disciplines (Batifoulier, Cordonnier and Zenou 1992), remindful of the selective appropriations of contents from psychology later characterizing the development of behavioural economics and its subfields (such as behavioural development economics) during an epoch of so-called "reverse imperialisms" (see Davis 2013a). In light of all this, the emerging general picture is one in which non-market behaviour cannot but ultimately appear as residual. The recent economic literature on gift-giving (see Van de Ven 2000, Reinstein 2014) could be better described, in effect, as a 'gift as residual' literature, trying to explain market imperfections or economic conundrums by calling gift-giving dynamics into support, while at the same time, though often implicitly, reaffirming the primacy of market relations. This latter ambition is evident in the work of Akerlof's co-author, Rachel Kranton, wherein the starting point is once again – as in Camerer's – the bizarre persistence, in modern societies, of "informal, personalized relationships . . . as modes of exchange despite the possibility of anonymous market alternatives" (Kranton 1996: 830). Differently from the 'reciprocity as insurance' literature initiated by Posner and Akerlof, Kranton suggests, as against the explanation of reciprocal gifts focusing on the difficulty to obtain goods and services through market channels, that market search costs increase with the proportion of people engaged in reciprocal exchange. For the market is thin, so that it becomes harder to locate trading partners, and this further diffuses personalized exchange despite its inefficiency. This way, gift-giving relationships are made dependent on the size of the market, as well as on agents' preferences – that is, on the value they place on future utility, which determines whether they are willing to provide goods in anticipation of reciprocal exchange.

Kranton's article represented an important attempt to identify the place of the gift in modern capitalist societies – that is, the issue around which the economic literature on altruism and reciprocity (in that joining the sociological literature on the gift in that same period) was debated in the 1990s. Andreoni's 1990 contribution on "warm glow giving" tried to answer this same question – Van de Ven 2000 categorizes both Kranton's and Andreoni's as studies of 'egoist' motivations for gift-giving – while looking at individuals' eventual taste for giving. While models of "pure" altruism presuppose that donors are exclusively interested that charities receive a certain amount of philanthropic donations, "impure altruists" are concerned with the sources of such funding (so that government donation cannot completely crowd out individuals' philanthropy): they aim at experiencing a "warm glow" from contributing to such causes. In a not-too-different perspective, Holländer (1990) focused on social approval as main motivation for giving, while Harbaugh (1998) directly spoke of "prestige".

In contrast to the theoretical character of studies like Kranton's and Andreoni's, however, the literature on reciprocity of the 1990s and 2000s openly participated in the applied/empirical turn in economics aptly detected by Backhouse and Cherrier (2014). The passing from the 'old' economics imperialism to an era of 'new economics imperialism', if we are to follow Fine and Milonakis (2009), or in any case of "reverse imperialisms" (Frey and Benz 2004) signals also a passing from theoretical and conceptual to concrete and experimental work: economics "became applied" (Backhouse and Cherrier 2014) after the 1970s. Before that date, there was widespread consensus on the primacy of economic theory over empirical work: extending the core model of maximizing behaviour to other social disciplines, old economics imperialism was an essential part of this story. Then, the shift from theoretical towards applied economics produced the 'empirical revolution' of the 1990s, and launched the process of continuous creation and institutionalization of new subfields which constitutes the salient trait of today's fragmentation (perhaps pluralism: see Davis 2006, 2008a) in (mainstream) economics (see Cedrini and Fontana 2015). The 'economics of reciprocity' is an important offspring of two of the most promising 'new' research programmes in mainstream economics: behavioural economics and evolutionary game theory.

7.4 The economics of reciprocity

In presenting the birth of a subfield, 'economics of reciprocity', to readers of the *Journal of Economic Perspectives* in 2000, Ernst Fehr and Simon Gächter denounced the limits of the purely self-interested individual of traditional neoclassical economics, and argued that, on the contrary, there is ample evidence that people reciprocate, in a positive or negative manner. While the economics of altruism had generally centred on forms of "unconditional kindness" (Fehr and Gächter 2000: 160), reciprocity is in response to others' concrete acts: "people repay gifts and take revenge even in interactions with complete strangers and even if it is costly for them and yields neither present nor future material rewards" (ibid.: 159). The economics of reciprocity uses in its support results from one-shot games, like the famous ultimatum bargaining game, where the proponent suggests a specific division of an amount of money received between her/himself and the respondent, who has the possibility to decline the offer – in which case neither players receive anything – or to accept it. Although conventional economic theory holds that the proponent should offer a minimum amount of money, which the respondent has an incentive to accept, experimental results show that responders tend to reject offers of less than 30 per cent of the available sum (see also Camerer and Thaler 1995). Likewise, in 'gift-exchange' games, wherein the amount that the proponent decides to offer to the respondent – who can then give a proportion back to the proponent) is multiplied by the experimenter – positive reciprocity prevails (see Gächter and Falk 2002). But as Fehr and Gächter remind us, experiments show that the propensity to punish opportunistic behaviour (negative reciprocity) is even stronger than the one to reward friendliness (see Charness and Rabin 2002).

The general idea is to subvert the conventional hypothesis that self-interested types win over reciprocal types whenever there is conflict between the two attitudes, and that in some quite general situations, such as the ones shaped by the presence of incomplete markets or when there are strong incentives to free-ride, individuals are willing to orient their behaviour to patterns of reciprocity, even to the detriment of their own material interest – so that they will punish opportunists even when punishment is costly. Fehr himself, with economists Herbert Gintis and Samuel Bowles, and anthropologist Robert Boyd, will later use the concept of "strong reciprocity" exactly to describe the predisposition to cooperate (conditional to the adoption of this same behaviour on the part of others) and punish (altruistically), "even when implausible to expect that these costs will be recovered at a later date" (Gintis et al. 2006: 8).

As in Kranton's theoretical model, size matters: the sizeable proportion of agents who base their behaviour on considerations of reciprocity may be decisive as regards, *in primis*, contributions to public goods, in contexts where negative reciprocal agents are given the possibility to observe other actors and directly sanction (punishment is costly for the punisher) free-riders, inducing these latter to act so as to avoid punishment (see Ostrom et al. 1992). Fehr and Gächter believe this bias toward reciprocal behaviour has important consequences for social stability. Reciprocal types' punishing behaviour can help to achieve cooperation, enhancing "the power to enhance collective actions and to enforce social norms" (Fehr and Gächter 2000: 160): social norms can be conceived as

> a sort of behavioural public good, in which everybody should make a positive contribution – that is, follow the social norm – and also where individuals must be willing to enforce the social norm with informal social sanctions, even at some immediate cost to themselves.
>
> (Ibid.: 166)

Social policy, write Gintis and colleagues, is more than, and probably something different from, "the goal of improving social welfare by devising material incentives that induce agents who care only for their own personal welfare to contribute to the public good" (2006: 4). Coming somehow close to Singer's philosophy, they rather observe that "effective policies are those that support socially valued outcomes not only by harnessing selfish motives to socially valued ends, but also by evoking, cultivating, and empowering public-spirited motives" (ibid.).

Moral Sentiments and Material Interests, the volume that perhaps more completely exposes this interdisciplinary assault on the *homo oeconomicus* paradigm and, at the same time, is a transdisciplinary attempt at establishing a new synthesis between human sciences, opens with the "Adam Smith problem" (on which see Part I of this volume). The endeavour to reduce to unity or integrate the "sympathy" of the *Theory of Moral Sentiments* and the material interests of *A Wealth of Nations* (on which see Kolm and Ythier 2006) is in fact (as the title itself makes evident) the main goal of a research path that identifies its "intellectual inheritance" (Gintis et al. 2006: 3) in the theoretical connections linking Smith, Hume, Malthus, Darwin, Durkheim, to Hamilton and Trivers.

The novelty of the approach is first of a methodological nature: a large interdisciplinary research team, composed of economists (Bowles, Camerer, Fehr, Gintis, and Abigail Barr), anthropologists (Joseph and Nathalie Henrich, Robert Boyd, Richard McElreath, Michael Alvard, Kim Hill, Michael Gurven, Frank Marlowe, John Patton, David Tracer), and other social scientists (Jean Ensminger, psychologist and anthropologist Francisco Gil-White) have tested the conventional "selfishness axiom" (Henrich et al. 2005: 796) – that is, "the assumption that individuals seek to maximize their own material gains in these interactions and expect others to do the same" (ibid.). The aim was to determine whether deviations heretofore found from the predictions of the selfish man model derive from "universal patterns of human behaviour" (ibid.: 795). To corroborate the hypothesis, the research team proposed to gather a different kind of experimental evidence from the one normally employed in the field – which usually consists of analyses of university students' behaviour in virtual laboratories – exhibiting low variety if compared to the diversity characterizing human social environments. Ultimatum, public good, and dictator games were thus performed recruiting subjects in fifteen small-scale societies (twelve countries, four continents were involved): three groups of foragers, six groups of slash-and-burn horticulturalists, four groups of nomadic herders, and two groups of small-scale agriculturalists. The tremendous impact of the research (see commentaries on ibid.: 815–55) owes to its main results:

> first, there is no society in which experimental behavior is fully consistent with the selfishness axiom; second, there is much more variation between groups than previously observed, although the range and patterns in the behavior indicate that there are certain constraints on the plasticity of human sociality; third, differences between societies in market integration and the local importance of cooperation explain a substantial portion of the behavioral variation between groups; fourth, individual-level economic and demographic variables do not consistently explain behavior within or across groups; and fifth, experimental play often reflects patterns of interaction found in everyday life.
>
> (Ibid.: 797–8)

Even more importantly, however, these findings would also show that the combination of economic theory with experimental techniques of behavioural sciences (a "unification of disciplinary methods") allows to "empirically test sophisticated models of human behavior in novel ways" (ibid.: 4). The resulting transdisciplinary-in-nature research, in other words, is also considered as the main driver for the desired reunification of behavioural sciences (see Gintis 2007, 2009), from which economics and human biology, in particular, are expected to gain the most. While the empirical, transdisciplinary turn can induce economics to consider not only the outcome, but also the process through which agents attain it (the model of strong reciprocity arguably favours this perspective), by emphasizing the other-regarding component of human behaviour, biology can now leave aside the "complacency" produced by "the simplicity and apparent explanatory power" of two most important theories, Hamilton's (1964) and William's (1966) "inclusive fitness" and Trivers's "reciprocal altruism", which Gintis and colleagues (2006) regard as the biological counterpart of economics' obsession with characterizing individuals as genuinely self-interested.

Remarkably, in discussing the "origins of strong reciprocity", Gintis and colleagues observe that "some behavioral scientists, including many sociologists and anthropologists, are quite comfortable with the notion that altruistic motivations are an important part of the human repertoire and explain their prevalence by cultural transmission" (2006: 22).

They recognize that their own recent experiments in small-scale societies (Henrich et al. 2005) provide support for the thesis whereby "a strong cultural element" (Gintis et al. 2006: 22) plays a fundamental role in forging altruistic cooperation and punishment, as well as in explaining (through the identification of social variables) variations of behaviour between such societies. Nevertheless, the model would rather favour gene-culture co-evolution over culture alone (which, it is argued, can explain positive but not negative reciprocity, this latter being stigmatized in most societies wherein charity, on the contrary, is extolled and culturally transmitted) in motivating kin altruism and reciprocal altruism, via "a significant genetic component" (ibid.). In this view, cultural change, in other words, makes specific genetic adaptations fitness-enhancing: cultural group selection and genetic group selection not only coexist but mutually reinforce; altruism is fitness-enhancing for the group practising it because it promotes cooperation, thereby strengthening "altruistic" groups as against (more) self-oriented groups: "Group level-characteristics that enhance group selection pressures – such as small group size, limited migration, or frequent intergroup conflicts – coevolved with cooperative behaviors" (ibid.: 23). Cooperation is thus seen to rest

> in part on the distinctive capacities of humans to construct institutional environments that limit within-group competition and reduce phenotypic variation within groups, thus heightening the relative importance of between-group competition and allowing individually-costly but ingroup-beneficial behaviors to coevolve within these supporting environments through a process of interdemic group selection.
>
> (Ibid.)

In this model, therefore, natural selection affects cultural evolution, while if this latter tends to promote prosocial norms, this owes to the presence of sufficient fractions of strong reciprocators in social groups. In general, the idea is that "under conditions plausibly characteristic of the early stages of human evolution" (ibid.: 10), that is in contexts characterized by the absence (as happens for "most of human history", ibid.: 30) of "schools, churches, books, laws or states" (ibid.), strong reciprocators manage to stabilize prosocial norms

> that could not be supported using principles of long-term self interest alone, because it is generally fitness-enhancing for an individual to punish only transgressions against the individual himself and then only if the time horizon is sufficiently lengthy to render a reputation for protecting one's interests.
>
> (Ibid.)

The most ambitious aim of Gintis and colleagues' research is to devise a "cogent political philosophy for the twenty-first century" (ibid.: 8), remedying the unnecessary biases at work in the writings of some great thinkers of the past. The strong reciprocity model is assumed to reveal fundamental insights into the structural deficits, in addressing modern social problems, of the "two preeminently anonymous modern institutions – the market and the state" (ibid.: 33), by throwing new light on social communities and the norms that govern interactions among individuals in harmonious social contexts, where tasks are essentially of a qualitative nature and do not lend themselves easily to be captured in contracts.

A note on the origins of human cooperation: Samuel Bowles and Herbert Gintis on primitive societies

In their *A Cooperative Species. Human Reciprocity and its Evolution*, Bowles and Gintis (2013) deal with the problem of the origin of human cooperation. Chapter 6 of their book offers a picture of the ancestral human condition, making inferences from recent available data from archaeology, ethnography, demography and genetics on the ages of the Late Pleistocene and the early Holocene. The key question addressed is whether strong reciprocity could be the legacy of an evolutionary past "in which individuals behaving in these ways had higher fitness than they would have had had they been entirely amoral and self-regarding" (Bowles and Gintis 2013: 93). In fact, Trivers's concept of reciprocal altruism is reputed to be unable to provide a sufficient explanation as regards life conditions of those eras:

> neither the likely size of groups, nor the degree of genetic relatedness within groups, nor the typical demography of the foraging bands is favorable to the view that Late Pleistocene human cooperation can be adequately explained by kin-based altruism or reciprocal altruism . . . Ancestral humans did not live in small closed groups in which family and self-interest with a long time horizon alone were the cement of society. Rather our ancestors were cosmopolitan, civic-minded, and warlike. They almost certainly benefited from far-flung coinsurance, trading, mating and other social networks, as well as coalitions and, if successful, warfare with other groups.
>
> (Ibid.: 94)

Data on genetic differentiation among foragers show that most humans had frequent contact with individuals beyond the immediate family:

> Inferences from . . . genetic data are . . . consistent with evidence of both long-distance exchange . . . and hostile conflict . . . among ancestral group, and among recent foragers thought to be plausible models of ancestral humans, significant levels of long-distance exchange and migration, occasional large scale seasonal agglomerations, and far-flung insurance partnership.
>
> (Ibid.: 101)

Ethnographic evidence confirms the presence of extensive contacts outside the group, of both beneficial and hostile kinds. Further evidence comes from cataclysmic demographic events, "frequent catastrophic mortality due to conflicts, environmental challenges" (ibid.: 97), "extraordinary climatic instability", "turbulent climatic conditions" that "probably" characterized the Late Pleistocene (ibid.).

An 'Hobbesian state of nature' condition is supposed to be typical of the Late Pleistocene, although Bowles and Gintis admit that "lethal intergroup conflict among hunter-gatherers during the Late Pleistocene and early Holocene remains a controversial . . . subject, with little agreement on either its extent or its consequences" (ibid.: 102). In spite of "few distinctive archeological traces", as well as ethnographic evidence, of a state of permanent war, Bowles and Gintis maintain that "conflict among hunter-gatherer groups was common and exceptionally lethal" (ibid.). This opinion is made stronger by the consideration, essentially based on Ember and Ember (1992), that

> the extraordinary volatility of climate . . . must have resulted in natural disaster and periodic resource scarcities, known strong predictors of group conflict . . . and undoubtedly forced long-distance migrations and occasioned frequent encounters between groups having no established political relations.
> (Bowles and Gintis 2013: 106)

These conditions – high level of mortality, population crashes, climatic instability, sudden social changes and warfare – were unfavourable, the authors write, to the evolution of reciprocal altruism. On the contrary, they maintain that:

> a particular form of altruism, often hostile towards outsiders and punishing towards insiders who violate norms, coevolved with a set of institutions – sharing food and making war are examples – that at once protected a group's altruistic members and made group-level cooperation the *sine qua non* of survival.
> (Ibid.: 110)

Was warfare truly necessary to the evolution of human altruism? Bowles and Gintis's answer is that "warfare, no doubt in conjunction with environmental challenges, played a critical role in the evolution of this particular cooperative species" (ibid.: 147).

Notes

1 Boulding was prone to recognize the importance of positive utility interdependence, although in a general conception of economics as moral science that necessarily rejects the neoclassical approach of personal or exogenous preferences, and has no consideration for culture as system; see Davis 2013b.

2 Reminiscent of both Gouldner's (1973) and Boulding's work, Robert Sugden (1982, 1984) later applied Sen's remarks concerning ethical behaviour to philanthropy, analysed through a game-theoretic approach.

8 A unified framework for behavioural sciences?

On Herbert Gintis's proposal

8.1 How to remedy the "scandalous" pluralism of social sciences

In 2007, in the same journal that had already hosted, in 2005, an exposition of the results of Henrich and colleagues' study of "economic man" in cross-cultural perspective, Herbert Gintis published a proposal for the unification of behavioural sciences. Later restated in the volume *The Bounds of Reason: Game Theory and the Unification of the Behavioral Sciences* (Gintis 2009), the proposal was more recently employed to suggest a theoretical bridge between the two disciplines of economics and sociology (Gintis and Helbing 2015). The aim of the general proposal is to integrate natural and social sciences by a "unifying bridge" (rather than "unified alternative", Gintis 2007: 46), "rendering coherent the areas of overlap of the various behavioral disciplines" (ibid.: 1). Gintis argues that "taken separately and at face value", behavioural disciplines "offer partial, conflicting, and incompatible models. From a scientific point of view, it is scandalous that this situation was tolerated throughout most of the twentieth century" (ibid.: 15). Today's "strong current of unification", resting on "both mathematical models and common methodological principles for gathering empirical data on human behavior and human nature" (ibid.), risks falling victim of disciplinary boundaries that, Gintis continues, are historically rather than logically determined.

Gintis wants to remedy the lack of effort to "repair this condition" (ibid.: 1) since the times of sociologist Talcott Parsons's (1937) attempt to provide a "formal modelling of modern societies" (Gintis and Helbing 2015: 2) through the AGIL model (Parsons's famous scheme of the four essential functions of a social system – adaptation, goal attainment, integration and latency). Parsons later proposed in 1951 with Edward Shils and Neil Smelser (Parson, Shils and Smelser 1965) and other scholars the road *Toward a General Theory of Action*. Gintis comments on the generally negative reception of this latter by pointing at the lack of both analytical decision theory and of "an appreciation for general equilibrium theory" à la Arrow-Debreu" (Gintis and Helbing 2015: 2). Moreover, Gintis stresses that Parsons's "forceful attack on utilitarian social thought" (Smelser and Swedberg 2005: 14) – wrongly, if Parsons had the ambition to construct a "general model of rational choice and social action" (Gintis and Helbing

2015: 2) – shared with Pareto the idea that preferences over economic values should be kept separate from those over socio-political and moral values.

More in general, however, Gintis recognizes another antecedent (which however offered no unifying principles) as most important for his own attempt to unify behavioural sciences, namely Edward O. Wilson's sociobiology. Remarkably, the three quotes opening the chapter of Gintis's *The Bounds of Reason* (2009) devoted to the topic of the unification of behavioural sciences are respectively from Edward Wilson, Gary Becker and Jack Hirshleifer.

The quote from Wilson – "each discipline of the social sciences rules comfortably within its own chosen domain . . . so long as it stays largely oblivious of the others" – introduces readers to the "semifeudal" (Gintis 2009: 247) conditions of behavioural disciplines. Game theorists themselves, Gintis writes, have often asserted the sufficiency of their own specialized branch of economics, the "feudal structure of the behavioural disciplines" (ibid.: 17) permitting them "to do social theory without regard for either the facts or the theoretical contributions of the other social sciences" (ibid.). On the contrary, game theory can become one of the two architects – the other one being the category of evolution, which covers ultimate causality, while game theory covers proximate causality – of the bridge required to integrate social and natural sciences. Provided it is conceived and used as "logical extension of evolutionary theory" (ibid.: 238), game theory – evolutionary game theory, avoiding the misrepresentation of human behaviour caused by classical game theory – can be raised to the status of "universal lexicon of life" (ibid.: 239), in a framework shaped by the evolutionary-biological perspective of gene-culture co-evolution (as developed by Cavalli-Sforza and Feldman 1982 and Boyd and Richerson 1985).

The quote from Becker reads "the combined assumptions of maximizing behaviour, market equilibrium, and stable preferences, used relentlessly and unflinchingly, form the heart of the economic approach" (Gintis 2009: 247). It is evidently functional to remind readers of the necessity of reforming the "canonical model" of individual choice behaviour, using recent laboratory and field behavioural research (see, respectively, Fehr and Gächter 2000, Henrich et al. 2005; in general, see Camerer 2001 and Gintis et al. 2005).

Gintis's unified framework rests on five "conceptual units". To gene-cultural co-evolution and evolutionary game theory, Gintis (2009) adds a "sociopsychological theory of norms", aiming at solving

> the contradictions between the sociological and economic models of social cooperation, retaining the analytical clarity of game theory and the rational actor model while incorporating the collective, normative, and cultural characteristics stressed in psychosocial models of norm compliance.
>
> (Ibid.: 233)

Then comes "the most important analytical construct in the behavioral sciences operating at the level of the individual" (ibid.: 222), that is, a rational actor model, called "beliefs, preferences and constraints" (BPC) model, based on choice consistency:

> General evolutionary principles suggest that individual decision-making can be modelled as optimizing a preference function subject to informational and material constraints. Natural selection ensures that content of preferences will reflect biological fitness, at least in the environments in which preferences evolved.
>
> (Gintis 2007: 2)

The BPC model would assist in avoiding the rigidity of biological theory and economics, that conceive cooperation as the result of "inclusive fitness" (Hamilton 1964) – cooperation among kin – or of individual self-interest, on the bases of Trivers's (1971) "reciprocal altruism". Likewise, the model runs counter to the preconceptions of "sociological, anthropological, and social psychological theory", which explain that "human cooperation is predicated upon affiliate behaviors among group members" (Gintis 2007: 14). Behavioural game theory – which Gintis and Helbing see as a "generalization of rational choice theory" allowing "to include moral, social and *other-regarding* values" (2015: 3; original emphasis) – assumes on the contrary that behaviour reveals underlying preferences, as implicit in Gintis's own (with others) studies on strong reciprocity as other-regarding. In response to his critics, Gintis clarified that the BPC model should not be intended as an explanation of choice behaviour, but rather as a "compact analytical representation of behavior", or an "analytical apparatus that exploits the properties of choice transitivity to discover a tractable mathematical representation of behavior" (ibid.: 48–9). Finally, complexity theory, that Gintis included in the list, oddly enough, only after criticisms to his target 2007 article on "Behavioral and Brain Sciences", notes that the characterization of societies as complex adaptive systems allows the use of powerful methods that are conversely of little use in non-complex systems.

Becker's epigraph may thus be said to serve multiple purposes. His "economic approach" is "the pure, if rough, road to economics imperialism" (Fine and Milonakis 2009: 32), celebrated in the motivation for the Nobel Prize winner as the successful extension of the "domain of economic theory to aspects of human behaviour which had previously been dealt with – if at all – by other social science disciplines".[1] Persuaded that economics should define itself by its own method rather than its subject matter, as seen, it was Becker's conviction that all behaviour can be thought of as rational and is therefore susceptible to economic analysis. The champion of the competing imperialism of sociobiology, Wilson, can thus modify the conventional perspective on Becker's imperialism (following, it must be admitted, Becker himself, who described – in his Nobel lecture – the essence of his own work as the attempt "to pry economists away from narrow assumptions about self-interest"), and safely credit him for having urged economists "to broaden their vista" to include "desires that are variously altruistic, loyal, spiteful, and masochistic. These too, he argued, are forces that govern rational choice" (Wilson 1998: 221). In general, writes Wilson:

> [Becker] cut more deeply than previous economists into the sources of human preferences. He recognized that most of economic reasoning is based on the implicit assumption that people are driven by basic biological needs for food, shelter, and recreation. But there are other incentives, he said, such as the type of housing and furniture, the restaurants, and forms of leisure they prefer, that lie outside the elemental imperatives. All these choices and more depend on variations in personal experience and social forces beyond individual control. If human behaviour is to be explained fully, the utility of the choices (that is, their value perceived by the consumer) must be entered into economics models.
>
> (Ibid.: 220)

Still, while positively aiming at both "parsimony" and "generality", Wilson finds economics (Becker's rational choice approach) guilty of having carried them too far, thereby forbidding any incursion into the biological and psychological foundations of human nature. Wilson (1998) believes that social sciences are still victim of an original sin, "ignorance of the natural sciences by design" (ibid.: 200), as "strategy fashioned by the founders, most notably Emile Durkheim, Karl Marx, Franz Boas, and Sigmund Freud, and their immediate followers" (ibid.). With the result that the continuing era of feudalism, to say it à la Gintis, in which behavioural disciplines operate, unwilling to abandon the "Standard Social Science Model" (whereby – in Wilson's interpretation – culture, orienting human behaviour in society, is regarded as independent of biology and psychology), still shows signs of "biophobia" (ibid.: 203).

As seen, Becker believed in the fruitfulness of combining the techniques of economics with those of sociobiology, but in Wilson's view, Becker's economics remains a missed opportunity. Interestingly, Wilson does not insist as he otherwise could on Hirshleifer's ambition to reform economics by adopting the "biological viewpoint" (Hirshleifer 1977; see Part I, sec. 2.3). This owes also to Hirshleifer's words in favour of moderating the assault on social Darwinism (which Wilson considers as the reason why social sciences – due in particular to Boas's followers, anthropologists Margaret Mead and Ruth Benedict – said "no" to biology).

Wilson writes:

> The goal of psychologically oriented analysts such as Becker, as well as Jack Hirshleifer, Thomas Schelling, Amartya Sen, George Stigler, and others of similar interests, is to strengthen microeconomics and draw from it more accurate predictions of macroeconomic behaviour. That, of course, is admirable.
>
> (Wilson 1998: 222)

But the strategy results in adopting "folk psychologies", that must be substituted for the true foundations of both individual and collective behaviour provided by biology and psychology. Now, the third epigraph of the "unity of science" chapter of Gintis's volume is a quote from Jack Hirshleifer (1985: 53): "While scientific work in anthropology, and sociology and political science will become increasingly indistinguishable from economics, economists will reciprocally have to become aware of how constraining has been their tunnel vision about the nature of man and social interaction."

Hirshleifer's (1977) prediction about "economics" being destined to become synonymous with "social science" is here evidently employed to strengthen the case of a common framework for the analysis of human behaviour, the "new synthesis" between natural and social sciences being jointly guided by the two formerly competing imperial sciences, economics and biology.

Becker's economics represents thus, at the same time, the unnecessarily restricted paradigm of the "economic man" to be replaced by a less pugilistic economic contribution to the unified framework, and the symbol of the analytical power of economics, one that can be greatly enhanced if only economics recognizes the need to discuss the non-economic origins of preferences. In this perspective, references to Hirshleifer's bioeconomics direct attention towards the problems of the inward-looking Chicago imperialism à la Becker, which was very strongly against, as Davis (forthcoming) argues, the idea that disciplines can have transformative effects on one another, and was muscularly in favour of a vision of the economic discipline as autonomous from contiguous sciences.

8.2 The socio(bio)logy of *homo socialis*

Under the impact of the recent transformation underwent by economics, whose mainstream is now populated by a variety of research programmes significantly deviating from the neoclassical core of the discipline, Gintis's framework clearly recognizes the limits of Chicago imperialism. It goes beyond Lazear's (2000) notion of economics imperialism (in times of threatening reverse imperialisms) as a trade in ideas – economics registering a "comparative advantage" (Lazear 2000: 103) that would result from its analytical rigour. The proposed framework seems in fact to accept, also on the bases of the interdisciplinary field researches Gintis himself actively promoted, that disciplines can have transformative effects, once the legitimacy of importing contents from other sciences is established. After all, the proposed framework adopts Hirshleifer's dictum on the impossibility "to carve off a distinct territory for economics, bordering upon but separated from other social disciplines. Economics interpenetrates them all, and is reciprocally penetrated by them" (1985: 53). Still, at the same time, and exactly as in the case of Hirshleifer's bioeconomics, the proposed common framework rests on well-identifiable pillars that do little to operationalize the possible overlaps between different disciplines. On one side, gene-cultural co-evolution is in fact presented as "the application of sociobiology" (Gintis 2009: 224), reviving (as noted by Getty 2007) Wilson's ambition to include the "last branches of biology", that is (recalcitrant) social disciplines, into the "Modern Synthesis" (Wilson 1975: 4). As some critics (see commentaries to Gintis 2007 as target article) have stressed, the proposal might truly aim at establishing the conditions for a "unified alternative" for all the behavioural disciplines, rather than the "unifying bridge" Gintis (2007: 46) declares to have in mind. On the other side, by pointing the finger at the incompatibility of behavioural disciplines' different models (see also Colander 2014), it is as if Gintis were conveying a crucial message about the revolutionary changes mainstream economics is undergoing under the impact of processes of radical specialization. This latter developed in reaction to the discipline's growth in size and diversity since the apogee of economics imperialism. But Gintis is also providing evidence that interdisciplinary research with specialists from biology, anthropology and sociology made economists achieve adequate awareness of the decreasing returns of economics imperialism itself (Hirshleifer 1985, Frey and Benz 2004, Fine and Milonakis 2009, Marchionatti 2012), a perception likely strengthened by today's reverse imperialisms (see Cedrini and Fontana 2015).

The unifying framework configures itself as a collage of many, if not all, today's mainstream research programmes: from behavioural economics to evolutionary game theory, from new institutional economics to complexity economics. Implicit in Gintis's proposal (see also Clarke 2007) seems the idea that economics will inaugurate a new, post-neoclassical era of 'dominance', replacing 'pluralism' only after the advent of a unified, 'transdisciplinary social science', able to reconcile the autonomous streams of today's 'mainstream pluralism' (all such expressions come from Davis 2006, 2008a, 2008b) with one another into a much larger general framework. The proposal would thus have the non-secondary aim of bringing economists working in the various programmes of mainstream economics to perceive unity in (and despite) this variety, somehow using other social sciences as sources of legitimacy for this belief. This is what emerges from a spin-off of the unified framework, that is, Gintis and physicist and sociologist Dirk Helbing's (2015) proposal of a new analytical core for sociology. As sociologist Michael Hechter argues, in presenting it, the two authors seem "principally interested in convincing economists to take at least some aspects of sociological theory seriously" (2015: 89). Moreover, that the proposal is published "in a behavioral economics journal is proof of the pudding". Cornell University sociologist Michael Macy is even more explicit: the authors, he writes, may be

> proposing an analytical core not for a discipline that needs one, but for a discipline that needs a new one. If so, then perhaps *homo socialis* is actually being offered as a Trojan horse to unsuspecting economists still wedded to the old one.
>
> (Macy 2015: 165)

The revised version of the rational actor model outlined in the new framework for behavioural disciplines rests, as said, on the last version, so to speak, of the sociobiological approach to human behaviour: gene-culture co-evolution. "Genes adapt to a fitness landscape of which cultural forms are a critical element, and the resulting genetic changes lay the basis for further cultural evolution" (Gintis 2007: 2) – which would explain why, contrary to what is assumed by the *homo oeconomicus* model, individuals preferences can be other-regarding.

Gintis (2010) is ready to admit, as he did on returning on Sahlins's (1976b) *The Use and Abuse of Biology*, that even Wilson's most recent attempt to reinforce the case of a (sociobiological) synthesis of natural and social sciences amounted, de facto, tot reducing culture to biology. But he defends the more modern version of sociobiology represented by gene-cultural co-evolution as a revised and correct form ("gene-cultural coevolution is an empirical fact, not a theory", Gintis and Helbing 2015: 14) of a general theory of social organization. One that can safely treat cultural transmission as niche construction, "the environmental change [being] that of the social structure within which individuals live out their lives" (ibid.: 13). Cultural transmission, in this perspective, occurs when "environmental conditions are positively but imperfectly correlated across generations" (ibid.: 14), so that valuable information about the environment cannot be transmitted genetically. To criticisms of the analogy between genes and units of culture, Gintis replies by noting that the two units are more similar – the former being more fluid and the latter more delimited and specific – than conventionally believed.

Culture is more aptly defined as fitness-enhancing "conformism":

> one might expect that the analytical apparatus for understanding cultural transmission, including the evolution, diffusion, and extinction of cultural forms, might come from sociology or anthropology, the disciplines that focus on cultural life; but such is not the case, Both fields treat culture in a static manner that belies its dynamic an evolutionary character. By recognizing the common nature of genes and culture as forms of information that are transmitted intergenerationally, biology offers an analytical basis for understanding cultural transmission.
>
> (Gintis 2007: 2)

Individual goals being socially programmable, culture is rather embedded into norms and values, that are in their turn incorporated into individual preferences functions through (the sociological notion of) socialization and (psychological) internalization (with internalized norms being treated as "ends in themselves – arguments in the preference function that the individual maximizes" (Gintis and Helbing 2015: 11). These latter mechanisms occupy the forefront of Helbing and Gintis's contribution on *homo socialis*, the suggested analytical core for sociology.

According to Helbert and Gintis (2015), sociology is one of the disciplines that lack a "core analytical model" (ibid.: 2): the legitimacy itself of its own existence as separate discipline, distinct from anthropology and social psychology is questioned, given that they share

> [the] same object of study – human society. There is no plausible justification for considering the focus of sociology on highly institutional societies and of anthropology on small-scale societies a good reason for maintaining contrasting and barely overlapping theoretical and empirical literatures. Moreover, the practice in social psychology of treating individual social behavior as

> capable of explanation independent of general social theory is not defensible. All these fields have suffered by separating themselves from sociobiology, which is the study of social life in general.
>
> (ibid.: 31)

In particular, Helbing and Gintis believe that to prevent sociologists from developing an analytical core "that is synergistic with economic theory" was the antagonism itself between economists and sociologists, which is also the reason why the former have substantially neglected the latters' contributions. The main novelties Helbing and Gintis propose for sociology come from economics. Schelling's (1960) notion of focal point equilibrium is understandably called upon to enrich the analysis of *homo ludens* (the term was introduced by Johan Huizinga, 1949 [1938]), able to construct new games and to satisfy both cognitive and moral requirements for game-playing. Among the most important pillars of the new model is rational decision theory. Helbing and Gintis (2015: 5) specify that maximization of utility is not to be conceived as either producing "utilitarian implications" or assuming "selfish, calculating, or amoral" agents, but, conversely, as "analytical convenience, akin to the least action principle in classical mechanics" (Helbing and Gintis 2015: 5). But critics of the proposal have rightly put an emphasis on a more contested pillar of the suggested new core for sociology, that is, the general equilibrium model (à la Arrow and Debreu).

This latter is seen as "capable of a surprisingly straightforward and plausible extension to a general social equilibrium model of considerable sophistication" (Helbing and Gintis 2015: 3). To construct such a model, it is necessary to enrich "the Walrasian general equilibrium model of economic theory" (ibid.: 7) with the characterization of actors as "rational decisions-makers who maximize their preference functions subject to the content of the social roles they occupy, and given a belief system that is context-dependent and governed by the expectations defined by the actor's social location" (ibid.). Thus,

> in general social equilibrium, each actor maximizes his preference function in the sense that no change of role will increase his expected payoff . . . and the pattern of supply and demand for social roles will be such that expected payoffs will not change over time.
>
> (Ibid.: 8)

Helbing and Gintis's proposal of general social equilibrium emphasizes (as against the received view in economics) the importance of moral commitments, which sociology has traditionally considered as the factors explaining the functioning of social rules, also for economic roles: by dropping the general-equilibrium-theory assumption of complete contracts, "moral commitments become as salient in economic life as they are in social life in general" (ibid.: 9).

Most scholars called upon to comment on Helbing and Gintis's suggestion of a Walrasian-in-nature model of general social equilibrium expressed doubts about the idea of combining a rational choice framework as general explanation with other-regarding preferences and, more in general, the search for motivations illustrating peculiar behaviours like altruism. More in general, it seems questionable that "research that challenges the presupposition that people generally act rationally would have been conducted in a unified behavioral science in which the BPC model was adopted", writes Clarke (2007: 22). Utility maximization as employed by Helbing and Gintis – the rational choice model expressing but not explaining preferences, as seen – is victim of the same criticism Coase (1978) made in observing that it tells us nothing about the aims pursued in economic activities. It is a non-falsifiable non-tautology, Hodgson writes, in that it is "conceivably false" – inconsistent behaviour, which would violate Helbing and Gintis's assumption of choice consistency, is evidently possible, but this cannot be established by employing empirical evidence. Hodgson refers to Posner's (1980: 53) description of rationality "as a matter of consequences" rather than "intentions", claiming that the differences between Helbing and Gintis's perspective and Posner's approach "may be on the degree to which preferences are to be taken as 'self-regarding', but not on their non-explanatory, non-motivational, and non-intentional characterization of rational choice theory" (Hodgson 2015: 96). By revamping general equilibrium theory, moreover, Helbing and Gintis appear to reinforce the case of the optimization-cum-general equilibrium nexus on which economics imperialism was based: the combination of rational choice with "the assumption that a state of society exists in which the choices of *all* individuals are mutually compatible" (Witt 2015: 196), with substantial neglect for key sociological concepts like power distribution, and even for the non-necessarily harmonious visions of the state of society advanced by, among others, Schumpeter and followers (ibid.).

Helbing and Gintis's gift to sociology, Geoffrey Hodgson believes, is thus a Trojan horse. If the rational choice framework implies separation between the economic and other spheres, in fact, it is inevitably at fault, just because Pareto (and other) never succeeded in establishing the conditions for such separateness, whereas Parsons came to accept Robbins's definition of economics as the science of choice, and was persuaded of a division of labour between sociology (investigating preferences) and economics (choice): had he studied general equilibrium theory and game theory, he "would still raise the problem of explaining preferences as the distinctive task of sociology" (Hodgson 2015: 108). More importantly, however, Gintis's work ends up with treating morality as "a matter of preference" to be expressed by the other-regarding preference function (ibid.: 100).[2] Following philosophers Mackie (1977) and Joyce (2006), Hodgson argues that:

> [Morality] surpasses questions of preference. It is a matter of right or wrong, or of duty, of 'doing the right thing', irrespective of whether we like it or not. This is part of what makes us human: we are capable of considering moral rules, and understanding that their observance is more than a matter of personal whim or satisfaction. This dimension is missing in much of economics. Moral values are either ignored or subsumed under matters of utility and preferences.
>
> (Hodgson 2015: 102–3)

In sum, by neglecting the specificity of morality, one would also miss its (social and biological) evolutionary character, as well as – being essentially a relational rather than individual phenomenon – the contribution it offers to human cooperation and social cohesion. Hodgson correctly maintains that, by inducing sociologists to "subsume all human motivation or behavior within the rational choice framework", the gift "threatens to undermine part of sociology's positive legacy, and it stops short of extending evolutionary theory to the explanation of moral and other motives" (ibid.: 109).

Notes

1 Thus reads the motivation given by the Sveriges Riksbank to grant Gary Becker the Prize in Economic Sciences in Memory of Alfred Nobel in 1992: see http://www.nobelprize.org/nobel_prizes/economic-sciences/laureates/1992/press.html.

2 Hodgson (2015: 101) accepts Darwin's view of morality as a "social phenomenon involving social relations and shared values". In general, see Hodgson 2013.

Part IV

The theoretical and practical relevance of Mauss's gift to the development of a non-imperialist economics

Part IV deals with the legacy of Marcel Mauss in social sciences, and attempts to throw light on the fertility of his analysis of the gift as vehicle of social bonds.

Chapter 9 analyses the most relevant contributions on the so-called paradox of the 'free gift', that is, on the ambiguities intrinsic to the modern perception of the gift in contemporary market societies, and more in general on the tension between 'gift' and 'reciprocity'. French philosopher Jacques Derrida's treatment of the gift as 'impossible', due to the inescapable contradiction between its being as far as removed from market exchange and the impossibility of escaping a "closing-the-circle", utilitarian logic of reciprocity is here employed as the starting point of the analysis. The chapter focuses in particular on the path covered by sociologist Alvin Gouldner in addressing the problems of reciprocity ("something for something") as the generalized social norm of modern societies, which led him to discover the importance of a "something for nothing" principle. The chapter closes with anthropologist Mary Douglas's proposal to reconsider Mauss's analysis of gift-giving in terms of social system, as a theoretical counterpart to Smith's invisible hand.

Chapter 10 is devoted to presenting the main theses of the group of intellectuals known as *Mouvement Anti-Utilitariste dans les Sciences Sociales*. Since the early 1980s, the group has been fostering an interpretation of the *Essai sur le don* as an alternative to the double reductionisms of methodological individualism of rational action theory, on one side, and the holism that typically affects sociological conceptions on the other. We thus expose, in the chapter, the main tenets of this interpretation, which identifies the gift as performer of social alliance. We then briefly elaborate, in Chapter 11, on a possible Maussian legacy for economics, while drawing from this perspective some suggestions for a general rethinking of economics as a 'moral' science (along lines popularized by John Maynard Keynes) in a milieu of social disciplines.

9 The gift in social sciences

9.1 Jacques Derrida's philosophy of the impossibility of the (modern) gift

> "When considering seemingly unselfish behavior, economists have perhaps underestimated the complexity of their endeavor."
>
> (Fontaine 2012: 196)

Fontaine's study on altruism economics demonstrated that in "elucidating the conditions under which altruism is possible with self-interested people", economists pointed at the expected benefits of unselfish behaviour, thus "making it just another form of self-interest" (ibid.). Fontaine is here making a parallel with French philosopher Jacques Derrida's (1992) famous words about the gift in modern societies, and the aporia that would necessary result from the attempt to define, and circumscribe, the concept of gift in opposition to the utilitarianism of the economic approach. The gift, in Derrida's terms, is "that which, in suspending economic calculation, opens the circle so as to defy reciprocity or symmetry, the common measure, and so as to turn aside the return in view of the no-return" (ibid.: 7). It is not, Derrida continues, "that it remains foreign to the circle, but it must *keep* a relation of foreigness to the circle, a relation without relation of familiar foreigness. It is perhaps in this sense that the gift is impossible" (ibid.). The gift *as gift* – that is, the gift as antidote to economic calculation – cannot in fact be followed by a counter-gift, not even in terms of expected symbolic reward in the form of gratitude or gratification, because this would amount to destroying the freedom wherein the act itself of giving takes life. But if restitution dissolves the gift, this implies that neither the donor nor the receiver should respectively conceive of and recognize the gift as gift. In short, the gift is not only impossible, but it is "*the* impossible", and rather "the very figure of the impossible" (ibid.; original emphasis).

In using Derrida's *Given Time I: Counterfeit Money* as the starting point of an analysis of the "incoherence" of the concept of gift, Mirowski (2001) brilliantly provides an access point to the difficulties economics faces in proclaiming its potential openness to interdisciplinarity. Waldfogel's (1993) extremely popular work (published in *The American Economic Review*) on "The Deadweight Loss of Christmas" is an exercise in pure neoclassical economics that limits itself to apply the neoclassical "dogma", says Mirowski (2001: 432), according to which a transfer of resources can be efficient (that is, economic; otherwise, it just configures a case of deadweight loss) only when and if corresponding to receiver's preferences: "By bequeathing people a stark yet seemingly paradoxical image of what they want, neoclassical economics can get what it wants, which is to subsume or displace all other academic social theory in the name of unified science" (ibid.: 433).

Yet neoclassical economics would thereby demonstrate also the futility of any criticism: "neoclassicism must also undermine every possible rival account of exchange by ruthlessly exposing its vulnerability to self-contradiction" (ibid.). The problem with such rivals would be that they are 'non-economic', whereas Waldfogel's not-simply-a-joke shows why neoclassicism "has become the icon of rational self-knowledge for academics and businessmen alike" (ibid.). Adopting Derrida's perspective, Mirowski observes that

> the concept of 'the gift' has been constitutive to any number of anti-neoclassical social theories in the twentieth century, but *all* the traditions that have relied upon it to explicate various forms of exchange have been ultimately vanquished *qua* social theory.
>
> (ibid.: 433).

The reason would be that the incoherence of the ("modern concept of the") gift makes it

> the weak link in the quest to define the 'non-economic'. From this we may extrapolate that all further attempts to capitalize on the gift will go the way of their predecessors, and worse, attempts to base social theory upon it actually serve to strengthen the neoclassical orthodoxy.
>
> (Ibid.: 433–4)

This amounts to recognizing, on one side, that – as Mirowski maintains with respect to Akerlof's use of Maussian gifts to describe the essence of the interaction between employers and employees – "an interdisciplinary neoclassical is an oxymoron" (ibid.: 451); but also that economic anthropologists since Mauss (Mauss included) have wrongly concentrated on the possibility of discovering an alternative theory of exchange, which left them, contrary to their intentions, vulnerable to neoclassical theory. Mirowski analyses Sahlins's own reservations about the exact meaning of "generosity" in his famous, cultural continuum from negative to positive reciprocity,[1] and Gregory's distinction between "exchange" and "gift economies" as the one between "objective quantitative relationships between the objects transacted" and "personal qualitative relationships between the subjects transacting" (1982: 41). He thus finds that economic anthropology ended up with predicating definitions of the gift "upon some . . . invariant", neglecting that "the gift corrodes and undermines all the posited invariants" (ibid.). Value invariance, Mirowski argues in opposition to neoclassical theory (which finds it in individual self-interested preferences), is rather socially constructed, with the double consequence, for the gift, that this latter is compelled to play an 'impossible' role in market societies, and that it cannot but acquire meaning if contrasted to payments system, with their own value invariance: "Gifts are an attempt to transcend the system of value; but that system transcendence already presupposes some form of monetary structure" (ibid.: 453).

Now, Derrida was clearly interested in disconnecting the concept of gift from Mauss's *The Gift* – "one can go so far as to say a work as monumental as Marcel Mauss's *The Gift* speaks of everything but the gift" (1992: 24) – since, as Osteen acutely observes, "his aim is rather to expose the limits of rationalism and empiricism, as well as to probe the limits of previous analysis of the gift" (2002: 15). Osteen finds two flaws in Derrida's reasoning. First, as Mirowski (2001) points out, Derrida equates intentionality and calculation, which do not necessarily present themselves as indissolubly connected. Second, even more importantly, he decides to subject to the "ideology of the 'perfect gift'" (Osteen 2002: 16) which is functional to his exposition of the aporias of rational thought, the duality disinterestedness/interestedness that Mauss recognizes, postulates and – in terms of ambiguous opposition between freedom and obligation – may be said to exalt (see Godbout 2004). Believing that the gift is but a camouflage, hiding behind subjective truths, the (undeclared) calculations made by both the giver and the receiver in (the objective truth of) the exchange, Bourdieu (1997) famously spoke of the gift as a concept that leaves aside the oppositions it nurtures. In antithesis to the French intellectual, Osteen reminds that humans are "quite capable of simultaneously entertaining conflicting ideas about their behavior" (2002: 16).

This introduces a further element of complexity into the discourse, one that may explain (on different bases than those upon which the reasoning rests) why Mirowski himself does not foresee "the death of the gift" and the concomitant need to herald "the triumph of the theorist of rational self-interest" (2001: 451). The solution to the various paradoxes of intentionality or of value invariance, he claims, must be of a social nature, and come from outside the "circle" (as happens, for instance in complexity theory, with "some results capable of being stated within the system [that] cannot be proven or even calculated within the system" (ibid.: 455).

9.2 Alvin Gouldner's sociology: the norm of reciprocity and the principle of 'something for nothing'

It was sociologist Alvin Gouldner (1920–80) who indicated how to solve the impasse of the "something for something", balanced-reciprocity (modern market) society. "The Norm of Reciprocity" (Gouldner 1996 [1960]) must be supplemented by one of beneficence, or of "Something for Nothing" (1973), "that requires men to do more than conform with the norm of reciprocity and, also, to do more that is required of them by the specific obligations of their concrete social statuses" (Gouldner 1973: 266).

The path Gouldner covered to reintroduce the gift into his analysis of reciprocity as social stabilizer provides useful insights into the sociological-anthropological discourse about the gift. Paradoxically as it may seem, it was Malinowski who launched what then developed as a sort of dichotomy in the literature between gift-giving and reciprocity (see Hann 2006, Aria 2008). Malinowski famously claimed, in *Argonauts of the Western Pacific*, that "the real native of flesh and bone differs from the shadowy Primitive Economic Man, on whose imaginary behaviour many of the scholastic deductions of abstract economics are based" (Malinowski (2002) [1922]: 61). Believing that "the study of extremely primitive economic institutions would no doubt prove very refreshing and fertilising to [economic] theory" (Malinowski 1921: 12), Malinowski made reciprocity the central notion of his *Crime and Custom in Savage Society* (1926), which he wrote after reading Mauss's *Essai sur le don*. As Parry observes, in recognizing the limits of the taxonomy of primitive transactions introduced in *Argonauts*, and in particular the concept of "free gift",[2] Malinowski de facto allowed the possibility "to see exchanges as essentially *dyadic* transactions between *self-interested individuals*, and as premissed on some kind of balance" (Parry 1986: 454). While in the *Argonauts*, he had described the "deep tendency to create social ties through exchange of gifts" (Malinowski 1922: 175), in *Crime and Custom* he spoke of the "inner symmetry of social transactions" (Malinowski 1926: 25), with reciprocity as "the basis of social structure" (ibid.: 46). In so doing, he abandoned the complexity inherent to Mauss's conception of the gift as inhabited by both interest and disinterest, freedom and obligation (Aria 2008; see Caillé 1998, Parry 1986, Panoff 1970).

In "The Norm of Reciprocity", Gouldner commented Malinowski's insistence on reciprocity as "mutually gratifying pattern of exchange" (1996 [1960]: 170), with some sort of long-run balance, "benefiting both sides equally" (Malinowski 1926: 40), emerging between the parts involved. Criticizing him (as well as Parsons) for failing to distinguish between complementarity of status rights and duties, on one side, and a norm of reciprocity, defining "certain actions and *obligations* as repayments for benefits received" (Gouldner 1996 [1960]: 170), Gouldner suggested a "generalized" form of the norm of reciprocity, a universal one whereby people should help those who have helped them ("we owe others certain things because of what they have previously done for us, because of the history of previous interaction we have had with them", ibid.: 170–71), and abstain from injuring them. This "engenders motives for returning benefits even when power differences might invite exploitation" (ibid.: 174). Between the giver's gratification and the receiver's repayment, "falls the shadow of indebtedness" (ibid.), Gouldner wrote:

> it is obviously inexpedient for creditors to break off relationships with those who have outstanding obligations to them. It may also be inexpedient for debtors to do so because their creditors may not allow them to run up a bill of social indebtedness. In addition, it is morally improper, under the norm of reciprocity, to break off relations or to launch hostilities against those to whom you are still indebted.
>
> (Ibid.: 175)

But then, it follows – in reason of the contribution reciprocity offers to social stability – that "we should also expect to find mechanisms which induce people to remain socially indebted to each other and which inhibit their complete repayment" (ibid.).

On revising, thirteen years later, his work on reciprocity, Gouldner will admit that for a number of structural reasons (variously related to the impossibility some may experience to reciprocate, to the uncertainty of future willingness and ability to repay, and the like), the norm cannot, in truth, produce the required moral requirements to ensure social stability: a "norm of beneficence" is thus needed, causing men to aid others even without consideration for the history of previous relations. It is this latter, not reciprocity itself, that can act as "'credit' mechanism for stopping vicious cycles of social interaction" (ibid.: 274), à la Mauss, Gouldner observes ("as Marcel Mauss noted, the beginnings of new social systems are often attended by the giving of gifts"). It is the norm of beneficence, that can "serve as a starting mechanism and launch a new and ongoing series of reciprocal exchange" (ibid.); it is "the ignition key that activates the starting engine (the norm of reciprocity) which, in turn, gets the motor – the ongoing cycle of mutual exchanges – to turn over" (ibid.: 275). Gouldner concludes that:

> to note that an exchange of reciprocities may be the *consequence* of a given action is, of course, no basis for interpreting that act as having been *motivated* by the norm of reciprocity. The 'earthy' consequences of mutual exchange may be activated by the 'heavenly' motive of an altruistic beneficence.
>
> (Ibid.)

Now, the very norm of reciprocity, "the norm that insists that men *must* give something in return for what they have received, is in some part a criticism of, a reply to, and an effort to control men's readiness to seek and to take, something for nothing" (ibid.: 267–8) – hence the obligatory character of the something for nothing, and the "beneficence of élites". But the interaction between reciprocity and beneficence is also, and above all, at the basis of what became known as "the paradox of the free gift":

> there is no surer way to stop a vicious cycle of social interaction than for one party to give the other something for nothing. There is no gift more certain to command attention than the gift that need not have been given because of our past indebtedness, our future ambitions, or our present sense of obligation. The paradox is this: there is no gift that brings a higher return than the free gift, the gift given with no string attached. For that which is truly given freely moves men deeply and makes them most indebted to their benefactors. In the end, it is beneficence that transcends this world and can make men weep the tears of reconciliation. If such prodigies of social interaction are rare, it is not for want of knowing how to produce them.
>
> (Ibid.: 277)

Gouldner's analysis has the merit of making the tension between reciprocity and gift-giving explicit, recognizing it as something that cannot be eliminated – unless one decides to concentrate on gift exchange as exchange of equivalents, on the symmetry of the exchange itself, thus running the risk of coming close to the reciprocity inherent to market exchange. Lévi-Strauss's structuralism – his introduction to Mauss's *Sociologie et anthropologie* (1987) [1950]) in particular – avoids this risk, by suggesting the symbolic origins of human social aggregates (as shown in Godelier 1996), nor can Sahlins's work be accused, as conversely Parry does, of openness to an "Indian" conception of the gift – one "for which an equivalent return is expected" (1986: 455). But it is a fact that "despite Sahlins's warning" – reciprocity is an ambiguous term, in primitive societies – "the principle of reciprocity has until recently dominated anthropological discourse about the gift" (Osteen 2002: 5). French philosopher Claude Lefort (1951) had already spoke in defence of Mauss's gift as central element in human relations, allowing the expression of both subjective and collective identity. But it was Sahlins himself, as seen, to separate the idea of reciprocity from a vision of exchange as involving equivalents only, and to rescue the gift itself – by connecting it to Hobbes's state of nature – by situating it at the very centre of primitive life, in its quality of being a vehicle of social alliance.

9.3 On Mauss again: anthropology in the 1980s and 1990s

The 1980s have been correctly described as the decade of "deconstruction" (Hart 2000: 1022) and, at the same time, of a "back to Mauss" cry, accompanied by the removal of the structuralist cover that had been spread over the *Essai sur le don* (see Aria 2008). This in its turn permitted an inquiry into the relevance of Mauss's philosophy for contemporary societies. Gregory's 1982 *Gifts and Commodities* (followed by Strathern 1988, Carrier 1991) signalled the beginning of a new era in economic anthropology, focusing on the concept of the gift's inalienability and its opposite, commodities' alienability, as criteria to distinguish between "two vastly different social systems and visions of identity" (Osteen 2002: 8). The gift came thus to be considered as a vehicle of social qualitative ties between persons, whereas commodities represent quantitative relationships between things. The resulting literature has been sometimes welcomed for the possibility it would offer to revisit the gift without the burden represented by the parallel with market reciprocity and rationality. Yet Gregory's dichotomy raised a variety of criticisms, all pinpointing the "Western" origins of the dichotomy itself. Appadurai (1986) suggested that things also can have a "social life", which may bring them, in some stages of their "biography", to acquire the status of commodities, for their value – which is mobile and culturally negotiated – depends on the desires it inspires. Others fostered, as in Parry and Bloch's (1989) case, the idea that both market exchange and the idea of a "pure" gift are in truth ideologies. As Wilk maintains, "gifts ultimately show that the dividing lines between rational choice, social goals, and morality are entirely our own creation" (1996: 155).

Subsequent refinements of Gregory's pioneering approach questioned the concept of reciprocity itself as universal norm. Weiner (1992) explored the possibility of locating the complex nature of the gift (that is, its interested and at the same time disinterested nature) upon the paradox of "keeping-while-giving", which brings attention towards objects one wants to protect from the "constant give and take" Malinowski referred to in *Argonauts*. Protected by a belt of alienable objects, inalienable possessions embody authority and power, which would then lie at the basis of exchange, as Godelier's (2002) research on sacred objects tend to confirm – that is, not reciprocity, therefore, but *in primis* the power of withholding such inalienable possessions from the circulation of things). The things one keeps with her/himself, rather than gifts and obviously commercial objects, are shown to preserve individual and collective identities over time, giving humans back both their laws, with (the myths of) their divine origins (factors that, in Godelier's view, Mauss had failed to consider).

It has been observed that the postmodern outlook of these works, and the potential of novelty represented by revisiting Mauss's *Essai* in the light of awareness of the Western origins of many of the categories heretofore employed to discuss the social relevance of the gift, have been somehow obfuscated by the difficulty of abandoning the presumed universality of the categories of inalienability and sacred (Aria 2008). Still, most relevant for our purposes, the gifts-commodities literature ended up with distorting Mauss's actual legacy (Hart 2007).[3] Once again, at stake is the polarization of the two notions, reciprocity and the gift, in the form of commercial self-interest and the 'free gift', which the gifts-commodities literature has somehow tended to reiterate under different vestiges. Although he cannot be said to be completely extraneous to the large variety of interpretations of his own *Essai*, Mauss "eliminates the two utilitarian ideologies" that had been advanced to illustrate the origins of human societies, obscuring "the non-contractual element in the contract", to say it with Durkheim (Hart 2007: 8) – namely, "'natural economy', Smith's idea that individual barter was aboriginal; and the notion that primitive communities were altruistic, giving way eventually to our own regrettably selfish, but more efficient individualism" (ibid.). As Hart puts it, on analysing the much-contested conclusions of the *Essai*,

> Mauss' chief ethical conclusion is that the attempt to create a free market for private contracts is utopian and just as unrealizable as its antithesis, a collective based solely on altruism. Humans institutions everywhere are founded on the unity of individual and society, freedom and obligation, self-interest and concern for others.
>
> (Ibid.: 9)

As Parry (1986) and then Laidlaw (2000) have argued, it was Mauss's ambition to avoid bringing his readers' attention to the concept of disinterested giving, which can be typical of certain religious doctrines or historical conditions, but not of primitive societies, where "the problem of altruism", as Hann (2006: 212) maintains, "simply cannot be posed". This stance is famously shared by social anthropologist Mary Douglas (1921–2007) in her foreword to the English translation of Mauss's *Essai*, where it is held that "the theory of the gift is a theory of human solidarity" (Douglas 2002 [1990]: 13). In his survey of the ethnographic and legal evidence, Douglas writes, Mauss shows that there are no free gifts:

> the whole idea of a free gift is based on a misunderstanding. There should not be any free gifts. What is wrong with the so-called free gift is the donor's intention to be exempt from return gifts coming from the recipient. Refusing requital puts the act of giving outside any mutual ties. Once given, the free gift entails no further claims from the recipient. The public is not deceived by free gift vouchers. For all the ongoing commitment the free-gift gesture has created, it might just as well never have happened. According to Marcel Mauss that is what is wrong with the free gift.
>
> (ibid.: ix–x)

Following Mauss, Douglas writes that "gift cycles engage persons in permanent commitments that articulate the dominant institutions" (ibid.: xiii). In the history of human civilization, the main transfer of goods "has been by cycles of obligatory returns of gifts" (ibid.: x). These gift cycles represent a mechanism "by which individual interests combine to make a social system, without engaging in market exchange". In this sense, the gift cycle echoes Adam Smith's invisible hand: "like the market it supplies each individual with personal incentives for collaborating in the pattern of exchanges" (ibid.).

However, the gift economy is more visible than the market. In fact, Douglas notes

> gifts are given in a context of public drama, with nothing secret about them. In being more directly cued to public esteem, the distribution of honour, and the sanctions of religion, the gift economy is more visible than the market.
>
> (Ibid.: xviii)

This has an important implication:

> Just by being visible, the resultant distribution of goods and services is more readily subject to public scrutiny and judgements of fairness than are the results of market exchange. In operating a gift system a people are more aware of what they are doing, as shown by the sacralization of their institutions of giving. Mauss's fertile idea was to present the gift cycle as a theoretical counterpart to the invisible hand.
>
> (Ibid.)

By adopting a fully Maussian perspective (but taking inspiration also from Lévi-Strauss's 1980 [1950] reading of the *Essai*), Douglas can conclude that the "gift exchange system is a 'visible hand'" (Douglas 2002 [1990]: xix). As Hann (2006) reminds us, Douglas's interpretation has been challenged both on the grounds of the universality (which some fieldworks would deny) of the Maussian categories employed, as well as on the idea itself that exchange and reciprocity can be taken as the bases of social life. The American anthropologist Stephen Gudeman (2001), in particular, believes that Mauss built upon his notions of reciprocity and gift-giving without noticing the pre-existing community employing (rather than being based upon them) them strategically, that is, to extend the community outside its borders.

Reciprocity, in Gudeman's vision, is the "badge" of society rather than its core, or a "part of a system of practices in which participants express, conserve, lose, and gain position in sphere of social value" (Gudeman 2001: 470). Gudeman thus comes to define the gift – "a foray across group boundaries" – as "a probe into uncertainty" (ibid.: 467): "if the gift is an unstable or uncertain category that is only because it is 'about' uncertainty itself" (ibid.: 473).

Notes

1 It is to be noted that Sahlins himself was explicit about his lack of interest in a theory of value.
2 As Douglas (2002 [1990]: x) remarks, Mauss's lesson is that "a free gift that does nothing to enhance solidarity is a contradiction."
3 Here is Gregory's self-defence: "My problem was to explain the paradox, brought about by colonization, of the efflorescence of gift exchange in a world dominated by commodity production and exchange" (1997: 47). But in so doing, he ended up denying the social aspect of any constitutive autonomy; see Wilk 1996.

10 Mauss's research programme revisited

The *Mouvement anti-utilitariste dans les sciences sociales (MAUSS)*

10.1 Utilitarianism and anti-utilitarianism

If one were to judge from the inherent variety of the constellation of recent approaches in social disciplines indebted, to a low or high degree, with Mauss's *Essai*, she should conclude, with Mirowski (2001), that social scientists are still trying – and will not cease trying – to make peace with Mauss himself. Or that the nephew of Durkheim had simply undervalued the difficulty of combining "a synthesis of anthropological research" with the ambition of producing a "history of culture and a work of moral philosophy" (Osteen 2002: 3) at the same time. But this would also amount to belittling, to say it with Douglas (2002 [1990]), the fundamental contribution (even with respect to Durkheim's insistence on "solidarity based on collective representations", Douglas (2002 [1990]: xii) Mauss continues to provide today, in times of ongoing "political debate" between "utilitarians" and critics of "the effects of unfettered individualism" (ibid.). It was Claude Lefort (1951), negatively reacting to Lévi-Strauss's structuralist reading of the *Essai sur le don*, who argued that by investigating the spirit of the gift, Mauss had addressed the social as totality and, at the same time, the problem of intersubjectivity. He was therefore not neglecting, but exalting that relational dimension of the gift (see also Douglas 2002 [1990]) which economists, as Prouteau (1999) argued, in general find difficult to reduce to instrumental rationality, which might explain, in part at least, the widespread adoption of the "altruism" perspective to illustrate its fundaments.

In this regard, it seems reasonable and fair to assert that if Mauss's research programme on the basis of social cohesion continues to exert an influence on contemporary social sciences, this owes mainly to the work of the "*Mouvement Anti-Utilitariste dans les Sciences Sociales*", better known with the acronym "MAUSS" and for its "Revue" (*La Revue du MAUSS*). In 1981, French sociologist Alain Caillé and Swiss sociologist Gérald Berthoud, who had met at a debate on gift-giving organized by the Centre Thomas-More at Arbresle, gathered together scholars from various disciplines interested in rescuing the anti-utilitarian perspective from the dominance of utilitarian thought. Devoting his activities to "a systematic attack on the philosophical underpinnings of economic theory", as anthropologist David Graeber (2000) notes, the group is generally recognized as the continuator of Mauss's "intellectual politics" (Hart 2007: 11). If "the *Essay on the Gift* was a part of an organized onslaught on contemporary political theory, a plank in the platform against utilitarianism", the MAUSS "fully recognizes" this intention, as Douglas (2002 [1990]: viii) writes.

The group initially concentrated on Chicago-style economics imperialism and its acceptance in mainstream sociology (as exemplified by James Coleman's and Raymond Boudon's work), but immediately enlarged its perspective by detecting in the broader philosophy of utilitarianism the theoretical bases of the (utilitarian) anthropology inspiring the "instrumental vision of man" (Caillé 2005: 1) that underlies economics imperialism. The "negative anti-utilitarianism" (Caillé 1998: 33, our translation) perspective employed by the *Revue du MAUSS* in its first years of life identified in the "dogmatique de l'égoïsme" (Halévy 1995 [1901]) not only, and simply, a theory of practical rationality, but a veritable political philosophy, of which economic theory represents the positive dimension. According to this dogmatics, actors are individuals interested in their own happiness, conceived as the only rational goal, and one to be pursued rationally, again, that is, by maximizing one's own utility, with altruism conceived as solution to the de facto unsolved problem of how to conciliate rational egoism with Bentham's utilitarian principle. The MAUSS group directed its criticism towards 'conditionalism' *tout court*, the vision whereby a principle of 'something for nothing' is simply unthinkable (with an imperative of generalized equivalence as practical consequence). Mauss's gift becomes, in this perspective, an indispensable potential factor of change for the renewal of both sociological theory and political economy.

The general proposal is to consider the gift as key to the construction of a "third paradigm" (Caillé 1998), opposing both the reductionism of the individualism of utilitarian conceptions and the reductionist anti-reductionism, so to speak, of holistic views (see also Adloff and Mau 2006):

> Modern times begin with the decision to split entirely and without hope of return what the ancient societies had tried to hold together – namely, the sacred and the profane, gods and men, the political and the economic, splendor and calculation, friendship and war, gift and interest.
>
> (Caillé 2001: 23)

Mauss's essay can be thus shown to provide an antidote to the modern conceptions of the gift as "pure", like those advanced by French philosophers Bourdieu (1997) and Derrida (1992), who end up by raising "to the standard and ethical norm of universal value exactly the Western and modern conception of the gift" (Caillé 2001: 30). Modernity separates egoism from altruism, with the result that it cannot reconcile them any longer with one another, unless altruism is conceived (*pace* Durkheim's thesis on the impossibility of deducting giving from egoistic calculations) as a derivation from egoism. And modernity refuses the gift with its "'background' of social obligation" (Godbout 1998: 161–2), from which modernity itself aims at freeing us. The "modern realist refuses to believe in the existence of the gift because the gift is seen as diametrically opposed to material, egoistic self-interest" (ibid.: 7). This would be because modernity has first compelled social bonds outside the sphere of production, during the transition from feudalism to capitalism, markets and their intermediaries between production and consumption, freeing circulating things from the obligation to vehicle emotional social bonds. Then, the whole utilitarian dimension of life acquired autonomy from emotional bonds. After a second 'liberation', operated by the state with the production of services, had stripped off their material content, emotional bonds found refuge in the pure realm of feelings: emancipation *of* social bonds was thus followed by emancipation *from* social bonds, which now exist only at a 'pure' state.

Hence the ideology of the free gift, and the appearance of the "gift between strangers" (the gift of blood, organ donation, and so on; see Godbout 1998), with its emphasis on freedom but not (or much less so) on obligation. Characterized by gratuity and spontaneity, the modern gift seems to nurture a shadow of indebtedness: the return of the gift is not guaranteed, and rather may even be absent, as in the case of gifts to strangers; usually, it coincides with the pleasure of giving (see also Hyde 1983). Or it is much greater than the gift itself, when this latter tends to produce a "positive reciprocal debt" between partners of the gift relationship, whereby debts are not liquidated (as in the case of market relationships) and, rather, donors do not expect restitution, continuously feeling indebted toward the partner.

10.2 The gift as a new paradigm for social sciences

The MAUSS rescues on the contrary the essence of the (non-modern) "circularity" of archaic gifts from which the "fertility", as Sahlins (engaged in the attempt to demonstrate the necessity – rather than "enigma" – of the "third person" in Maori informant Ranaipiri's account of the *hau*) called it, of gifts conceived as vehicles of social bonds derive (see Hyde 1983). For paradoxical as it may appear, the MAUSS makes the "visible hand" of gift exchanges appear when focusing explicitly on the latent tension – better, on the impossibility to separate the two elements – between the dimension of freedom and the burden of obligation implied by gift exchanges – themselves an irreducible mix of obligation and freedom, social norms and individual interests, as even a textual analysis of Mauss's *Essai* (revealing that the emphasis on freedom is gradually accentuated, and the one on obligation progressively reduced, in the course of the volume; see Godbout 2004) can show.

Confirming Sahlins's (1972: 170) motto: the gift is "no sacrifice of equality and never of liberty", the Movement concentrates on the complexity of a social environment characterized by uncertainty and want of freedom. It emphasizes the fundamental role played by "unconditional" gifts, that is, voluntarily offered, without guarantee of return; gifts that are in truth situated in chains of reciprocity, whose circularity (accompanied by spontaneity and indebtedness) is antithetical, in truth, to the closeness of the "give and take", of the prestation/counter-prestation dynamic (see Gasché 1997 [1972]). The use which Godbout and Caillé (2000) make of the metaphor of the spiral reminds readers of the "priority" to be accorded to giving (as sort of "strange attractor") over receiving and reciprocating. This owes to the "return" of an opening gift lying in a second gift made by the receiver her/himself, who – as Anspach 2002 suggests when considering gifts as embedding the positive reversal of the logic of revenge – does not limit her/himself to reciprocate, and rather gives in her/his turn (see also Godbout 2004), according to the "principle of alternance that characterizes most horizontal gifts" (Godbout 1998: 140). In the MAUSS interactionist (political) perspective, the gift serves to play a role in creating and sustaining social bonds and alliances between partners previously regarding each other as potential enemies.

Gifts are therefore to be defined as exchanges of goods and services "without the expectation of a determined return and in view of strengthening the social nexus" (Caillé 2001: 37), of creating, maintaining and nourishing social bonds (see also Godbout and Caillé 1998), by preserving – rather than suppressing – debts. If "the question of the gift is also a question of value" (Osteen 2002: 23), therefore, this latter is a "bonding-value" (Godbout and Caillé 1998: 188), that in modern societies is expressed by the element of uncertainty and indeterminacy (as well as of play) arising out of the "rule of the implicit" (ibid.: 186), of the fact itself of playing with rules as constitutive of the gift. Outside both the paradigm of individualism – accepting the market as a device to liquidate, immediately and permanently, debts – and of holism – whereby action is fully constrained by adhesion to social rules – the gift gives its name to a "third", interactionist paradigm, positing an atmosphere of uncertainty (in the form of the complex play of freedom and obligation which characterizes the gift as vehicle of alliance) as absolutely indispensable, if it is to produce trust. Gifts cannot tolerate being reduced to the one and only of the multiple dimensions that permeate social interactions; or, when approaching only one of the poles (interest and disinterest, freedom and obligation, and so on), they end up with denying their own essence, to transform into pure love and altruism, economic exchange, sacrifice, and so on. All this evidently reinforces the symbolic dimension of the gift, which is also the one of society (see Tarot 1996): a symbolic dimension which exceeds the utilitarian one, and promotes continuity between individuals and the society they live in. It is in this sense that Caillé can describe the obligation of the gift as a choice of freedom: "the obligation to give is a paradoxical obligation to be free and to oblige others to be free too" (2005: 6). Social bonds are built "through an interactionist logic of alliance and association which is the very logic of the political. Maussian gift is a political gift" (ibid.: 7): "gift" is the performer, Caillé (1998) writes, of the (micro-sociological level of) alliance between persons, "association" is the performer (at the meso-sociological level) of relationships between persons and groups, and between groups themselves, while "politics" is the performer, at the macro-sociological level, of the relationships between persons and groups with the "symbolic" totality of the society they belong to and shape: "Each one of these three terms – gift, association, and politics – is a metaphor, a symbol, and a tool for interpreting the others" (ibid., 236; translation by O. Romano, in Romano 2015).

11 A new Maussian perspective in economics[1]

11.1 On complexity and economics

If altruism appears as a more tractable and less troublesome concept for economics, this is likely because its assumptions about human nature are simply too strong to resist the reductionism of interdependent utility functions, wherewith altruism is reconciled with the standard egoism of neoclassical economics. Conversely, if economics has voluntarily left aside the gift, it is because the revolutionary essence of Mauss's work lies in

> posing as morally desirable just what the whole of known societies seems to consider exactly as such: an invariant core which is common to all ethics. What men must do is no longer intrinsically different from what they in fact do.
>
> (Caillé 1998: 30; our translation)

Both the power of the gift, which helps to explain the enormous interest it has excited in the other social disciplines, and its weakness, which causes it to be an easy victim of the reductionism of economics, owe to the same fundamental factor: the gift does not make any unnecessarily demanding assumption about human nature.

To grasp this point, however, economics should denounce the limits of what economists perceive as a key advantage of the discipline, justifying its imperialism: the ability to "strip off" social complexity, intended as an obstacle to "seeing what is essential" (Lazear 2000: 100). Two main strands have been quarrelling in economics as concerning the adequate methodology for treating complex objects. First, the orthodox tradition established by John Stuart Mill and Carl Menger, resulting in the adoption of methodological individualism; second, the approach developed in modern economics by a series of pioneers in social sciences, from Marx to Pareto, to Alfred Marshall and John Maynard Keynes, who expressly addressed the problem of how to deal with social complexity, to institutional economists. In *System of Logic*, Mill (1843) assigns due importance to social relations, and even argues that complexity is a key issue in social sciences, but ultimately uses the term to denote a context characterized by a large number of interacting variables and multiplicity of behavioural motivations (general economic equilibrium). He in fact believed that the laws of complex social wholes can be deducted from those ruling individual behaviour. Mill's proposal of a concrete-deductive method of analysis instead of the inductive methods of hard sciences, which would clash against the lack of adequate tools available to economists and the impossibility to conduct controlled experiments, was meant to overcome the limitations affecting human computational powers. Walras's and Robbins's conceptions of economics draw on Mill's famous expedient, the *homo oeconomicus*, and on his argument in favour of deduction.

On the contrary, outside the neoclassical field, Marxian and "old" institutionalist economists saw the economy as complex. But also in the mainstream of those times, Marshall and Keynes took a radically different stance from the orthodox approach, although only recently has the great potential of their legacy (see Marchionatti 2002, 2004) been fully acknowledged, especially in relation to modern complexity science (Foster 2006, Marchionatti 2010). Marshall's perspective suggests that today's mainstream approach is necessarily unable to grasp the complexity of the real world, essentially because it traces precise borders exactly where borders are uncertain, concepts are ill-defined and cannot be captured in one-dimensional definitions. In Marshall's *Principles*, economics is a science of human and social complexity: "Abstract reasoning", he wrote, is essential, but inadequate "to disentangle the interwoven effects of complex causes" (reported in Whitaker 1996, II: 393), and must be supplemented by "trained common sense". Rooted in Marshall's methodological stance was Keynes's conception of economics as a non-positivist "moral" science, dealing with introspection and ethical values. Pioneering works in the 1980s and contributions that followed (see Carabelli and Cedrini 2014) have brought attention to the continuity between the early epistemological concern of Keynes's work on probability (*A Treatise on Probability*, 1973b [1921]) and his reflections on the method, theory and practice of economics in the *General Theory* (1973a [1936]). Economics is to Keynes (1983: 856) a "technique of thinking" required to cope with a complex economic material made of "motives, expectations, psychological uncertainties" (1973c: 300) and, in general, with a social world which is not simply explicable in terms of the individual behaviour of its presumedly separable parts. The "atomic hypothesis" – underlying much of neoclassical economics as well as the "blind" manipulation of unqualified, "pseudo-mathematical methods" (1973a: 297)

> breaks down in psychics. We are faced at every turn with the problems of organic unity, of discreteness, of discontinuity – the whole is not equal to the sum of the parts, comparisons of quantity fail us, small changes produce large effects, the assumptions of a uniform and homogeneous continuum are not satisfied.
>
> (Keynes 1972 [1933]: 262)

Keynes's reflections, along Marshallian lines, on economic reasoning, and the conditions to capture the complexity of economic process beyond the limits of simplistic theorizing, offer theoretical support for the construction of a transdisciplinary perspective on human behaviour, and insights that modern complexity economics can legitimately and profitably put to use in attempting to achieve significant developments in this regard. These authors were in fact concerned with the problem of building a theoretical framework able to resist the comfort of methodological individualism. It is this peculiar perspective, coupled with heterodox economists' concerns for the complex nature of the socio-historical world, that allows revisiting and reformulating the issue of interdisciplinarity.

11.2 Back to the future with Mauss

11.2.1 The gift as the basis of a new economic discourse

Adam Smith's *Wealth of Nations* is the beginning of two stories, rather than one only: that of economics, but also that of economics imperialism. By actively encouraging the "bartering savage" paradigm, Smith ended up with expelling himself from a pioneering research programme (launched by ethnographic sources which were available to him) on the historical origins of modern societies. Shedding light on the historicity of market exchange, on the contrary, Marcel Mauss helps us recognize the political aim of Smith's theoretical construction: the a-historical path towards emancipation from the serfdom of necessity ends with reaching exactly the societal context that allows man to fully express his "bartering" essence, that is, a market society. He himself a promoter of a (radically different) political project, Mauss re-introduces historicity exactly where Smith had removed it, with the result of dissolving the notion of history in that of nature, from the analysis of primitive societies. As if he were discussing Smith's stage theory, Mauss notes:

> Societies have progressed in so far as they themselves, their subgroups, and lastly the individuals in them, have succeeded in stabilizing relationships, giving, receiving, and finally, giving in return. To trade, the first condition was to be able to lay aside the spear . . . Only then did people learn how to create mutual interests, giving mutual satisfaction, and, in the end, to defend them without having to resort to arms. *Thus the clan, the tribe, and peoples have learnt how to oppose and to give to one another without sacrificing themselves to one another.*
>
> (1990: 82; emphasis added)

Here lies the primitives' lesson for our times: "This is what tomorrow, in our so-called civilized world, classes and nations and individuals also, must learn. This is one of the enduring secrets of their wisdom and solidarity" (Mauss 1990 [1923–24]: 82–3).

Mauss intercepts the *homo oeconomicus* not at the beginning but at the (provisional) end of history. In the beginning, he finds human beings engaged in the attempt to escape the state of nature. He finds not a natural propensity to truck, barter and exchange elaborated on the model of modern, free-market societies ("*Homo oeconomicus* is not behind us, but lies ahead . . . For a very long time man was something different; and he has not been a machine for very long, made complicated by a calculating machine", Mauss 1990: 76), but a social contract. Primitives apply a sort of "substantial" rationality, which includes rationality à la Robbins but transfers it into a context of perceived abundance with socially limited material needs, with a view to preserving the ecological equilibrium. In this context, gift exchange protects both tribes' independence in a Hobbesian world, and a tradition of socially preferred equality (hence the prohibition of hoarding and the marginalization of market exchange) threatened by the traditional pattern of resolution of such conflict, that is, the state. What Mauss finds, in the end, is the *visible hand* of gift exchange, that is, the socio-political foundation of societies, on which their economic dimension (and its rationality) depends. The dark side of economic exchange, gift exchange is truly a missed opportunity for economics. Owing to the (ab)use Smith made of the conjectural method in studying the evolution towards free market societies, economics lost sight of the non-contractual element of the social contract, and erroneously came to perceive self-regulation as a natural quality of market exchange. The attention Mauss focused on the complexity of both social practices and human motivations, as well as on the political-symbolical representation of society, might conversely be a chance for a discipline currently aspiring to become a non-imperialistic partner of sciences investigating social complexity.

11.2.2 An illustration of the fertility of the concept of gift: The political essence of Keynes' plans of global reform

It is well known that the current troubled times of crisis brought unprecedented attention to John Maynard Keynes's global reform plans of the 1940s. Much less known is that Keynes's international economics and diplomacy can throw light on the still-to-be-explored potential of the political anthropology of the gift in today's economic discourse. At the end of both World Wars, in fact, Keynes suggested the need to resort to a gift dynamic to favour international adjustment to a more balanced economic world. It is in particular his somewhat heretical 1945 proposal of an American gift (which then became, to Keynes's disappointment, a loan of "business as usual" character) to a highly indebted Britain that strikes the imagination. The literature has mainly regarded this surprising episode of Keynes's diplomacy as a desperate attempt to save Britain from financial decline, even more so in the transition to a new international system, which would have relegated Britain to the status of second-order power (see, for example, Skidelsky 2000). But the suggestion to reconsider and redistribute the costs of war, in 1945, in such a way as to strongly limit the evils their burden could produce for the transition to the new order, is not a *unicum* in Keynes's work of international diplomacy. Rather, the proposal provides direct continuity with the recommendations he had made at the end of the First World War to cancel inter-Allied debts as a preliminary and indispensable requirement for a more viable solution to the problem of German reparations. The literature has mainly focused on Keynes's presumed political *naïveté* and identified an abuse of moral arguments in his First World War diplomacy. A methodological reading of *The Economic Consequences of the Peace* as an essay in the complexity of international economic relations (see Carabelli and Cedrini 2010a), to the contrary, provides reasons to believe that the concept of gift plays a fundamental role in Keynes's vision.

Keynes considered the impasse of German reparations as a situation of general conflict within a Continental economy characterized by organic interdependence, a fallacy of composition between particular and general interests, reflected and fostered by the uncertain economic prospects of European countries. The conflict was nurtured by inter-Allied debts: it was mainly because of their burden that European policymakers could not recede from asking for impossible reparations to Germany, thereby inviting their own destruction as well. The Cambridge economist believed that the only possibility to overcome the Continent's debt impasse lay in a starting gift in the form of generous inter-Allied debt cancellation on the part of the two only creditor countries (the United States and Britain). This would have induced European countries, in their turn, to moderate their requests upon Germany to the advantage of the whole Continent and its future trade partners. The gift, in Keynes's vision, was the triggering mechanism of a spiral of "generosity" progressively enlarging the spectrum of countries disposed to take part in the adjustment to a more equilibrated world.

Twenty-six years later, at the end of the Second World War, Keynes recovered this line of reasoning when suggesting that only creditors' generosity could provide a chance of restoring a multilateral world of free trade after the economic disasters and international animosity of both the war and the interwar period. In discussing the proposal of an American gift to an exhausted Britain (overburdened with the costs of the Allies' war, and highly indebted vis-à-vis the sterling area and the US) in a correspondence with the Treasury Official in Washington Robert H. Brand in the spring of 1945, Keynes referred to the "psychological atmosphere of the free gift" (Keynes 1979: 340). He described this latter as the decisive factor to induce sterling countries, which were the main creditors of Britain and the only nations who could revive multilateral trade in the post-war period by stimulating American exports, to participate in the adjustment to the Bretton Woods world (see Carabelli and Cedrini 2010b).

Keynes had an "extraordinarily clear understanding of how *pieces of global economy* interact, driven by the policies of autonomous nations, in an only partly coherent manner" (Vines 2003: 339). He had acute awareness of the problem of freedom in a complex international society, to say it à la Polanyi, wherein economic interdependence seems to require a strong degree of discipline and a general tendency towards uniformity of policy. Keynes avoided assimilating nations to the utility-maximizers actors of rational choice theory (ibid.), and rather saw them as social actors who can and should cooperate internationally in the name of mutual respect for each other's freedom, if the opportunities of global interdependence must exceed its threats. Now, Mallard (2011) has recently stressed the affinity between Keynes's and Mauss's reasoning about German reparations and the European economic conflict at the end of the First World War – it is to be noted that Mauss was then drafting *The Gift*. This comparison offers therefore a fundamental starting point for a highly promising research on Keynes's attempt to promote a desired social dimension in international relations.

An interdisciplinary study of the non-purely economic aspects of Keynes's desired new world order shows in fact that the "American gift" proposal rests on the complex play of freedom and obligation which characterizes Maussian gift dynamics. This tension allows gifts to perform a role in creating socio-political alliances intended to defend individual autonomy, as stressed by the research tradition stemming from Mauss's work. Moreover, Keynes's gift proposal helps to grasp the revolutionary principles that inspire his lifelong effort to endow the world with public-spirited institutions promoting "shared responsibilities" approaches to global equilibrium. The culminating stage of this work, the International Clearing Union scheme designed for the Bretton Woods world, sheds light on the overall political essence of Keynes's desired reform. Designed to avoid the insurgence of excessive debt and credit positions, Keynes's rules for symmetric adjustment limited creditor countries' license to adopt rentier-like attitudes, but granted them the possibility to reap the fruits of the proposed recycling of surpluses. Yet this criterion of economic efficiency was indissolubly associated with a full political vision centred on the need to defend debtors' policy space from the presumed inevitability of austerity solutions, and more generally their right to heterogeneity and diversity in devising road-maps toward growth and development (see Kirshner 2009). Expressly building on the peculiar social dimension of the gift as against the purely instrumental rationality of a market loan, the American gift proposal is a telltale sign of this general, political vision of the international economic order (see Carabelli and Cedrini 2010b).

The Maussian character of Keynes's new order – wherein, as Sahlins (1972: 162) observed in relation to gift exchange in archaic societies, "the freedom to gain at others' expense is not envisioned by the relations and form of exchange" – may be profitably put to use in trying to devise the political foundations of a possible alternative to the current international disorder. The emphasis Keynes posed on policy space and his vision of the global order as a happy mix of international discipline and national freedom may in fact offer the foundations for constructing the "new Bretton Woods compromise" which Rodrik (2011), among others, posits as the only viable solution for today's world. And the interdisciplinary character of Keynes's approach to the complexity of international economic relations, coupled with the use he made of ethical arguments when defending the right to policy heterogeneity, supplies a powerful alternative of thought to the currently prevailing moralistic vision of intra-European imbalances.

Note

1 This chapter is based on Cedrini and Marchionatti 2016.

Conclusions

The myth of economics imperialism and the possibility of a non-imperialist economics

Simplicity is a requirement of science, writes Dani Rodrik on defending economists from criticisms of reductionism: "Every explanation, hypothesis, causal account is necessarily an idealization; it leaves many things out so that it can focus on the essence" (2015: 179). Fair enough; and it is equally true that "simple need not mean simplistic" (ibid.). Among the various research programmes of today's 'mainstream pluralism' is evidently one – Bowles 1998, Akerlof and Kranton 2010 are the first two references of the "sampling of this work" cited by Rodrik (2015: 229) that tries to remedy the traditional, substantial neglect of "the social and cultural roots of people's preferences and constraints" (ibid.: 181). "There is no reason", the Harvard economist continues, "the [most basic benchmark] models cannot be extended to incorporate these influences and to work out their implications" (ibid.). Economists' models are "well-equipped" to analyse constraints faced by agents who actively take decisions concerning actions to take: "From the perspective of good social analysis, the contrast between individual- and societal-level analyses sets up a largely false and unhelpful dichotomy" (ibid.: 182).

Rodrik is one of the smartest economists of our times, and a most required (though less influential than deserved) voice in the 'waste land' of mainstream economists who are versed in, and willing to discuss, lines of reasoning and methods of other social disciplines. This explains the considerable weight we are here assigning to his recent inquiry into what exactly economic models are and should do: the argument, as seen, rests on a correct appreciation of the variety that currently characterizes economics, and it is recognized that economists are unduly hiding this diversity of models. While acknowledging economists' narrow-mindedness and scarce concern for the social dimension of economic processes, Rodrik (2015: x) rejects "standard criticisms of economics" coming from outside the discipline. He rather points at "the kind of attention to analytic argumentation and evidence that is the bread and butter of economists" as something other social sciences should emulate to "improve" their own practices (ibid.: ix), provided "humility" helps economists to become "better citizens in the broader academic community of social science" (ibid.: 209).

Still, understandably, Rodrik's defence of economics omits the problem of the discipline's imperialism, since the argument is inward looking. The problem is that this conception of democratic exchange (a trade in ideas) between economics and other social sciences is contradicted by the historical evolution of the dismal science since Robbins's systematization. It was exactly Robbins's characterization of economics as the science of rational choice to grant economics the possibility of an ever-growing scope. It is therefore generally held that economics imperialism ultimately rests (at least this is what the narrative exposed by its practitioners suggests) on a form of "economic hubris" (Mäki 2009: 25), on a presumption of 'superiority' (see Fourcade et al. 2015) which is the opposite of the 'humility' called for by Rodrik in his recent volume *Economics Rules*. Yet, to restate the argument, one could legitimately object to the reassuring idea of a 'division of labour' between disciplines with economics as an exception to a general rule of peaceful trade in contents and methods. Would an unpretentious economics truly confirm the rule and participate in a grandiose scheme for the reorganization of behavioural disciplines in the name of compatibility (of approaches), along the lines Gintis (2007) has recently suggested?

This book has tried to establish that the imperialistic character of the economic science is not an innovation brought about by neoclassical economics, but a salient feature of classical economics since the birth of the discipline with Adam Smith. Economics imperialism has deep roots. Evidence of this comes from a key issue in the foundations of economics, that is the study of ancient, pre-market societies, and in particular of primitive economic life. Classical economics is built on a hypothesis of generality, and universality of applicability of its fundamental categories. This acts to superimpose a peculiar perspective in the understanding of human history, one that assigns Western societies a role of touchstone. Economic science is thus called upon to define the place of the various societies and economies in history. The most evident confirmation of the abuse Smith made of the conjectural method, namely the bartering-savage stereotype, reduces exchange in archaic societies to market exchange, thereby denying any theoretical relevance to the major form of primitive exchange, the gift, expressing the essence itself of archaic societies and, at the same time, signalling a fundamental discontinuity with modern societies. Here, in the elimination of the 'other', lies the original sin of economics.

Despite a variety of characterizations, the general theoretical framework erected by the economic science for studying archaic societies presupposes a linear view of history, and a view of this latter as progress, primitive societies representing the initial, backward stage. It is such presumed backwardness that permits underestimating or even neglecting those positive characteristics of archaic societies that have most disturbed non-trained Western eyes: as the French philosopher Volney remarked, the price to be paid for savage freedom is simply too high.

There is widespread conviction that economics imperialism can grasp the essentiality of social issues, all the more so after proposals of 'new syntheses' combining the economic approach with neo-Darwinian strands. In truth, while reflecting upon the relationships between economic science and primitive societies, it becomes relatively easy to realize that these latter – which economics takes as the foundational element of the economicist approach that binds together the theory of economics as developed since the eighteenth century, of its strength, relevance and practical influence – constitute a complex object, one that does not tolerate being made the object of reductionist interpretations. Economics can offer, at best, a partial, inadequate representation of such societies, and one that is substantially extraneous to the object itself of the analysis. As Mauss appropriately put it, the category of *homo oeconomicus* does not simply belong to the imaginary of primitive societies. The economicist interpretation is intriguing, since its reductionism grants unity and logical consistency to the facts it is intended to explain, but in the end, little or no gain appears to result in interpretative power.

In the end, in fact, the strength of economics' analysis of archaic societies is also its weakness: the idea of detecting an unequivocal, natural law or character in human beings, upon which to found the generality of its vision. The universality of economic science, which is often regarded as the reason for its primacy over other social sciences, derives not so much from rigour and scientificity, as from the – ideological in character – assumption that man is essentially a *homo oeconomicus*. Economics imperialism is, to put it differently, a myth that stems fundamentally from the ideology that the *homo oeconomicus* embodies.

If economics imperialism is a myth, the *Homo oeconomicus* is its hero, the founding type in the worldview of a community. Economists perfectly recognize the supernatural character of the 'rational fool', and the "critical" nature of this basic assumption – in Rodrik's terms, "an assumption is critical if its modification in an arguably more realistic direction would produce a substantive difference in the conclusion produced by the model" (Rodrik 2015: 27). But the mainstream of economics is much less disposed to disavow this hero, exactly because this latter delineates the psychology, traditions, way of thinking and ideals of the community of economists, which it protects, at the same time, from the potentially perilous impact of more structured relationships with other social sciences. The hubris, in the sense of excessive self-confidence, of the *homo oeconomicus* hero exalts economics' autonomy, economics imperialism being at once the weapon to be used in colonizing heretofore unexplored territories and a virtually invincible declaration of independence from the methods, scopes and style (see Mäki 2009) of other disciplines.

All this may explain both, on one side, the insularity of economics, and on the other, the apparent U-turn made by the discipline in recent decades. Somehow, the historical evolution of economists' interpretation of archaic societies reflects – it might even be said, more precisely, to anticipate – the trajectory covered by the discipline itself in its interchanges with other disciplines. The insularity implicit in Robbins's systematization of economics as the science of rational choice finds an important antecedent in Smith's decision to tackle the complexity of the forms and reasons of exchange in archaic societies. Economics imperialism, which entered the mainstream of economics in the 1970s, reached its apogee in economics with the rise and success of the formalist strand. While Posner's 'transaction costs' theory of primitive societies participates in the revolution of the 'information-theoretic approach', which re-embedded the 'social' into the 'economic' by considering the former as the institutionalization of rational reactions to market failures. The era of 'reverse imperialisms' by other social sciences is precognized by the appropriation of some key concepts and theoretical frameworks of economic anthropology in mainstream economists, in the 1980s, when anthropological and sociological insights were found to be functional to the analysis of the most surprising aspects of economic coordination and of its most spectacular failures. Whereas the recent 'economics of reciprocity', rooted in interdisciplinary fieldworks of enormous impact, attempts at remedying economics' failure to participate constructively in the multidisciplinary debate; this is likely to be the most important discussion of the twentieth century in social sciences, on the socio-political and ethical foundations of modern societies.

The development of this peculiar research programme, and the groundbreaking results it suggests, should ideally induce a profound revision of the *homo oeconomicus*, and replace the hero of the myth of economics' primacy and imperialism with a less contestable multifaceted man. Still, this potential revolution in economics (the possibility of a post-neoclassical mainstream) is rather presented as a historical opportunity to make the historically constructed, alternative disciplinary approaches of behavioural sciences compatible with one another. The resulting 'end-of-(scientific) history' perspective (see Steve Clarke's 2007 philosophical criticism of Gintis's 2007 proposal for a qualified theoretical bridge unifying behavioural sciences) evidently mirrors, once again, a view of economics as *primus inter pares*, a status it shares with sociobiology. The two formerly competing imperialist sciences are now called upon to cooperate with a view to realizing the 'new synthesis' invoked by Edward O. Wilson in the mid-1970s, which found in Hirshleifer a most influential supporter in economics, and in Sahlins's substantivist anthropology (another anticipation) a strenuous opponent.

There is little doubt that a general reorganization of behavioural sciences would compel economics to revisit its basic tenets and, above all, its pugilistic habitus towards other sciences. But for the resulting post-neoclassical mainstream to represent a true departure, a reconsideration of the cultural and political (rather than biological) origins of the '*homo reciprocans*' seems necessary. It is first in this sense that Mauss's legacy might help economics reconfigure its relationships with other social sciences. Mauss's discovery of the primitive social contract allows the understanding of the place of the economy (and the 'economic') in archaic societies exactly by positing political independence and internal equality to be vigorously defended as common goods *par excellence*. This is the element required to substantiate the recently found alternative to *homo oeconomicus*, also in its characterization as the hero of economics imperialism. When Mauss's analysis of primitive exchange is read in terms of the 'political miracle' (as Leibniz called it) separating human societies from the artificial nightmare of Hobbes' 'natural' war of all against all, the *homo oeconomicus* can finally appear as the 'natural', for the sake of paradox, that is, the pre-social condition of human beings.

But gift exchange, writes sociologist Helmuth Berking, "is not only the significant form in which archaic societies reproduce themselves; giving and taking are also the elementary activities through which sociability became rich in evolutionary chances, and upon which any community-building process still rest" (1999: 31). Berking rightly approves of German philosopher Georg Simmel's perspective, whereby giving is "one of the strongest sociological functions. Without constant giving and taking within society . . . no society would have come into existence. For giving is . . . exactly what is required of a sociological function: it is interaction" (1958 [1908]: 444). Mauss's gift is required to absolve a complex task, namely to create and nurture social bonds. This complexity – as against the simplicity of market exchange and the underlying, reductionist notion of reciprocity (which permits the redefinition of gifts in terms of deferred payments; see Callari 2002, Osteen 2002) – provides therefore, even from a symbolical point of view, insights into the place of economics in the plurality of social sciences. For there is, as Caillé (2005: 7) observes, a fundamental epistemological lesson Mauss can offer at an epoch when such pluralism of (rather than in) social sciences is accused of being "dysfunctional" (Colander 2014: 517). "Economics, sociology, anthropology, philosophy etc. must not be thought, taught, learned and practiced as totally separate and alien disciplines", warns Caillé

> but as moments of a *general social science* the main question of which is: which part of social and human activities is and must be devoted to satisfying needs, to functional, instrumental and utilitarian activities? And which to producing meaning, making sense of life, to symbolic, ritual, political and anti-utilitarian activities.
>
> (Caillé 2005: 7)

Despite the intrinsic limits of the operation, Gintis's suggested framework for the unification of behavioural sciences intercepts a possible crossroad in the history of economics. Today's 'mainstream pluralism', or even simply the fragmentation of economics into a variety of divergent research programmes, might provide an opportunity to bypass the historically proven impossibility of an interdisciplinary neoclassical economics (perfectly exemplified by the 'Titmuss affair' discussed in Part III). On one side, the recent incursions of other disciplines into economics have de facto compelled economics imperialists to retract the substantial (and structural) neglect of old-style imperialism for interdisciplinarity, as is shown in Lazear's defence of Chicago imperialism, which, as Davis (forthcoming) remarks, makes necessarily use of a trade-in-ideas theory. On the other, it has become difficult to ascribe economics imperialism to the entire discipline (see Davis 2013a): social sciences are actively fostering the fragmentation that characterizes today's mainstream pluralism. Gintis's work can thus be considered, also, as a reaction to the 'disintegration' of the mainstream of economics, with the concomitant attempt at reorganizing the mainstream itself by exploiting the contribution that other social sciences can offer in this regard. *Mutatis mutandis*, this perspective is shared by more heterodox approaches like the evolutionary/institutionalist strand in economics. As Geoffrey Hodgson and Jan-Willem Stoelhorst (2014: 680) argue, only a "paradigmatic evolutionary social science" will produce the desired revolution in economics, so that, to achieve this latter, institutionalist and evolutionary economists should be "willing to cast themselves as evolutionary social scientists first, and as economists only second" (ibid.: 679).

A non-secondary aim of this volume is to demonstrate that Mauss's gift can help revisiting economics in its quality of social science. An obvious shortcoming of economics imperialism is that it considers complexity – which, one can note *en passant*, is evidently the main motive why interdisciplinarity is required – not as the fundamental issue at stake when dealing with social contexts, but as an unnecessary complication that economists luckily manage to get rid of in progressing toward better understanding of human behaviour. To overcome the obstacles posed by disciplinary boundaries, a non-imperialist economics should rather bring social complexity to the fore. As seen, the anthropological-sociological literature on the gift opposes the idea of naturality of market exchange. This book has largely insisted on the two alternative paths traced by Smith and Mauss to discovering the socio-political foundations of modern societies. It is worth noting that while failing to remedy Smith's neglect for the complexity of the social dimension embedded in gift relationships, economics has also voluntarily opted for a reductionist route to complexity itself. When light is thrown on these two radically alternative ways of implementing a common general research programme, it becomes evident that any reflection on the nature and method of economics should necessarily address the issues Mauss identified as problematic in his account of the evolution of human societies. The Maussian approach makes the gift appear both a triggering mechanism for the creation of social bonds and a vehicle of such ties. Social cohesion is ensured exactly by practices of gift exchange, which appear to protect individual autonomy from the potentially excessive discipline of social norms, through the complex – and paradoxical only to the eyes of contemporary economists – mix of freedom and obligation on which the act of giving rests.

The author of a famous critique of modern development economics, Swiss political scientist and sociologist Gilbert Rist invokes the necessity for a heretofore 'deluding' economic science to pass "from reductionism to complexity" (Rist 2010: 20). It is evident that to achieve this result, economics must fully accept the challenge of interdisciplinarity. Economic imperialism configures a clear case of decreasing returns – that is, it loses explanatory power when applied to societies and phenomena whose complexity resists its reductionism. While proclaiming the primacy of economics, imperialists are compelled to reject, to the detriment of economics itself, the variety and diversity of economic practices. Yet it is true that mainstream economics is changing face, under the impact of field and laboratory research on human sociality, but also because of the willingness to investigate a series of black boxes of economic theory (endogenous preferences, intrinsic motivations, complexity of micro-macro relations), and of widespread awareness of the limits of neoclassical reductionism. Time will tell whether economics can successfully face the now pressing challenges of complexity, morality, political philosophy. If economics is to contribute to transdisciplinary framework for analysing behaviour, however, economics reformers should first address the original, historical, 'Smithian' sin of their discipline, and possibly remove the deep roots of economics imperialism. Second, they should rediscover and update a methodological approach soon left aside, conceiving economics as a science of social complexity and the economic material as made up of human actions, beliefs and feelings shaping a social scenario. Third, they should explore the benefits stemming from adopting the Maussian approach to analyse inherently complex social facts; benefits that include the possibility to rethink economics' potential contribution to a shared, interdisciplinary and democratic theoretical framework for behavioural sciences.

Bibliography

Adloff, F. and Mau, S. (2006) 'Giving Social Ties, Reciprocity in Modern Society', *Archives Européennes de sociologie*, 47(1): 93–123.

Akerlof, G. A. (1970) 'The Market for "Lemons": Quality Uncertainty and the Market Mechanism', *Quarterly Journal of Economics*, 84(3): 488–500.

Akerlof, G. A. (1982) 'Labor Contracts as Partial Gift Exchanges', *Quarterly Journal of Economics*, 97(4): 543–69.

Akerlof, G. A. (1984) 'Gift Exchange and Efficiency-Wage Theory: Four Views', *American Economic Review*, 74(2): 79–83.

Akerlof, G. A. (1990) 'George A. Akerlof', in R. Swedberg (ed.), *Economics and Sociology, Redefining their Boundaries: Conversations with Economists and Sociologists*, Princeton, NJ: Princeton University Press, 61–77.

Akerlof, G. and Kranton, R. (2010) *Identity Economics: How Our Identity Shape Our Work, Wages, and Well-Being*, Princeton, NJ: Princeton University Press.

Alchian, A. A. (1950) 'Uncertainty, Evolution, and Economic Theory', *Journal of Political Economy*, 58(3): 211–21.

Alchian, A. A. and Allen, W.R. (1964) *University Economics*, Belmont, CA: Wadsworth.

Altman, J. (1984) 'Hunter-gatherers' Subsistence Production in Arnhem Land: The Original Affluence Hypothesis Re-examined', *Mankind*, 14(3): 179–90.

Andreoni, J. (1988) 'Privately Provided Public Goods in a Large Economy: The Limits of Altruism', *Journal of Public Economics*, 35(1): 57–73.

Andreoni, J. (1990) 'Impure Altruism and Donations to Public Goods: A Theory of Warm-Glow Giving', *Economic Journal*, 100(401): 464–77.

Anspach, M. R. (2002) *A charge de revanche. Figures élémentaires de la réciprocité*, Paris: Seuil.

Appadurai, A. (ed.) (1986) *The Social Life of Things: Commodities in Cultural Perspective*, Cambridge: Cambridge University Press.

Archard, D. (2002) 'Selling Yourself: Titmuss' Argument Against a Market in Blood', *The Journal of Ethics*, 6(1): 87–103.

Aria, M. (2008) "*Dono*, hau e reciprocità. Alcune riletture antropologiche di Marcel Mauss", in M. Aria and F. Dei (eds), *Culture del dono,* Roma: Meltemi, 181–219.

Arnell, B. (1996), *John Locke and America. The Defence of English Colonialism*, New York: Oxford University Press.

Arrow, K. J. (1963) 'Uncertainty and the Welfare Economics of Medical Care', *American Economic Review*, 53(5): 941–73.

Arrow, K. (1972) 'Gifts and Exchanges', *Philosophy & Public Affairs,* 1(4): 343–62.

Ault, D. E. and Rutman, G. L. (1980) 'The Development of Individual Rights to Property in Tribal Africa', *Journal of Law and Economics*, 22(1): 163–82.

Axelrod, R. (1984) *The Evolution of Cooperation*, New York: Basic Books.

Axelrod, R. and Hamilton, W. D. (2010) [1981] 'The Evolution of Cooperation', in A. Rosenberg and R. Arp (eds), *Philosophy and Biology: An Anthology*, Malden, MA: Wiley-Blackwell, 347–57.

Backhouse R. E. and Cherrier, B. (2014) 'Becoming Applied: The Transformation of Economics after 1970', The Center for the History of Political Economy Working Paper Series, No. 2014–15. Available at: http://hope.econ.duke.edu/sites/default/files/Backhouse%20and%20Cherrier%20-%20Becoming%20applied%20version%201%2012.pdf.

Bardhan, P. and Ray, I. (2015) 'Methodological Approaches in Economics and Anthropology', in J. B. Davis and W. Dolfsma (eds), *Elgar Companion to Social Economics*, Cheltenham: Edward Elgar, 497–515.

Barnard, A. and Woodburn, J. (1988) 'Property, Power and Ideology in Hunter-gathering Societies: An Introduction'. In T. Ingold, D. Riches and J. Woodburn (eds), *Hunters and Gatherers: Property, Power and Ideology*, Oxford: Berg Publishers, 4–31.

Batifoulier, P., Cordonnier, L. and Zenou, Y. (1992) 'L'emprunt de la théorie économique à la tradition sociologique. Le cas du don contro-don', *Revue économique*, 43(5): 917–46.

Becker, G. S. (1961) 'Notes on an Economic Analysis of Philanthropy', mimeograph (April). NBER (reported in Fontaine 2007).

Becker, G. S. (1974) 'A Theory of Social Interaction', *Journal of Political Economy*, 82(6): 1063–93.

Becker, G. S. (1976a). *The Economic Approach to Human Behaviour*, Chicago, IL: University of Chicago Press.

Becker, G. S. (1976b) 'Egoism, and Genetic Fitness: Economics and Sociobiology', *Journal of Economic Literature*, 14(3): 817–26.

Benet, F. (1957) "Explosive Markets: The Berber Highlands", in K. Polanyi, C. M. Arensberg and H. W. Pearson (eds), *Trade and Market in the Early Empires. Economies in History and Theory*, Glencoe, IL: The Free Press 188–216.

Benot, Y. (1970) *Diderot, de l'athéisme à l'anticolonialisme*, Paris: Maspero.

Berking, H. (1999) *Sociology of Giving*, London: Sage.

Bernheim, B. D., and Bagwell, K. (1988) 'Is Everything Neutral?', *Journal of Political Economy*, 96(2): 308–38.

Bettinger, R. L. (1991) *Hunter-Gatherers: Archeological and Evolutionary Theory*, New York: Plenum Press.

Binembaum, E. (2005) 'Knight versus Herskovits. A Methodologically Charged Debate in the 1940s', Working Paper no. 8, School of Economics, University of Adelaide.

Binmore, K. (2005) 'Economic Man – or Straw Man? Commentary on Henrich et al.: Economic Behavior in Cross-cultural Perspective', *Behavioral and Brain Sciences*, 28: 817–18.

Bird-David, N. (1992) 'Beyond "The Original Affluent Society": A Culturalist Reformulation, *Current Anthropology*, 33(1): 25–47.

Blaney, D. L. and Inayatullah, N. (2010) *Savage Economics: Wealth, Poverty, and the Temporal Walls of Capitalism*, London: Routledge.

Boas, F. (1896) 'The Limitation of Comparative Method of Anthropology', *Science*, 4: 901–8.

Boas, F. (1897) *The Social Organization and the Secret Societies of the Kwakiutl Indians*, Report of National Museum of National History for 1885.

Boas, F. (1921) *Ethnology of the Kwakiutl*, Thirty-fifth Annual Report of the Bureau of American Ethnography.

Boas, F. (1966) *Kwakiutl Ethnography*, H. Codere ed., Chicago, IL: University of Chicago Press.

Bohannan, D. and Dalton, G. (eds) (1965) *Markets in Africa*, Chicago, IL: Northwestern University Press.

Bonar, J. (1966) [1932] *A Catalogue of the Library of Adam Smith*, New York: August M. Kelly.

Boulding, K. (1958) *Principles of Economic Policy*, Englewood Cliffs, NJ: Prentice-Hall.

Boulding, K. (1962) 'Notes on a Theory of Philanthropy', in F. G. Dickinson (ed.), *Philanthropy and Public Policy*, New York: NBER, 57–71.

Boulding, K. (1963) 'Towards a Pure Theory of Threat Systems', *American Economic Review*, 53(2): 424–34.

Boulding, K. (1967) 'The Boundaries of Social Policy', *Social Work*, 12(1): 3–11.

Boulding, K. (1968) *Beyond Economics: Essays on Society, Religion and Ethics*, Ann Arbor: University of Michigan Press.

Boulding, K. (1973) *The Economy of Love and Fear: A Preface to Grants Economics*, Belmont, CA: Wadsworth.

Bourdieu, P. (1997) 'Selections from "The Logic of Practice"', in A. Schrift (ed.), *The Logic of the Gift: Toward an Ethic of Generosity*, New York: Routledge, 190–230.

Bowles, S. (1998) 'Endogenous Preferences: The Cultural Consequences of Markets and Other Economic Institutions', *Journal of Economic Literature*, 36(1): 75–111.

Bowles, S. and Gintis, H. (2013) *A Cooperative Species: Human Reciprocity and its Evolution*, Princeton, NJ: Princeton University Press.

Boyd, R. and Richerson, P. J. (1985) *Culture and the Evolutionary Process*, Chicago, IL: University of Chicago Press.

Buchanan, J. (1972) 'Toward Analysis of Closed Behavioral Systems', in J. Buchanan and R. Tollison (eds), *Theory of Public Choice: Political Applications of Economics*, Ann Arbor: University of Michigan Press, 11–23.

Buchanan, J. (1975) 'The Samaritan's Dilemma', in E. Phelps (ed.) *Altruism, Morality, and Economic Theory*, New York: Russell Sage Foundation, 71–85.

Buchanan, J. (1979) [1969] 'Professor Alchian on Economic Method', in J. Buchanan, *What Should Economists Do?*, Indianapolis, IN: Liberty Press, 65–97.

Bucher, K. (1893) *Die Entstehung der Volkswirtsehaft*, Tubingen: Verlag der H. English translation: *Industrial Evolution*, New York: Henry Holt and Company, 1901.

Buckley, P. and Casson, M. (1993) 'Economics as an Imperialist Social Science', *Human Relations*, 46(9): 1035–52.

Buffon, G.-L. (1826–28) [1749–89] *Histoire naturelle, générale et particulière, avec la description du Cabinet du Roi,* 36 vols. Paris: Imprimerie Royale, then in *Oeuvres completes*, Paris: Richard.

Caillé, A. (1998) *Anthropologie du don. Le tiers paradigme*, Paris: P. Desclée de Brouwer.

Caillé, A. (2001) 'The Double Inconceivability of the Free Gift', *Angelaki: Journal of Theoretical Humanities*, 6(1): 23–39.

Caillé, A. (2005) 'Anti-utilitarianism, Economics and the Gift-paradigm', *Revue du MAUSS permanente*, available at: www.revuedumauss.com.fr/media/ACstake.pdf.

Callari, A. (2002) 'The Ghost of the Gift: The Unlikelihood of Economics', in M. Osteen (ed.) *The Question of the Gift: Essays across Disciplines*, London: Routledge, 248–65.

Camerer, C. F. (1988), 'Gift as Economic Signals and Social Symbols', *The American Journal of Sociology*, 94 (Suppl.): 180–214.

Camerer, C. F. (2001) *Behavioral Economics*, Princeton, NJ: Princeton University Press.

Camerer, C. F. and Thaler, R. H. (1995) 'Anomalies: Ultimatums, Dictators and Manners', *Journal of Economic Perspectives*, 9(2): 209–19.

Carabelli, A. M., and Cedrini, M. A. (2010a) 'Keynes and the Complexity of International Economic Relations in the Aftermath of World War I', *Journal of Economic Issues*, 44(4): 1009–28.

Carabelli, A. M., and Cedrini, M. A. (2010b) 'Global Imbalances, Monetary Disorder, and Shrinking Policy Space: Keynes's Legacy for Our Troubled World', *Intervention. European Journal of Economics and Economic Policies*, 7(2): 303–23.

Carabelli, A. M. and Cedrini, M. A. (2014) 'Chapter 18 of the General Theory "Further Analysed": Economics as a Way of Thinking', *Cambridge Journal of Economics*, 38(1): 23–47.

Carrier, J. (1991) 'Gifts, Commodities, and Social Relations: A Maussian View of Exchange', *Sociological Forum*, 6(1): 119–36.

Cashdan, E. (1989) 'Hunters and Gatherers: Economic Behavior in Bands', in S. Plattner (ed.), *Economic Anthropology*, Palo Alto, CA: Stanford University Press, 21–48.

Cassirer, E. (1951) [1932] *Die Philosophie der Aufklärung*, Tübinen: Morh. English Translation: *The Philosophy of the Enlightenment*. Princeton, NJ: Princeton University Press, 1951.

Cavalli-Sforza, L. and Feldman, M. W. (1982) 'Theory and Observation in Cultural Transmission', *Science*, 218(4567): 19–27.

Cedrini, M. and Fontana, M. (2015) 'Just Another Niche in the Wall? How Specialization Is Changing the Face of Mainstream Pluralism", revised version of the Department of Economics and Statistics "Cognetti de Martiis" Working Paper 2015/10, University of Turin.

Cedrini, M. and Marchionatti, R. (2016) 'On the Theoretical and Practical Relevance of the Concept of Gift to the Development of a Non-Imperialist Economics', *Review of Radical Political Economics*, forthcoming, doi: 10.1177/0486613416635040.

Champlain, S. (1619) *Voyages et decouvertes faites en la Nouvelle France . . . par le Sieur de Champlain*. Paris: Claude Collet.

Champlain, S. (1632) *Les Voyages de la Nouvelle France occidentale, dicte Canada, faits par le Sr de Champlain . . .*, Paris: Louis Sevestre.

Champlain, S. (1922–36) *The Works of Samuel de Champlain*, H. P. Biggar general ed., 6 vols, Toronto: The Champlain Society.

Charlevoix, P. F. X. (1744) *Histoire et description générale de la Nouvelle France*, Paris: Pierre-François Giffart.

Charness, G. and Rabin, M. (2002) 'Understanding Social Preferences with Simple Tests', *Quarterly Journal of Economics*, 117(3): 817–69.

Chayanov, A. (1966) [1925, original Russian edn] *The Theory of Peasant Economy*, D. Thorner ed., Homewood, IL: Basile Kerblay and R. E. F. Smith.

Choi, B. C. K. and Pak, A. W. P. (2006) 'Multidisciplinarity, Interdisciplinarity and Transdisciplinarity in Health Research, Services, Education and Policy: 1. Definitions, Objectives, and Evidence of Effectiveness', *Clinical and Investigative Medicine* 29(6): 351–64.

Churchill, A. and J. (eds) (1704), *A Collection of Voyages and Travels, some now first printed from original MSS., others translated out of foreign languages and now first published in English; in four volumes, with an original preface giving an account of the progress of navigation, &c.*, 4 vols, London: Awnsham and John Churchill at the Black Swan.

Clarke, S. (2007) 'Against the Unification of the Behavioral Social Sciences', *Behavioral and Brain Sciences*, 30(1): 21–2.

Clastres, P. (1974) *La société contre l'état*, Paris: Editions de Minuit. English translation: *Society Against the State. Essays in Political Anthropology*, Cambridge, MA.: The MIT Press.

Clastres, P. (1994) [1980] *Recherches d'anthropologie politique*, Paris: Editions du Seuil.

Clastres, P. (1994) [1980], *Archeology of violence*, New York: Semiotext(e).

Coase, R. (1978) 'Economics and Contiguous Disciplines', *Journal of Legal Studies*, 7(2): 201–11.

Cohen, P. S. (1967) 'Economic Analysis and Economic Man', in R. Firth (ed.) *Themes in Economic Anthropology*, London: Tavistock.

Colander, D. (2000), 'The Death of Neoclassical Economics', *Journal of the History of Economic Thought*, 22(2): 127–43.

Colander, D. (2014) 'The Wrong Type of Pluralism: Toward a Transdisciplinary Social Science', *Review of Political Economy*, 26(4): 516–25.

Colander, D., Holt, R. and Rosser Jr., J. B. (2004), 'The Changing Face of Mainstream Economics', *Review of Political Economy*, 16(4): 485–99.

Colden, C. (1727) *History of the Five Indian Nations Depending on the Province of New York in America*, New York: William Bradford.

Conley, T. (2005) 'The *Essays* and the New World', in *The Cambridge Companion to Montaigne*, U. Langer ed., Cambridge: Cambridge University Press, 74–95.

Cook, S. (1966) 'The Obsolete "Anti-Market" Mentality: A Critique of the Substantive Approach to Economic Anthropology', *American Anthropologist*, 68(2): 323–45.

Cook, S. (1969) 'The Anti-Market Mentality Re-examined: A Further Critique of the Substantive Approach to Economic Anthropology', *Southwestern Journal of Anthropology*, 25(4): 378–406.

Cooper, M. and Culyer, A. (1968) *The Price of Blood*, London: Institute of Economic Affairs.

Cordonnier, L. (1997), *Coopération et réciprocité*, Paris: Presses Universitaires de France.

Davis, J. B. (2006) 'The Turn in Economics: Neoclassical Dominance to Mainstream Pluralism?', *Journal of Institutional Economics*, 2(1): 1–20.

Davis, J. B. (2008a) 'Heterodox Economics, the Fragmentation of the Mainstream, and Embedded Individual Analysis', in J. T. Harvey and R. F. Garnett (eds), *Future Directions for Heterodox Economics*, Ann Arbor: University of Michigan Press, 53–72.

Davis, J. B. (2008b) 'The Turn in Recent Economics and Return of Orthodoxy', *Cambridge Journal of Economics*, 32(3): 349–66.

Davis, J. B. (2013a) 'Mäki on Economics Imperialism', in A. Lehtinen, J. Kuorikosky and P. Ylikoski (eds), *Economics for Real. Uskali Mäki and the Place of Truth in Economics*, New York: Routledge, 213–19.

Davis, J. B. (2013b) 'Economics Imperialism under the Impact of Psychology: The Case of Behavioral Development Economics', *Oeconomia*, 3(1): 119–38.

Davis, J. (forthcoming) 'Economics Imperialism vs. Multidisciplinarity', *History of Economic Ideas*.

Dawkins, R. (1976) *The Selfish Gene*, Oxford: Oxford University Press.

De Brosses, C. (1756) *Histoire des navigations aux terres australes*, 3 vols, Paris: Durand.

Defoe, D. (1945) [1719] *The Life and Strange Surprising Adventures of Robinson Crusoe*, London: Dent & Sons.

De Léry, J. (1994) [1578] *Histoire d'un voyage faict en la terre du Brésil*, Paris: Bibliothèque classique du Livre de Poche. English translation: *History of a Voyage to the Land of Brazil* (1990), Translation and introduction by J. Whatley, Oakland: University of California Press.

Demsetz, H. (1997) 'The Primacy of Economics: An Explanation of the Comparative Success of Economics in the Social Sciences', *Economic Inquiry*, 35(1): 1–11.

Derrida, J. (1992) *Given Time: I. Counterfeit Money*, Chicago, IL: University of Chicago Press.

Diderot, D. (1992) [1772] *Supplément au voyage de Bougainville et autres œuvres morales*, E. Tassin ed., Paris: Presses Pocket.

Douglas, M. (1971) 'Review of The Gift Relationship: From Human Blood to Social Policy', *Man*, 6(3): 499–500.

Douglas, M. (1990) 'Foreword' to M. Mauss, *The Gift*, translated by W. D. Halls, London and New York: Routledge.

Duchet, M. (1971) *Anthropologie et Histoire au siècle des Lumières*, Paris: Maspero.

Duchet, M. (1978) *Diderot et l'«Histoire des deux Indes» ou L'écriture fragmentaire*, Paris: A. G. Nizet.

Eibl-Eibesfeldt, I. (1991) 'On Subsistence and Social Relations in the Kalahari', *Current Anthropology*, 32(1): 55–7.

Ellingson, T. (2001) *The Myth of the Noble Savage*, Berkeley: University of California Press.

Ember, C. and Ember, M. (1992) 'Resource Unpredictability, Mistrust, and War', *Journal of Conflict Resolution*, 32(2): 242–62.

Engels, F. (1990) [1884] *Der Ursprung der Familie, des Privateigentums und des Staats (The Origin of the Family, Private Property and the State*, in K. Marx and F. Engels, *Collected Works,* Vol. 26: Frederick Engels, 1882–89. New York: International Publishers.

Eyre, E. J. (1845), *Journals of Expeditions of Discovery into Central Australia, and Overland from Adelaide to King George's Sound, in the Years 1840–41*, 2 vols, London: Boone.

Feest, C. (2001) 'Father Lafitau as Ethnographer of the Iroquois', *European Review of Native American Studies*, 15(2): 19–25.

Fehr, E. and Gächter, S. (2000) 'Fairness and Retaliation: The Economics of Reciprocity', *Journal of Economic Perspectives*, 14(3): 159–81.

Fenton, W. N. (1965) *'The Iroquois Confederacy* in the Twentieth Century: A Case Study on the Theory of Lewis H. Morgan in Ancient Society', *Ethnology*, 4(3): 251–65.

Fenton, W. N. (1969) 'J. F. Lafitau, Precursor of Scientific Anthropology', *Southwestern Journal of Anthropology*, 25(2): 173–87.

Ferguson, A. (1793) [1767] *Essays on the History of Civil Society*, London: T. Cadell, in the Strand, and W. Creech, and Edinburgh: Bill and Bradfute.

Fine, B. (2000) 'Economics Imperialism and Intellectual Progress: The Present as History of Economic Thought?', *History of Economics Review*, 32(1): 10–36.

Fine, B, and Milonakis, D. (2009) *From Economics Imperialism to Freakonomics: The Shifting Boundaries Between Economics and Other Social Sciences*, London and New York: Routledge.

Finley, M. I. (1973) *The Ancient Economy*, Berkeley and Los Angeles: University of California Press.

Firth, R. (1965) [1939, 1st edn], *Primitive Polynesian Economy*, London: Routledge & Sons.

Fontaine, P. (2002) 'Blood, Politics, and Social Science: Richard Titmuss and the Institute of Economic Affairs, 1957–1973', *Isis*, 93(3): 401–34.

Fontaine, P. (2007) 'From Philanthropy to Altruism: Incorporating Unselfish Behavior into Economics, 1961–1975', *History of Political Economy*, 39(1): 1–46.

Fontaine, P. (2012) 'Beyond Altruism? Economics and the Minimization of Unselfish Behavior, 1975–93', *History of Political Economy*, 44(2): 195–233.

Foster, J. (2006) 'Why is Economics not a Complex System Science?', *Journal of Economic Issues*, 40(4): 1069–92.

Fourcade, M., Ollion, E. and Algan, Y. (2015) 'The Superiority of Economists', *Journal of Economic Perspectives*, 29(1): 89–114.

Fournier, M. (1994) *Marcel Mauss*, Paris: Fayard. English translation: *Marcel Mauss. A Biography*, Princeton, NJ: Princeton University Press, 2006.

Fowler, C. S. and Turner, N. J. (2001) 'Ecological/Cosmological Knowledge and Land Management among Hunter-Gatherers', in R. B. Lee and R. Daly (eds), *The Cambridge Encyclopedia of Hunters and Gatherers*, Cambridge: Cambridge University Press, 419–25.

Fraser, L. M. (1937) *Economic Thought and Language*, London: Macmillan.

Frey, B. S. (1997) *Not Just for the Money*, Cheltenham: Edward Elgar.

Frey, B. S. and Benz, M. (2004) 'From Imperialism to Inspiration: A Survey of Economics and Psychology', in J. B. Davis, A. Marciano and J. Runde (eds), *The Elgar Companion to Economics and Philosophy*, Cheltenham: Elgar, 61–83.

Friedman, M. (1953) *Essays in Positive Economics*, Chicago, IL: University of Chicago Press.

Gächter, S., and Falk, A. (2002) 'Reputation and Reciprocity: Consequences for the Labour Relation', *Scandinavian Journal of Economics*, 104(1): 1–26.

Garrett, A. (2003) 'Anthropology: The "Original" of Human Nature', in A. Broadie (ed.), *The Cambridge Companion to The Scottish Enlightenment*, Cambridge: Cambridge University Press, 79–93.

Gasché, R. (1997) [1972] 'Heliocentric Exchange', *L'Arc*, 48: 70–84, reprinted in A.D. Schrift (ed.), *The Logic of the Gift: Toward an Ethic of Generosity*, New York: Routledge, 1997, 100–17.

Geertz, C. (1978) 'The Bazaar Economy: Information and Searching Peasant Marketing', *The American Economic Review*, 68(2): 28–32.

Gerbi, A. (1973) *The Dispute of the New World: The History of a Polemic, 1750–1900*, Pittsburgh, PA: University of Pittsburgh Press.

Getty, T. (2007) 'In Evolutionary Games, Enlightened Self-interests are Still Ultimately Self-Interests', *Behavioral and Brain Sciences*, 30(1): 25–6.

Ghiselin, M. T. (1974), *The Economy of Nature and the Evolution of Sex*, Berkeley: University of California Press.

Ghiselin, M. T. (1978) 'The Economy of the Body', *The American Economic Review*, 68(2): 233–7.

Gintis, H. (2007) 'A Framework for the Integration of the Behavioral Sciences', *Behavioral and Brain Sciences*, 30(1): 1–16.

Gintis, H. (2009) *The Bounds of Reason: Game Theory and the Unification of the Behavioral Sciences*, Princeton, NJ: Princeton University Press.

Gintis, H. (2010) 'Review of Marshall Sahlins, The Use and Abuse of Biology: An Anthropological Critique of Sociobiology (University of Michigan Press, 1977)'. Available at: http://www.umass.edu/preferen/gintis/Sahlins%20on%20Sociobiology.docx.

Gintis, H. and Helbing, D. (2015) 'Homo Socialis: An Analytical Core for Sociological Theory', *Review of Behavioral Economics,* 2(1): 239–53.

Gintis, H., Bowles, S., Boyd, R. and Fehr, E. (2006) *Moral Sentiments and Material Interests. The Foundations of Cooperation in Economic Life*, Cambridge, MA: The MIT Press.

Glazer, N. (1971) 'Blood', *The Public Interest*, 24: 86–94.

Godbout, J. T. (1998) *The World of the Gift*, Montreal and Ithaca, NY: McGill-Queen's University Press.

Godbout, J. T. (2000) *Le don, la dette et l'identité. Homo donator versus homo oeconomicus*, Paris/Montréal: Editions La Découverte/MAUSS.

Godbout, J. T. (2004) 'L'actualité de l'«Essai sur le don»', *Sociologie et sociétés*, 36(2): 177–88.

Godbout, J. T., in collaboration with A. Caillé (1998) *The World of the Gift*, Montreal and Ithaca, NY: McGill-Queen's University Press.

Godelier, M. (1996) *L'Enigme du don*, Paris: Fayard.

Godelier, M. (2002) 'Some Things You Give, Some Things You Sell, but Some Things You Must Keep for Yourselves: What Mauss Did not Say About Sacred Objects, in E. Wyschogrod, J.-J. Goux, and E. Boynton (eds), *The Enigma of Gift and Sacrifice*, New York: Fordham University Press, 19–37.

Gouldner, A. (1996) [1960] 'The Norm of Reciprocity: A Preliminary Statement', in A. Komter (ed.), *The Gift: An Interdisciplinary Perspective*, Amsterdam: Amsterdam University Press, 49–66.

Gouldner, A. (1971) 'The Gift Relationship', *New York Times*, March 21.

Gouldner, A. (1973) 'The Importance of Something for Nothing', in A. Gouldner (ed.), *For Sociology. Renewal and Critique in Sociology Today*, London: Allen Lane, 260–99.

Graeber D. (2000) 'Give It Away', *In These Times.com*, August 21. Available at: http://inthesetimes.com/issue/24/19/graeber2419.html.

Green, J. (ed.) (1745–47) *New General Collections of Voyages and Travels*, 4 vols, London: Thomas Astley.

Gregory, C. A. (1982) *Gifts and Commodities*, San Diego, CA: Academic Press.

Gregory, C. A. (1997) *Savage Money: The Anthropology and Politics of Commodity Exchange*, London: Taylor & Francis.

Grey, J. (1841) *Journal of Two Expeditions of Discovery in North-West and Western Australia. During the Years 1837, 38, and 39 . . .*, 2 vols. London: Boone.

Grinde, D. A. and Johansen, B. E. (1991) *Exemplar of Liberty: Native America and the Evolution of Democracy*, Los Angeles, CA: American Indian Studies Center, UCLA.

Griswold, C. L. (2006) 'Imagination: Morals, Science, and Arts' in K. Haakonssen (ed.), *The Cambridge Companion to Adam Smith*, Cambridge: Cambridge University Press, 22–56.

Groethuysen, B. (1956) *Philosophie de la Révolution française*, Paris: Gallimard.

Gross, N. and Simmons, S. (2007) 'The Social and Political Views of American Professors', available at: http://www.wjh.harvard.edu/~ngross/lounsbery_9–25.pdf.

Grossbard, A. (1978) 'Towards a Marriage Between Economics and Anthropology and a General Theory of Marriage', *The American Economic Review*, 68(2): 33–7.

Grossbard-Shechtman, S. and Clague, C. (2001a) 'Symposium on the Reorientation of Economics: What Is Economics?', *Journal of Socio-Economics*, 30(1): 1–6.

Grossbard-Shechtman, S. and Clague, C. (2001b) *The Expansion of Economics: Towards a More Inclusive Social Science*, Armonk, NY: M. E. Sharpe.

Gudeman, S. (2001) 'Postmodern Gifts', in S. Cullenberg, J. Amariglio and D. F. Ruccio (eds), *Postmodernism, Economics and Knowledge*, London and New York: Routledge, 459–74.

Hakluyt, R. (1850) [1582] *Divers Voyages Concerning the Discovery of America London*, J. W. Jones ed., London: Hakluyt Society.

Hakluyt, R. (1965) [1589] *Principal Navigations, Voyages, Traffiques, and Discoveries of the English Nation*, 2 vols, Cambridge: Cambridge University Press for Hakluyt Society.
Halévy E. (1995) [1901] *La formation du radicalisme philosophique*, 3 vols, Paris: PUF.
Hamilton, W. D. (1964) 'The Genetical Evolution of Social Behaviour', *Journal of Theoretical Biology*, 7(1): 1–16.
Hammond, J. D. (1991) 'Frank Knight's Antipositivism', *History of Political Economy*, 23(3): 359–81.
Hann, C. (2006) 'The Gift and Reciprocity: Perspectives from Economic Anthropology', in S.-C. Kolm and J. M. Ythier (eds), *Handbook of the Economics of Giving, Altruism and Reciprocity, Volume I*, Amsterdam: Elsevier, 207–23.
Harbaugh, W. T. (1998) 'The Prestige Motive for Making Charitable Transfers', *American Economic Review*, 88(2): 277–82.
Harkin, M. (2005) 'Adam Smith's Missing History, Primitives, Progress and Problems of Genre', *English Literary History*, 72(2): 429–51.
Harrod, R. F. (1948) *Towards a Dynamic Economics*, London: Macmillan.
Hart, K. (2000) 'Comment on Pearson's "Homo Economicus Goes Native"', *History of Political Economy*, 32(4): 1017–26.
Hart, K. (2007) 'Marcel Mauss: In Pursuit of the Whole: A Review Essay', *Comparative Studies in Society and History*, 49(2): 473–85.
Harvey, D. A. (2008) 'Living Antiquity: Lafitau's Moeurs des Sauvages Amériquains and the Religious Roots of the Enlightenment Science of Man', *Proceedings of the Western Society for French History*, 36: 75–92.
Harvey, D. A. (2010) 'The Noble Savage and the Savage Noble: Philosophy and Ethnography in the "Voyages" of the Baron de Lahontan', *French Colonial History*, 11: 161–91.
Hawkes, K. and O'Connell, J. (1981) 'Affluent Hunters? Some Comments in Light of the Alyawara Case', *American Anthropologist*, 83(3): 622–26.
Hawkes, K., O'Connell, J. F. and Blurton Jones, N. G. (1991) 'Hunting Income Patterns Among the Hadza: Big Game, Common Goods, Foraging Goals, and the Evolution of the Human Diet', *Philosophical Transactions of the Royal Society, London, Series B*, 334: 243–51.
Hechter, M. (2015) 'Why Economists Should Pay Heed to Sociology', *Review of Behavioral Economics*, 2(1–2): 89–92.
Henrich, J., Boyd, R., Bowles, S., Camerer, C., Fehr, E., Gintis, H., McHlreath, R., Alvard, M., Barr, A., Ensminger, J., Smith Henrich, N., Hill, K., Gil-White, F., Gurven, M., Marlowe, F. W., Patton, J. Q., Tracer, D. (2005) '"Economic Man" in Cross-cultural Perspective: Behavioral Experiments in 15 Small-scale Societies', *Behavioral and Brain Sciences*, 28: 795–855.
Herskovits, M. (1940) *The Economic Life of Primitive Peoples*, New York: Knopf.
Herskovits, M. (1941) 'Economics and Anthropology: A Rejoinder', *Journal of Political Economy*, 49(2): 269–78.
Herskovits, M. (1952) *Economic Anthropology, New York: Knopf.*
Hirshleifer, J. (1977) 'Economics from a Biological Viewpoint', *Journal of Law and Economics*, 20(1): 1–52.
Hirshleifer, J. (1978a) 'Competition, Cooperation, and Conflict in Economics and Biology', *The American Economic Review*, 68(2): 238–43.
Hirshleifer, J. (1978b) 'Natural Economy versus Political Economy', *Journal of Social and Biological Structures*, I: 319–37.
Hirshleifer, J. (1985) 'The Expanding Domain of Economics', *The American Economic Review*, 75(6): 53–68.

Hirshleifer, J. (1987) [1967] 'Disaster Behavior: Altruism or Alliance?' in J. Hirshleifer, *Economic Behaviour in Adversity*, Chicago, IL: University of Chicago Press, 134–41.

Hobsbawn, E. J. (1965) 'Introduction', in K. Marx (1965) *Pre-capitalist Economic Formations*, E. J. Hobsbawn ed., New York: International Publishers, 9–65.

Hodgkinson, C. (1845) *Australia, from Port Macquarie to Moreton Bay, with Description of the Natives,* London: Boone.

Hodgson, G. M. (2007) 'Evolutionary and Institutional Economics as the New Mainstream?', *Evolutionary and Institutional Economics Review*, 4(1): 7–25.

Hodgson, G. M. (2013) *From Pleasure Machines to Moral Communities: An Evolutionary Economics without Homo Economicus*, Chicago, IL: University of Chicago Press.

Hodgson, G. M. (2015) 'A Trojan Horse for Sociology? Preferences versus Evolution and Morality', *Review of Behavioral Economics*, 2(1–2): 93–112.

Hodgson, G. M., and Stoelhorst, J. W. (2014) 'Introduction to the Special Issue on the Future of Institutional and Evolutionary Economics', *Journal of Institutional Economics,* 10(4): 513–40.

Hoebel, E. A. (1960) 'William Robertson: An 18th Century Anthropologist-Historian', *American Anthropologist*, 62(4): 648–55.

Holländer, H. (1990) 'A Social Exchange Approach to Voluntary Cooperation', *American Economic Review*, 80(5): 1157–67.

Homans, G. C. (1954) 'The Cash Posters: A Study of a Group of Working Girls', *American Sociological Review*, 19(6): 724–33.

Huizinga, J. (1949) [1938], *Homo ludens. A Study of the Play Element in Culture*, London: Routledge & Kegan Paul.

Hyde, L. (1983) *The Gift: Imagination and the Erotic Life of Poetry*, New York: Vintage.

Ingold, T. (1990) 'Comment on "Foragers, Genuine or Spurious: Situating the Kalahari San in History", by J. Solway and R. Lee', *Current Anthropology*, 31(2): 130–31.

Insel, A. (1991) 'L'enchâssement problématique du don dans la théorie néoclassique', *La Revue du MAUSS*, 12: 110–19, 2e trimestre.

Jefferson, T. (1787) *Notes on the State of Virginia*, London: Stockdale.

Joyce, J. (1964) [1912] *Daniel Defoe* (transl. by J. Prescott), *Buffalo Studies*, 1(1): 1–27

Joyce, R. (2006) *The Evolution of Morality*, Cambridge, MA: The MIT Press.

Kelly, R. L. (2004) *The Foraging Spectrum: Diversity in Hunter-Gatherer Lifeways*, New York: Percheron Press.

Kaplan, D. (2000) 'The Darker Side of the Original Affluent Society', *Journal of Anthropological Research* 56(3): 301–24.

Keynes J. M. (1972) [1933] *Essays in Biography*, in *The Collected Writings of John Maynard Keynes*, E. Johnson and D. E. Moggridge eds, Vol. 10, London: Macmillan.

Keynes, J. M. (1973a) [1936] *The General Theory of Employment, Interest and Money*, in *The Collected Writings of John Maynard Keynes*, E. Johnson and D. E. Moggridge eds, Vol. 7, London: Macmillan.

Keynes, J. M. (1973b) [1921] *A Treatise on Probability*, in *The Collected Writings of John Maynard Keynes*, E. Johnson and D. E. Moggridge eds, Vol. 8. London: Macmillan.

Keynes, J. M. (1973c) *The General Theory and After. Part II: Defence and Development*, *The Collected Writings of John Maynard Keynes*, E. Johnson and D. E. Moggridge eds, Vol. 14, London: Macmillan.

Keynes, J. M. (1979) *Activities 1944–1946: The Transition to Peace*, *The Collected Writings of John Maynard Keynes*, E. Johnson and D. E. Moggridge eds, Vol. 24, London: Macmillan.

Keynes, J. M. (1983) *Economic Articles and Correspondence: Investment and Editorial, The Collected Writings of John Maynard Keynes*, E. Johnson and D. E. Moggridge eds, Vol. 12, London: Macmillan.

Kirshner, J. (2009) 'Keynes, Legacies and Inquiries', *Theory and Society*, 38(5): 527–41.

Knight, F. (1941) 'Economics and Anthropology', *Journal of Political Economy,* 49(2): 247–68.

Kolm, S.-C. and Ythier, J. M. (2006), *Handbook of the Economics of Giving, Altruism and Reciprocity*, 2 vols, Amsterdam: North-Holland/Elsevier.

Krader, L. (ed.) (1974) *The Ethnological Notebooks of Karl Marx*, Assen: Van Gorcum & Comp.

Kranton, R. E. (1996) 'Reciprocal Exchange: A Self-sustaining System', *American Economic Review*, 86(4): 830–51.

Lafitau, J.-F. (1724) *Moeurs des sauvages americains*, Paris: Saugrain et Hochereau. English translation: *Customs of the American Indians compared with the customs of primitive times*, W. N. Fenton and E. L. Moore eds., 2 vols. Toronto: Champlain Society, 1974.

Lafitau, J.-F. (1974) [1733] *Histoire des découvertes e des conquetes des Portugais dans le Nouveau Monde*, Genève: Slatkine reprints.

Lahontan, L.-A. (1703) *Les Nouveaux voyages dans l'Amérique septentrionale avec Mémoires de l'Amerique septentrionale*, La Haye: chez les frères l'Honoré. English translation: *New Voyages to North America,* R. G. Thwaites ed., 2 vols. Chicago, IL: A. C. McClurg & Co., 1905, reprinted from the English edition of 1703.

Lahontan, L.-A. (1704) *Dialogues de Monsieur le Baron de Lahontan et d'un Sauvage, dans l'Amérique*, Amsterdam: Veuve de Boeteman.

Lahontan, L.-A. (1990) *Œuvres complètes*, édition critique par Réal Ouellet, avec la collaboration d'Alain Beaulieu, 2 vols, Montréal: Presses de l'Université de Montréal.

Laidlaw, J. (2000) 'A Free Gift Makes No Friends', *Journal of the Royal Anthropological Institute*, 6(4): 617–34.

Landes, W. M. and Posner, R. A. (1978) 'Altruism in Law and Economics', *American Economic Review* 68(2): 417–21.

La Page du Pratz, A.-S. (1758) *Histoire de la Lousiane*, Paris: Chez de Bure: La veuve Delaguette: Lambert. English translation: *History of Louisiana*, ed. with an introduction by Joseph G. Tregle, Jr. London: T. Becket, 1774; reprint, Baton Rouge: Louisiana State University Press, 1975.

Lazear, E. P. (2000) 'Economic Imperialism', *The Quarterly Journal of Economics*, 115 (1): 99–146.

Lee, R. B. and DeVore, I. (eds.) (1968) *Man the Hunter*, Chicago, IL: Aldine.

Lee, R. B. (1968) 'What Hunters Do for a Living, or, How to Make out on Scarce Resources', in R. B. Lee and I. DeVore (eds), *Man the Hunter*, Chicago, IL: Aldine, 30–48.

Lee, R. (1969), '!Kung Bushman Subsistence: an Input-Output Analysis', in A. P. Vayda (ed.), *Environment and Cultural Behavior*, New York: Natural History Press (47–79).

Lee, R. (1979) *The !Kung San: Men, Women and Work in a Foraging Society*, Cambridge: Cambridge University Press.

Lee, R. (1984) *The Dobe !Kung*, New York: Holt, Rinehart & Winston.

Lee, R. (1992) 'Art, Science or Politics? The Crisis in Hunter-Gatherers Studies', *American Anthropologist*, 94(1): 31–54.

Lee, R. B. and Daly, R. (eds) (2001) *The Cambridge Encyclopedia of Hunters and Gatherers*, Cambridge: Cambridge University Press.

Lefort, C. (1951) 'L'échange et la lutte des hommes', Les *Temps modernes*, 64(6): 1401–17; then in Lefort, C. *Les formes de l'histoire*, Paris: Gallimard.

Leibenstein, H. (1976) *Beyond Economic Man*, Cambridge, MA: Harvard University Press.

Leibenstein, H. (1982) 'The Prisoners' Dilemma in the Invisible Hand: An Analysis of Intrafirm Productivity', *American Economic Review*, 72(2): 92–7.

Leibenstein, H. (1987) *Inside the Firm: The Inefficiencies of Hierarchy*, Cambridge, MA: Harvard University Press.

Lescarbot, M. (2013) [1619], *Histoire de la Nouvelle France Paris Adrian Perier,* English Translation: *The History of New France*, W. L. Grant ed., Toronto: The Champlain Society.

Lévi-Strauss, C. (1959) *Les Structures élémentaires de la parenté*, Paris: Presses universitaires de France. English translation: *The Elementary Structures of Kinship*, London: Eyre and Spottiswoode, 1969.

Lévi-Strauss, C. (1987) [1950] *Introduction to the Works of Marcel Mauss*, London: Routledge & Kegan Paul.

Lindbeck, A., and Weibull, J. W. (1988) 'Altruism and Time Consistency: The Economics of Fait Accompli', *Journal of Political Economy*, 96(6): 1165–82.

Locke, J. (1824) [1689] *Two Treatises of Government,* vol. IV of *The Works of John Locke*, London: Rivington.

Lodewijks, J. (1994) 'Anthropologists and Economists: Conflict or Cooperation?', *Journal of Economic Methodology*, 1(1): 81–104.

Mackie, J. L. (1977) *Ethics: Inventing Right and Wrong*, Harmondsworth: Penguin.

Macy, M. W. (2015) 'Big Theory: A Trojan Horse for Economics?', *Review of Behavioral Economics*, 2(1–2), 161–6.

Mäki U. (2009) 'Economic Imperialism: Concept and Constraints', *Philosophy of the Social Sciences*, 39(3): 351–80.

Mäki, U. (2013) 'Scientific Imperialism: Difficulties in Definition, Identification, and Assessment', *International Studies in the Philosophy of Science*, 27(3): 325–39.

Malinowski, B. (1921) 'The Primitive Economics of the Trobriand Islanders', *The Economic Journal*, 31(121): 1–16.

Malinowski, B. (2002) [1922] *Argonauts of the Western Pacific. An Account of Native Enterprise and Adventure in the Archipelagoes of Melanesian New Guinea*, London: G. Routledge & Kegan Paul; New York: E.P. Dutton & Co.

Malinowski, B. (1926) *Crime and Custom in Savage Society*, London: Routledge & Kegan Paul.

Mallard, G. (2011). 'The Gift Revisited: Marcel Mauss on War, Debt, and the Politics of Reparations', *Sociological Theory*, 29(4): 225–47.

Marchionatti, R. (2002) 'Dealing with Complexity: Marshall and Keynes on the Nature of Economic Thinking', in R. Arena and M. Quéré (eds), *The Economics of Alfred Marshall. Revisiting Marshall's Legacy*, London: Palgrave-Macmillan, 32–52.

Marchionatti, R. (2003) 'On the Methodological Foundation of Modern Microeconomics. Frank Knight and the Cost Controversy in the 1920s', *History of Political Economy*, 35(1): 49–75.

Marchionatti, R. (2004) 'What Don't Economists Know Now That Marshall Knew a Century Ago? A Note on Marshall's "Sophisticated Informality"', *Journal of Post Keynesian Economics*, 26(3): 441–60.

Marchionatti, R. (2008) *Gli economisti e i selvaggi. L'imperialismo della scienza economica ed i suoi limiti*, Milano: Bruno Mondadori.

Marchionatti, R. (2010) 'J. M. Keynes, Thinker of Economic Complexity', *History of Economic Ideas*, 18(2): 115–46.

Marchionatti, R. (2012) 'The Economists and the Primitive Societies. A Critique of Economic Imperialism', *Journal of Socio-Economics*, 41(5): 529–40.

Marchionatti, R. (2013) 'La riflessione sulla libertà selvaggia di Pierre Clastres', in P. Clastres, *L'Anarchia Selvaggia*, Milano: Eléuthera.
Marchionatti, R. and Cassata, F. (2011) 'A Transdisciplinary Perspective on Economic Complexity. Marshall's Problem Revisited', *Journal of Economic Behavior & Organization*, 80(1): 122–36.
Marouby, C. (2007) 'Adam Smith and the Anthropology of the Enlightenment. The Ethnographic Sourses of Economic Progress', in L. Wolff and M. Cipolloni (eds), *The Anthropology of the Enlightenment*, Stanford, CA: Stanford University Press, 85–102.
Marshall, A. (1890) *Principles of Economics*, London: Macmillan.
Marshall, L. (1961) 'Sharing, Talking, and Giving: Relief of Social Tensions Among !Kung Bushmen', *Africa*, 31(3): 231–49.
Marshall, P. J. and Williams, G. (1982) *The Great Map of Mankind*, Dent: London.
Marx, K. (1973) [1857–58], *Grundrisse der Kritik der politischen Okonomie*, Berlin: Dietz Verlag. English translation: *Outlines of the Critique of Political Economy*, Londra: Penguin, 1973.
Marx, K. (1951) [1859] *Zur Kritik der Politischen Okonomie*, Berlin: Dietz Verlag.
Marx, K. (1867, 1885, 1894), *Das Kapital*, 3 vols, Hamburg: Meissner. English translation: *Capital*, Moscow: Progress Publishers.
Marx, K. and F. Engels (1953) [1845] *Die Deutsche Ideologie*, Berlin: Berlin: Dietz Verlag.
Marx K. (1965) *Formen, die der kapitalistichen Production vorhergehen*, in Marx, K. (1973). English translation: *Pre-capitalist Economic Formations*, E. J. Hobsbawn ed., New York: International Publishers.
Mauss, M. (1904–05), 'Essai sur le variations saisonnières des sociétés eskimos', in *Année Sociologique*, 9: 387–478.
Mauss, M. (1990) [1923–24] 'Essai sur le don. Forme et raison de l'échange dans les sociétés arcaiques', *Année Sociologique*, second série. English translation: *The Gift. The Form and Reason for Exchange in Archaic Societies*, translated by W. D. Halls, London and New York: Routledge.
McCarthy, F. and McArthur, M. (1960) 'The Food Quest and the Time Factor in Aboriginal Economic Life', in C. P. Mountford (ed.), *Records of the American-Australian Scientific Expedition to Arnhem Land*, Vol. 2, Anthropology and Nutrition, Melbourne: Melbourne University Press, 145–94.
McKenzie, R., and Tullock, G. (1978) *The New World of Economics: Explorations into the Human Experience*, Homewood, IL: Richard D. Irwin, Inc.
Meek, R. L. (1976) *Social Science and the Ignoble Savage*, Cambridge: Cambridge University Press.
Metha, P. B. (2006) 'Self-Interest and Other Interests', in K. Haakonssen (ed.) *The Cambridge Companion to Adam Smith*, Cambridge: Cambridge University Press, 246–69.
Mill, J. S. (1843) *A System of Logic, Ratiocinative and Inductive: Being a Connected View of the Principles of Evidence, and the Methods of Scientific Investigation*, London: John W. Parker.
Mirowski, P. (1994) 'Tit for Tat: Concepts of Exchange, Barter, and Higgling in Two Episodes in the History of Economic Anthropology', *History of Political Economy*, 26 (suppl. 1): 1–22.
Mirowski, P. (2000) 'Exploring the Fault Lines: Introduction to the Minisymposium on the History of Economic Anthropology', *History of Political Economy*, 32(4): 919–32.
Mirowski, P. (2001) 'Refusing the Gift', in S. Cullenberg, J. Amariglio and D. F. Ruccio (eds), *Postmodernism, Economics and Knowledge*, London and New York: Routledge, 431–58.

Montaigne, M. de (1580–88) *Essais*, Bordeaux: Simon Millanges. English translation: *Essays*, translated by C. Cotton, W. C. Hazlitt ed., London: Reeves and Turner, 1877.

Montesquieu (1750) *Défence de l'esprit des lois,* Genève: Barrillot & Fils.

Montesquieu (2001) [1748] *De l'esprit del lois*, 2 vols, Genève: Barrillot & Fils. English translation: *The Spirits of Laws*, translated by T. Nugent, Kitchener: Batoche Books.

Moravia, S. (1970) *La scienza dell'uomo nel Settecento*, Roma-Bari: Laterza.

Morgan, L. H. (1851) *The League of the Ho-de-no-sau-nee or Iroquois*, Rochester, NY: Sage and Brothers.

Morgan, L. H. (1877) *Ancient Society or Researches in the Lines of Human Progress from Savagery through Barbarism to Civilization*, London: MacMillan & Company.

Mueller, D. C. (1973), 'Constitutional Democracy and Social Welfare', *Quarterly Journal of Economics*, 87(1): 60–80.

Muthu, S. (2003) *Enlightenment against Empire*, Princeton, NJ: Princeton University Press.

Napoleoni, C. (1973) *Valore*, Milano: ISEDI.

Nettle, D., Gibson, M. A., Lawson, D. W. and Sear, R. (2013) 'Human Behavioral Ecology: Current Research and Future Prospects', *Behavioral Ecology*, 24(5): 1031–40.

Nik-Khah, E. and Van Horn, R. (2012) 'Inland Empire: Economics Imperialism as an Imperative of Chicago Neoliberalism', *Journal of Economic Methodology*, 19(3): 251–74.

North, D. (1977) 'Markets and Other Allocation Systems in History: The Challenge of Karl Polanyi', *Journal of European Economic History*, 6(3): 703–16.

Olson, M. (1965) *The Logic of Collective Action: Public Goods and the Theory of Groups*, Cambridge, MA: Harvard University Press.

Osteen, M. (ed.) (2002) *The Question of the Gift: Essays across Disciplines*, London: Routledge.

Ostrom, E, Walker, J. and Gardner, R. (1992) 'Covenants With and Without a Sword: Self-governance Is Possible', *American Political Science Review*, 86(2): 404–17.

Ouellet, R. (1983), *Sur Lahontan. Comptes rendus et critiques (1702–1711)*, Quebec: L'Hetrière.

Pagden A. (1982) *The Fall of Natural Man: the American Indian and the Origins of Comparative Anthropology*, Cambridge: Cambridge University Press.

Panoff, M. (1970) 'Marcel Mauss's "The Gift" Revisited', *Man*, 5(1): 60–70.

Parry, J. (1986) 'The Gift, the Indian Gift and the "Indian Gift"', *Man*, 21(3): 453–73.

Parry, J., and Bloch, M. (eds) (1989) *Money and the Morality of Exchange*, Cambridge, MA: Cambridge University Press.

Parsons, T. (1937) *The Structure of Social Action*, New York: McGraw-Hill.

Parsons, T., Shils, E. A. and Smelser, N. J. (eds) (1965) *Toward a General Theory of Action: Theoretical Foundations for The Social Sciences*, London: Transaction Publishers.

Pauchant, T. (2015) 'Adam Smith's Socio-cultural Theory of Evolution. New Insights from his 1749 Lecture', *The Adam Smith Review*, 9, forthcoming.

Pauw, C. (1768) *Recherches philosophiques sur les Américains*, Londres: s.n.

Pearson, H. (2000) 'Homo Economicus Goes Native, 1859–1945: The Rise and Fall of Primitive Economics', *History of Political Economy*, 32(4): 933–89.

Phelps, E. (ed.) (1975) *Altruism, Morality, and Economic Theory*, New York: Russell Sage Foundation.

Polakoff, M. E. (1953) 'Economic Methodology and the Significance of the Knight-Herskovits Controversy', *American Journal of Economics and Sociology*, 12(2): 201–10.

Polanyi, K. (2001) [1944] *The Great Transformation*, New York: Holt, Rinehart & Winston.

Polanyi, K. (1977) *The Livelihood of Man*, H. W. Pearson ed., New York: Academic Press.

Polanyi, K., Arensberg, C. M. and Pearson, H. W. (1957) *Trade and Market in the Early Empires. Economies in History and Theory*, Glencoe, IL: The Free Press.

Posner, R. A. (1973) *Economic Analysis of Law*, Boston, MA: Little Brown and Company.

Posner, R. A. (1980) 'A Theory of Primitive Society, with Special Reference to Law', *Journal of Law and Economics*, 23(1): 1–53; then in Posner, R. (1981) *The Economics of Justice*, Cambridge, MA: Harvard University Press.

Posner, R. A. (1987) 'The Law and Economics Movement', *The American Economics Review*, 77(2): 1–13.

Preti, G. (1977) *Alle origini dell'etica contemporanea. Adamo Smith*, Firenze: La Nuova Italia.

Prévost, A. F. (Abbé Prévost) (1747–59) *Histoire général des voyages*, 15 vols, La Haye: Pierre de Hondt.

Price, J. A. (1962) *Washo Economy*, Anthropological Papers n. 6, Carson City: Nevada State Museum.

Prouteau, L. (1999) *Économie du comportement bénévole: Théorie et étude empirique*, Paris: Economica.

Radnitzky, G. and Bernholz, P. (eds) (1987) *Economic Imperialism: The Economic Method Applied Outside the Field of Economics*, New York: Paragon House.

Rawls, J. (1971) *A Theory of Justice*, Cambridge, MA: Cambridge University Press.

Raynal, G. T. F. (2006) [1780, 3rd edn) *Histoire philosophique et politique des établissements et du commerce des Européens dans les deux Indes*, 5 vols, Paris: Bibliothèque des introuvables. English translation: *A Philosophical and Political History of the Settlements and Trade of the Europeans in the East and West Indies*, 6 vols, London: Strahan, 1798.

Reinstein, D. (2014) 'The Economics of the Gift', Economics Discussion Papers of the University of Essex, Department of Economics, Colchester. Available at: http://repository.essex.ac.uk/10009/1/dp749.pdf.

Rist, G. (2010) *The Delusions of Economics. The Misguided Certainties of a Hazardous Science*, London and New York: Zed Books.

Robbins, L. (1932) *An Essay on the Nature and Significance of Economic Science*, London: Macmillan.

Robertson W. (1842) [1777] The *History of the Discovery and Settlement of America*, Edinburgh: Thomas Nelson.

Robson, A. (2001) 'The Biological Basis of Economic Behavior', *Journal of Economic Literature*, 39(1): 11–33.

Rodrik, D. (2011) *The Globalization Paradox. Democracy and the Future of the World Economy*, New York and London: W. W. Norton.

Rodrik, D. (2015) *Economic Rules: The Rights and Wrongs of the Dismal Science*, New York and London: W. W. Norton.

Romano, O. (2015) 'Anti-utilitarianism' in G. D'Alisa, F. Demaria and G. Kallis (eds), *Degrowth. A Vocabulary for a New Era*, London: Routledge, 21–4.

Rothschild, E. and Sen, A. (2006) 'Adam Smith's Economics', in Knud Haakonssen (ed.), *The Cambridge Companion to Adam Smith*, Cambridge: Cambridge University Press, 319–65.

Rousseau, J. J. (1755) *Discours sur l'origine et les fondements de l'inégalité parmi les hommes*, Géneve: Marc-Michel Rey.

Rubiés, J. P. (2002) 'Travel writing and ethnography', in P. Hulme and T. Youngs (eds), *The Cambridge Companion to Travel Writing*, Cambridge: Cambridge University Press, 242–60.

Sackett, R. (1996) Time, Energy, and the Indolent Savage. A Quantitative Cross-cultural Test of the Primitive Affluence Hypothesis, PhD diss., University of California.

Sagard-Theodat, G. (1632) Le *Grand Voyage au pays des Huron*, Paris: Denys Moreau. English translation: *The Long Journey to the Country of the Hurons*, G. Wrong and H. Langton, eds., Toronto: Champlain Society, 1939.

Sahlins, M. (1969) 'Economic Anthropology and Anthropological Economics', *Social Science Information*, 8(5): 13–33.

Sahlins, M. (1972) *Stone Age Economics*, Chicago, IL: Aldine.

Sahlins, M. (1976a) *Cultural and Practical Reason*, Chicago, IL: University of Chicago Press.

Sahlins, M. (1976b) *The Use and Abuse of Biology. An Anthropological Critique of Sociobiology*, Ann Arbor: University of Michigan Press.

Sahlins, M. (1993) 'Goodbye to Tristes Tropes: Ethnography in the Context of Modern World History', *Journal of Modern History*, 65(1): 1–25.

Sahlins, M. (1994) 'Cosmologies of Capitalism: The Trans-Pacific Sector of the World System', in N. B. Dirks, G. Eley, and S. B. Ortner (eds), *A Reader in Contemporary Social Theory*, Princeton, NJ: Princeton University Press, 412–56.

Sahlins, M. (1996) 'The Sadness of Sweetness: The Native Anthropology of Western Cosmology', *Current Anthropology*, 37(3): 395–428.

Sahlins, M. (2008a) *The Western Illusion of Human Nature*. Chicago, IL: Prickly Paradigm Press.

Sahlins, M. (2008b) 'Interview with Marshall Sahlins', *Anthropological Theory*, 8(3): 319–28.

Sahlins, M. (2013) *What Kinship Is—and Is Not*, Chicago, IL: University of Chicago Press.

Sandel, M. J. (2012) *What Money Can't Buy: The Moral Limits of Markets*, London: Macmillan.

Schelling, T. C. (1960) *The Strategy of Conflict*, Cambridge, MA: Harvard University Press.

Schneider, H. K. (1974) *Economic Man: The Anthropology of Economics*, New York: Free Press.

Schumacher, E. F. (1973) [1966] 'Buddhist Economics', in E. F. Schumacher, *Small Is Beautiful: A Study of Economics As If People Mattered*, London: Blond & Briggs.

Seldon, A. (ed.) (1973) *The Economics of Charity: Essays on the Comparative Economics and Ethics of Giving and Selling with Applications to Blood*, IEA Readings 12, London: Institute of Economic Affairs.

Seligman, C. G. (1910) *The Melanesians of British New Guinea*, Cambridge: Cambridge University Press.

Sen, A. K. (1977). 'Rational Fools: A Critique of the Behavioural Foundations of Economic Theory', *Philosophy and Public Affairs*, 6(4): 317–44.

Sen, A. K. (1988) *On Ethics and Economics*, Oxford: Blackwell.

Shaw, W. H., (1984) 'Marx and Morgan', *History and Theory*, 23(2): 215–28.

Shearmur, J. (2001) 'Trust, Titmuss and Blood', *Economic Affairs*, 21(1): 29–33.

Simmel, G. (1958) [1908] *Soziologie. Untersuchungen über die Formen der Vergesellschaftung*, Berlin: Duncker & Humblot.

Singer, P. (1973) 'Altruism and Commerce: A Defense of Titmuss Against Arrow', *Philosophy and Public Affairs*, 2(3): 312–20.

Skidelsky, R. (2000) *John Maynard Keynes: Fighting for Britain 1937–1946*, London: Macmillan.

Skinner, A. S. (1975) 'Adam Smith: An Economic Interpretation of History', in A. S. Skinner and T. Wilson (eds), *Essays on Adam Smith*. Oxford: Clarendon Press, 154–78.

Smelser, N. J. and Swedberg, R. (2005) *The Handbook of Economic Sociology*, Princeton, NJ: Princeton University Press.

Smith, A. (1975) [1759] *The Theory of Moral Sentiments*, in *Glasgow Edition of the Works and Correspondence of Adam Smith*, Vol. I, D. D. Raphael and A. L. Macfie eds, Oxford: Clarendon Press.

Smith, A. (1976) [1776] *An Inquiry into the Nature and Causes of the Wealth of Nations,* in *Glasgow Edition of the Works and Correspondence of Adam Smith*, Vol. II, R. H. Campbell and A. S Skinner eds, Oxford: Clarendon Press.

Smith, A. (1982) [1762–63] *Essays on Philosophical Subjects*, in *Glasgow Edition of the Works and Correspondence of Adam Smith*, Vol. III, W. P. D. Wightman ed., Oxford: Clarendon Press.

Smith, A. (1975) [1762] *Lectures on Jurisprudence*, in *Glasgow Edition of the Works and Correspondence of Adam Smith*, Vol. V, R. L. Meek, D. D. Raphael and P. G. Stein eds, Oxford: Clarendon Press.

Smith, A. (1975) [1763] 'Early Draft of Part of *The Wealth of Nations*' in *Lectures on Jurisprudence*, R. L. Meek, D. D. Raphael and P. G. Stein eds, Oxford: University Press, 562–81.

Smith, E. A. and Winterhalder, B. (eds) (1992) *Evolutionary Ecology and Human Behavior*, New York: Aldine de Gruyter.

Smyth, R. B. (1878) *The Aborigines of Victoria*, 2 vols, Melbourne: Government Printer.

Solow, R. (1971) 'Blood and Thunder', *Yale Law Journal*, 80(8): 1696–711.

Souter, R. (1933) *Prolegomena to a Relativity Economics: An Elementary Study in the Mechanics and Organics of an Expanding Economic Universe*, New York: Columbia University Press.

Spencer, B. and Gillen, F. J. (1899) *The Natives Tribes of Central Australia*, London: Macmillan.

Steiner, P. (2003) 'Gifts of Blood and Organs: The Market and "Fictitious" Commodities', *Revue française de sociologie*, 44(5): 147–62.

Steward, J. H. (1955) *Theory of Cultural Change: The Methodology of Multilinear Evolution*, Urbana: University of Illinois Press.

Stewart, D. (1982) [1793] *Account of the Life and Writings of Adam Smith*, in A. Smith, (1982) [1762–63] *Essays on Philosophical Subjects*, in *Glasgow Edition of the Works and Correspondence of Adam Smith*, Vol. III, W. P. D. Wightman ed., Oxford: Clarendon Press, 269–351.

Stigler, G. (1984) 'Economics: The Imperial Science?', *The Scandinavian Journal of Economics*, 86(3): 301–13.

Stiglitz, J. E. (2000) 'The Contributions of the Economics of Information to Twentieth Century Economics', *Quarterly Journal of Economics*, 115(4): 1441–78.

Strathern, M. (1988) *The Gender of the Gift: Problems with Women and Problems with Society in Melanesia*, Berkeley, University of California Press.

Sugden, R. (1982) 'On the Economics of Philanthropy', *Economic Journal*, 92(366): 341–50.

Sugden, R. (1984) 'Reciprocity: The Supply of Public Goods through Voluntary Contributions', *Economic Journal*, 94(376): 772–87.

Tarot, C. (1996) 'Du fait social de Durkheim au fait social total de Marcel Mauss', *Revue du MAUSS*, 4: 57–69.

Thevet, A. (1557) *Les singularitez de la France antarctique, autrement nommee Amerique, & de plusieurs terres et isles decouvertes de nostre temps*, Paris: Heritiers de Maurice de la Porte.

Thurnwald (1912) *Forschungen auf den Salomo-Inseln und dem Bismarck-Archipel*, Berlin: Dietrich Reimer.

Thurnwald, R. (1932) *Economics in Primitive Communities,* London: Oxford University Press.

Titmuss, R. M. (1963) 'Ethics and Economics of Medical Care', *Medical Care*, 1(1):16–22.

Titmuss, R. M. (1966) 'Choice and "The Welfare State"', in R. Titmuss (ed.), *Commitment to Welfare*, London: Allen & Unwin (1968), 138–52.

Titmuss, R. M. (1967) 'The Subject of Social Administration', in R. Titmuss (ed.), *Commitment to Welfare*, London: Allen & Unwin (1968), 13–24.

Titmuss, R. (1970) *The Gift Relationship: From Human Blood to Social Policy*, New York: Pantheon Books.

Trivers, R. L. (1971) 'The Evolution of Reciprocal Altruism', *The Quarterly Review of Biology*, 46(1): 35–57.

Trivers, R. L. (1972), 'Parental Investment and Sexual Selection', in B. Campbell (ed.), *Sexual Selection and the Descent of Man, 1871–1971*, Chicago, IL: Aldine-Atherton, 136–79.

Tullock, G. (1972) 'Economics Imperialism', in J. Buchanan and R. Tollison (eds), *Theory of Public Choice: Political Applications of Economics*, Ann Arbor: University of Michigan Press, 317–29.

Tullock, G. (1978), 'Altruism, Malice and Public Goods', *Journal of Social and Biological Structures*, 1(1): 3–9.

Valeri, V. (2013) [1966] 'Marcel Mauss and the New Anthropology', *HAU: Journal of Ethnographic Theory*, 3(1): 262–86.

Van de Ven, J. (2000) 'The Economics of the Gift', CentER Discussion Paper 2000–68, Tilburg University. Available at: https://pure.uvt.nl/ws/files/536205/68.pdf.

Various Authors (1632–73) *Relation de ce qui s'est passé de plus remarquable aux Missions des Pères de la Compagnie de Jésus en la Nouvelle France, les années et Envoyée au R.P. Provincial de la Province de France [Relations des Jesuites de la Nouvelle-France]*, Paris, Sébastien Cramoisy, 41 vols. English translation: *The Jesuit Relations and Allied Documents: Travels and Explorations of the Jesuit Missionaries in New France, 1610–1791*, Reuben Gold Thwaites ed., 73 vols, Cleveland, OH: Burrows Bros. Co., 1896–1901.

Vikrey, W. S. (1962) 'One Economist's View of Philanthropy', in F. G. Dickinson (ed.), *Philanthropy and Public Policy*, New York: NBER, 31–56.

Vines, D. (2003) 'John Maynard Keynes 1937–1946: The Creation of International Macroeconomics', *Economic Journal*, 113(488): F338–F361.

Volney (C. F. Chasseboeuf) (1803) *Observations générales sur les Indiens ou sauvages de l'Amérique du Nord,* Appendix of *Tableau du climat et du sol des Etats-Unis d'Amérique*, in *Oeuvres de C. F. Volney*, Paris: Parmentier, 1826.

Vromen, J. (2011) 'Allusions to Evolution: Edifying Evolutionary Biology rather than Economic Theory', in R. Van Horn, P. Mirowski and T. A. Stapleford (eds), *Building Chicago Economics: New Perspectives on the History of America's Most Powerful Economics Program*, Cambridge: Cambridge University Press, 208–36.

Waldfogel, J. (1993) 'The Deadweight Loss of Christmas', *The American Economic Review*, 83(5): 1328–36.

Weiner, A. B. (1992) *Inalienable Possessions: The Paradox of Keeping-While Giving*, Berkeley: University of California Press.

Whitaker, J. K. (ed.) (1996) *The Correspondence of Alfred Marshall Economist*, 3 vols, Cambridge: Cambridge University Press.

Wilk, R. R. (1996), *Economies and Cultures: Foundations of Economic Anthropology*, Boulder, CO: Westview Press.

Williams, G. C. (1966) *Adaptation and Natural Selection*, Princeton, NJ: Princeton University Press.

Wilson, E. O. (1975) *Sociobiology: The New Synthesis*, Cambridge, MA: Harvard University Press.

Wilson, E. O. (1998) *Consilience: The Unity of Knowledge,* New York: Alfred A. Knopf.

Winterhalder, B. (1981) 'Foraging Strategies in the Boreal Forest: An Analysis of Cree Hunting and Gathering', in B. Winterhalder and E. A. Smith (eds), *Hunter-Gatherer Foraging Strategies: Ethnographic and Archaeological Analyses*, Chicago, IL: University of Chicago Press, 13–35.

Winterhalder, B. (1992) 'Work, Resources and Population in Foraging Society', *Man,* 28: 321–40.

Winterhalder, B. (2001) 'The Behavioral Ecology of Hunter-Gatherers', in C. Panter-Brick, R. H. Layton and P. Rowley-Conwy (eds), *Hunter-Gatherers: An Interdisciplinary Perspective*, Cambridge: Cambridge University Press, 12–38.

Winterhalder, B. and Smith, E. A. (2000) 'Analyzing Adaptive Strategies: Human Behavioral Ecology at Twenty-five', *Evolutionary Anthropology*, 9(2): 51–72.

Witt, U. (2015) 'Sociology and the Imperialism of Economics', *Review of Behavioral Economics*, 2(1–2): 195–202.

Woodburn, J. (1968) 'An Introduction to Hadza Ecology', in R. B. Lee and I. DeVore (eds), *Man the Hunter*, Chicago, IL: Aldine, 49–55.

Index

Note: 'n' denotes chapter notes.